FINANCIAL INSTITUTIONS AND SERVICES SERIES

SECURITIZATION OF SUBPRIME MORTGAGES

Financial Institutions and Services Series

Stock Exchanges, IPO's and Mutual funds
E. Klein (Editor)
2004 ISBN: 1-59454-173-6

Global Banking Issues
E. Klein (Editor)
2005 ISBN: 1-59454-172-8

Financial Institutions and Development
E. Klein (Editor)
2005 ISBN: 1-59454-177-9

Capital Formation, Governance and Banking
E. Klein (Editor)
2005 ISBN: 1-59454-191-4

U. S. Coins: The Price of a Penny
Walter M. Carvalho (Editor)
2009 ISBN: : 978-1-60692-939-1

Hedge Funds: Regulation and Nonregulation
Yeram E. Torrey (Editor)
2009. ISBN: 978-1-60692-041-1

Reforming Risk in Financial Markets
Melvin R. Turley (Editor)
2009 ISBN: 978-1-60692-445-7

Information Sellers and Resellers
Shane C. Leger (Editor)
2009. ISBN: 978-1-60692-228-6

Econometric Modeling of Value-at-Risk
Timotheos Angelidis and Stavros Degiannakis
2009. ISBN: 978-1-60741-040-9

Liquidity, Interest Rates and Banking
Jeffrey Morrey and Alexander Guyton (Editors)
2009. ISBN: 978-1-60692-775-5

Global Banking Regulation and Supervision: What are the Issues and What Are the Practices?
James R. Barth, Jie Gan and Daniel E. Nolle
2009. ISBN: 978-1-60741-315-8

Securitization of Subprime Mortgages
Milton R. Spotgeste (Editor)
2009. ISBN: 978-1-60692-200-2

FINANCIAL INSTITUTIONS AND SERVICES SERIES

SECURITIZATION OF SUBPRIME MORTGAGES

MILTON R. SPOTGESTE
EDITOR

Nova Science Publishers, Inc.
New York

For permission to use material from this book please contact us:
Telephone 631-231-7269; Fax 631-231-8175
Web Site: http://www.novapublishers.com

LIBRARY OF CONGRESS CATALOGING-IN-PUBLICATION DATA

Securitization of subprime mortgages / editor, Milton R. Spotgeste.
p. cm.
Includes index.
ISBN 978-1-60692-200-2 (hbk.)
1. Subprime mortgage loans--United States. 2. Mortgage-backed securities--United States. I. Spotgeste, Milton R.
HG2040.5.U5S42 2009
332.7'2--dc22
2009027059

Published by Nova Science Publishers, Inc. ✦ New York

CONTENTS

PREFACE

In this book, the authors provide an overview of the subprime mortgage securitization process and the seven key informational frictions that arise. They discuss the ways that market participants work to minimize these frictions and speculate on how this process broke down. They continue with a complete picture of the subprime borrower and the subprime loan, discussing both predatory borrowing and predatory lending. They present the key structural features of a typical subprime securitization, document how rating agencies assign credit ratings to mortgage-backed securities, and outline how these agencies monitor the performance of mortgage pools over time.

Chapter 1 - In this paper, the authors provide an overview of the subprime mortgage securitization process and the seven key informational frictions that arise. The authors discuss the ways that market participants work to minimize these frictions and speculate on how this process broke down. The authors continue with a complete picture of the subprime borrower and the subprime loan, discussing both predatory borrowing and predatory lending. The authors present the key structural features of a typical subprime securitization, document how rating agencies assign credit ratings to mortgage-backed securities, and outline how these agencies monitor the performance of mortgage pools over time. Throughout the paper, the authors draw upon the example of a mortgage pool securitized by New Century Financial during 2006.

Chapter 2 - Using loan-level data, the authors analyze the quality of subprime mortgage loans by adjusting their performance for differences in borrower characteristics, loan characteristics, and house price appreciation since origination. The authors find that the quality of loans deteriorated for six consecutive years before the crisis and that securitizers were, to some extent, aware of it. The authors provide evidence that the rise and fall of the subprime mortgage market follows a classic lending boom-bust scenario, in which unsustainable growth leads to the collapse of the market. Problems could have been detected long before the crisis, but they were masked by high house price appreciation between 2003 and 2005.

Chapter 3 - Substantial growth in the mortgage market in recent years has helped many Americans become homeowners. However, as of the latest quarterly data available, June 2007, more than 1 million mortgages were in default or foreclosure, an increase of 50 percent compared with June 2005. Defaults and foreclosures on home mortgages can impose significant costs on borrowers, lenders, mortgage investors, and neighborhoods. Additionally, recent increases in defaults and foreclosures have contributed to concern and increased volatility in certain U.S. and global financial markets. These developments have raised questions about the extent and causes of problems in the mortgage market.

Chapter 4 - Subprime mortgages are loans extended to borrowers with weak credit profiles. Subprime mortgages entail higher risk of delinquency and default. Recent increases in subprime borrower foreclosures and lender bankruptcies have prompted concerns that some lenders' underwriting guidelines are too loose and that some borrowers may not have fully understood the risks of the mortgage products they chose. Regulatory agencies are revisiting the guidance they provide lenders and are reevaluating required disclosures to consumers. In addition, Congress is holding hearings on the subject and may consider consumer protection legislation. Subprime foreclosures have reached the highs of the 2000-2001 recession but delinquency rates are not the same across mortgage features. The adjustable interest rate (ARM) feature is currently associated with higher delinquency rates than comparable fixed rate loans. However, the delinquency rate of loans with the negative amortization (NegAm) feature has remained below 1%, the range normally associated with less risky loans. NegAm is a loan that allows a monthly payment less than the current interest on the loan with the remaining interest added to the principal, thus increasing the loan balance.

Financial regulators issued a guidance for alternative mortgage products in October 2006 and issued a proposed statement for subprime lending in March 2007. The guidances require that consumers be given plain-language explanations of the risks of their mortgages. Borrowers must be qualified for mortgage loans based on the ability to repay the loan, not based on speculation about future increases in the value of the real estate collateral. The proposed guidance also seeks to limit payment shock and prepayment penalties. Policymakers are faced with the challenge of balancing the benefits of access to credit against the costs of potential foreclosures.

Chapter 5 - Problems in the housing and mortgage markets have now spread to a broader array of financial markets. At this point, the nation faces a serious disruption to the functioning of its financial markets that could substantially impair economic activity in the near term. Since the end of the unusual housing boom from 2003 to early 2006, delinquencies and foreclosures on mortgages have risen, particularly on subprime adjustable-rate mortgage loans (ARMs), reflecting a retreat of house prices from unsustainable levels, the use of lax credit standards to make the loans, weak local economies, and in some cases, higher interest rates on ARMs whose interest rates had reset as scheduled in their loan contracts. (Subprime loans are made to borrowers with low credit scores or other impairments to their credit histories.) The problems are not limited to subprime ARMs, however. Delinquencies have also risen for prime ARMs and on so-called alt-A mortgage loans, which are often made on the basis of little or no documentation of the borrower's income and may include low-downpayment loans, loans that are not for the owner's principal residence, interest-only loans, and loans whose balances rise over time. Because most mortgages are resold as mortgage-backed securities (MBSs), the rise in delinquencies has caused the value of MBSs to decline, in some cases quite sharply.

The problems in mortgage markets have spread to the wider financial markets for several reasons. Although highly uncertain, the number of bad mortgages and, consequently, losses on MBSs are expected to be large. The use of complex instruments to fund subprime lending, such as collateralized debt obligations (CDOs), also has made it difficult for participants in financial markets to identify the magnitude of the exposure of other participants to losses.

Moreover, a number of financial institutions borrowed heavily to finance their mortgage holdings, further increasing their risk exposure.

Those losses on mortgage assets, and the resulting contraction of the availability of credit to businesses and households, pose a significant threat to the pace of economic activity. Given the elevated uncertainty about their exposure to risk, financial institutions have tightened their lending standards and pulled back from all types of risky lending, preferring to conserve capital to guard against potential losses. Following a period in which the risk premium (the higher return required to compensate investors for assuming the risk of default) had been unusually low, the price of risk has risen, in some cases significantly. That pullback has extended to short-term lending between banks. In response, the Federal Reserve and some foreign central banks have intervened to provide large infusions of liquidity (that is, short-term financing) to keep financial markets from freezing up. Moreover, large numbers of foreclosures could trigger a downward spiral of house prices that could take them below what would be justified on the basis of normal relationships to income and production costs. Such a downward spiral would exacerbate the problems in the financial markets and could reduce consumption spending by reducing household wealth, increasing the likelihood and severity of a recession.

In: Securitization of Subprime Mortages
Editor: Milton R. Spotgeste
ISBN: 978-1-60692-200-2

Chapter 1

FEDERAL RESERVE BANK OF NEW YORK STAFF REPORTS: UNDERSTANDING THE SECURITIZATION OF SUBPRIME MORTGAGE CREDIT*

Adam B. Ashcraft† and Til Schuermann

This paper presents preliminary findings and is being distributed to economists and other interested readers solely to stimulate discussion and elicit comments. The views expressed in the paper are those of the authors and are not necessarily reflective of views at the Federal Reserve Bank of New York or the Federal Reserve System. Any errors or omissions are the responsibility of the authors.

ABSTRACT

In this paper, we provide an overview of the subprime mortgage securitization process and the seven key informational frictions that arise. We discuss the ways that market participants work to minimize these frictions and speculate on how this process broke down. We continue with a complete picture of the subprime borrower and the subprime loan, discussing both predatory borrowing and predatory lending. We present the key structural features of a typical subprime securitization, document how rating agencies assign credit ratings to mortgage-backed securities, and outline how these agencies monitor the performance of mortgage pools over time. Throughout the paper, we draw upon the example of a mortgage pool securitized by New Century Financial during 2006.

---

* This is an edited, reformatted and augmented edition of a Federal Reserve Bank of New York Staff Report, No. 318 dated March 2008

† Ashcraft: Federal Reserve Bank of New York (e-mail: adam.ashcraft@ny.frb.org). Schuermann: Federal Reserve Bank of New York (e-mail: til.schuermann@ny.frb.org). The authors would like to thank Mike Holscher, Josh Frost, Alex LaTorre, Kevin Stiroh, and especially Beverly Hirtle for their valuable comments and contributions. The views expressed in this paper are those of the authors and do not necessarily reflect the position of the Federal Reserve Bank of New York or the Federal Reserve System.

Keywords: subprime mortgage credit, securitization, rating agencies, principal agent, moral hazard
JEL classification: G24, G28

EXECUTIVE SUMMARY

Section numbers containing more detail are provided in [square] brackets.

- Until very recently, the origination of mortgages and issuance of mortgage-backed securities (MBS) was dominated by loans to prime borrowers conforming to underwriting standards set by the Government Sponsored Agencies (GSEs) [2]

  1) By 2006, non-agency origination of $1.480 trillion was more than 45% larger than agency origination, and non-agency issuance of $1.033 trillion was 14% larger than agency issuance of $905 billion.

- The securitization process is subject to seven key frictions.

  1) Fictions between the mortgagor and the originator: predatory lending [2.1.1]

     - Subprime borrowers can be financially unsophisticated
     - *Resolution*: federal, state, and local laws prohibiting certain lending practices, as well as the recent regulatory guidance on subprime lending

  2) Frictions between the originator and the arranger: Predatory borrowing and lending [2.1.2]

     - The originator has an information advantage over the arranger with regard to the quality of the borrower.
     - *Resolution*: due diligence of the arranger. Also the originator typically makes a number of representations and warranties (R&W) about the borrower and the underwriting process. When these are violated, the originator generally must repurchase the problem loans.

  3) Frictions between the arranger and third-parties: Adverse selection [2.1.3]

     - The arranger has more information about the quality of the mortgage loans which creates an adverse selection problem: the arranger can securitize bad loans (the lemons) and keep the good ones. This third friction in the securitization of subprime loans affects the relationship that the arranger has with the warehouse lender, the credit rating agency (CRA), and the asset manager.
     - *Resolution*: haircuts on the collateral imposed by the warehouse lender. Due diligence conducted by the portfolio manager on the arranger and originator.

CRAs have access to some private information; they have a franchise value to protect.

4) Frictions between the servicer and the mortgagor: Moral hazard [2.1.4]

- In order to maintain the value of the underlying asset (the house), the mortgagor (borrower) has to pay insurance and taxes on and generally maintain the property. In the approach to and during delinquency, the mortgagor has little incentive to do all that.
- *Resolution*: Require the mortgagor to regularly escrow funds for both insurance and property taxes. When the borrower fails to advance these funds, the servicer is typically required to make these payments on behalf of the investor. However, limited effort on the part of the mortgagor to maintain the property has no resolution, and creates incentives for quick foreclosure.

5) Frictions between the servicer and third-parties: Moral hazard [2.1.5] ¾ The income of the servicer is increasing in the amount of time that the loan is serviced. Thus the servicer would prefer to keep the loan on its books for as long as possible and therefore has a strong preference to modify the terms of a delinquent loan and to delay foreclosure.

- In the event of delinquency, the servicer has a natural incentive to inflate expenses for which it is reimbursed by the investors, especially in good times when recovery rates on foreclosed property are high.
- *Resolution*: servicer quality ratings and a master servicer. Moody's estimates that servicer quality can affect the realized level of losses by plus or minus 10 percent. The master servicer is responsible for monitoring the performance of the servicer under the pooling and servicing agreement.

6) Frictions between the asset manager and investor: Principal-agent [2.1.6]

- The investor provides the funding for the MBS purchase but is typically not financially sophisticated enough to formulate an investment strategy, conduct due diligence on potential investments, and find the best price for trades. This service is provided by an asset manager (agent) who may not invest sufficient effort on behalf of the investor (principal).
- *Resolution*: investment mandates and the evaluation of manager performance relative to a peer group or benchmark 7) Frictions between the investor and the credit rating agencies: Model error [2.1.7]
- The rating agencies are paid by the arranger and not investors for their opinion, which creates a potential conflict of interest. The opinion is arrived at in part through the use of models (about which the rating agency naturally knows more than the investor) which are susceptible to both honest and dishonest errors.
- *Resolution*: the reputation of the rating agencies and the public disclosure of ratings and downgrade criteria.

- Five frictions caused the subprime crisis [2.2]

  1) Friction #1: Many products offered to sub-prime borrowers are very complex and subject to mis-understanding and/or mis-representation.
  2) Friction #6: Existing investment mandates do not adequately distinguish between structured and corporate ratings. Asset managers had an incentive to reach for yield by purchasing structured debt issues with the same credit rating but higher coupons as corporate debt issues.[1]
  3) Friction #3: Without due diligence of the asset manager, the arranger's incentives to conduct its own due diligence are reduced. Moreover, as the market for credit derivatives developed, including but not limited to the ABX, the arranger was able to limit its funded exposure to securitizations of risky loans.
  4) Friction #2: Together, frictions 1, 2 and 6 worsened the friction between the originator and arranger, opening the door for predatory borrowing and lending.
  5) Friction #7: Credit ratings were assigned to subprime MBS with significant error. Even though the rating agencies publicly disclosed their rating criteria for subprime, investors lacked the ability to evaluate the efficacy of these models.
  6) We suggest some improvements to the existing process, though it is not clear that any additional regulation is warranted as the market is already taking remedial steps in the right direction.

- An overview of subprime mortgage credit [3] and subprime MBS [4]

- Credit rating agencies (CRAs) play an important role by helping to resolve many of the frictions in the securitization process

  1) A credit rating by a CRA represents an overall assessment and opinion of a debt obligor's creditworthiness and is thus meant to reflect only credit or default risk. It is meant to be directly comparable across countries and instruments. Credit ratings typically represent an unconditional view, sometimes called "cycle-neutral" or "through-the-cycle." [5.1]
  2) Especially for investment grade ratings, it is very difficult to tell the difference between a "bad" credit rating and bad luck [5.3]
  3) The subprime credit rating process can be split into two steps: (1) estimation of a loss distribution, and (2) simulation of the cash flows. With a loss distribution in hand, it is straightforward to measure the amount of credit enhancement necessary for a tranche to attain a given credit rating. [5.4]
  4) There seem to be substantial differences between corporate and asset backed securities (ABS) credit ratings (an MBS is just a special case of an ABS – the assets are mortgages) [5.5]

     - Corporate bond (obligor) ratings are largely based on firm-specific risk characteristics. Since ABS structures represent claims on cash flows from a *portfolio* of underlying assets, the rating of a structured credit product must take into account systematic risk.

[1] The fact that the market demands a higher yield for similarly rated structured products than for straight corporate bonds ought to provide a clue to the potential of higher risk.

- ABS ratings refer to the performance of a static pool instead of a dynamic corporation.
- ABS ratings rely heavily on quantitative models while corporate debt ratings rely heavily on analyst judgment.
- Unlike corporate credit ratings, ABS ratings rely explicitly on a forecast of (macro)economic conditions.
- While an ABS credit rating for a particular rating grade should have similar expected loss to corporate credit rating of the same grade, the volatility of loss (i.e. the *un*expected loss) can be quite different across asset classes.
- Rating agency must respond to shifts in the loss distribution by increasing the amount of needed credit enhancement to keep ratings stable as economic conditions deteriorate. It follows that the stabilizing of ratings through the cycle is associated with pro-cyclical credit enhancement: as the housing market improves, credit enhancement falls; as the housing market slows down, credit enhancement increases which has the potential to amplify the housing cycle. [5.6]
- An important part of the rating process involves simulating the cash flows of the structure in order to determine how much credit excess spread will receive towards meeting the required credit enhancement. This is very complicated, with results that can be rather sensitive to underlying model assumptions. [5.7]

1. Introduction

How does one securitize a pool of mortgages, especially subprime mortgages? What is the process from origination of the loan or mortgage to the selling of debt instruments backed by a pool of those mortgages? What problems creep up in this process, and what are the mechanisms in place to mitigate those problems? This paper seeks to answer all of these questions. Along the way we provide an overview of the market and some of the key players, and provide an extensive discussion of the important role played by the credit rating agencies.

In Section 2, we provide a broad description of the securitization process and pay special attention to seven key frictions that need to be resolved. Several of these frictions involve moral hazard, adverse selection and principal-agent problems. We show how each of these frictions is worked out, though as evidenced by the recent problems in the subprime mortgage market, some of those solutions are imperfect. In Section 3, we provide an overview of subprime mortgage credit; our focus here is on the subprime borrower and the subprime loan. We offer, as an example a pool of subprime mortgages New Century securitized in June 2006. We discuss how predatory lending and predatory borrowing (i.e. mortgage fraud) fit into the picture. Moreover, we examine subprime loan performance within this pool and the industry, speculate on the impact of payment reset, and explore the ABX and the role it plays. In Section 4, we examine subprime mortgage-backed securities, discuss the key structural features of a typical securitization, and, once again illustrate how this works with reference to the New Century securitization. We finish with an examination of the credit rating and rating monitoring process in Section 5. Along the way we reflect on differences between corporate and structured credit ratings, the potential for pro-cyclical credit enhancement to amplify the housing cycle, and document the performance of subprime ratings. Finally, in Section 6, we review the extent to which investors rely upon on credit rating agencies views, and take as a typical example of an investor: the Ohio Police & Fire Pension Fund.

We reiterate that the views presented here are our own and not those of the Federal Reserve Bank of New York or the Federal Reserve System. And, while the paper focuses on subprime mortgage credit, note that there is little qualitative difference between the securitization and ratings process for Alt-A and home equity loans. Clearly, recent problems in mortgage markets are not confined to the subprime sector.

2. Overview of Subprime Mortgage Credit Securitization

Until very recently, the origination of mortgages and issuance of mortgage-backed securities (MBS) was dominated by loans to prime borrowers conforming to underwriting standards set by the Government Sponsored Agencies (GSEs). Outside of conforming loans are non-agency asset classes that include Jumbo, Alt-A, and Subprime. Loosely speaking, the Jumbo asset class includes loans to prime borrowers with an original principal balance larger than the conforming limits imposed on the agencies by Congress;[2] the Alt-A asset class involves loans to borrowers with good credit but include more aggressive underwriting than the conforming or Jumbo classes (i.e. no documentation of income, high leverage); and the Subprime asset class involves loans to borrowers with poor credit history.

Table 1 documents origination and issuance since 2001 in each of four asset classes. In 2001, banks originated $1.433 trillion in conforming mortgage loans and issued $1.087 trillion in mortgage-backed securities secured by those mortgages, shown in the "Agency" columns of Table 1. In contrast, the non-agency sector originated $680 billion ($190 billion subprime + $60 billion Alt-A + $430 billion jumbo) and issued $240 billion ($87.1 billion subprime + $11.4 Alt-A + $142.2 billion jumbo), and most of these were in the Jumbo sector. The Alt-A and Subprime sectors were relatively small, together comprising $250 billion of $2.1 trillion (12 percent) in total origination during 2001.

A reduction in long-term interest rates through the end of 2003 was associated with a sharp increase in origination and issuance across all asset classes. While the conforming markets peaked in 2003, the non-agency markets continued rapid growth through 2005, eventually eclipsing activity in the conforming market. In 2006, non-agency production of $1.480 trillion was more than 45 percent larger than agency production, and non-agency issuance of $1.033 trillion was larger than agency issuance of $905 billion.

Table 1-1. Origination and Issue of Non-Agency Mortgage Loans

Year	Sub-prime Origina-tion $	Sub-prime Issu-ance $	Sub-prime Ratio %	Alt-A Origin-ation $	Alt-A Issu-ance $	Alt-A Ratio %	Jumbo Origina-tion $	Jumbo Issu-ance $	Jumbo Ratio %	Agency Origin-ation $	Agency Issu-ance $	Agency Ratio %
2001	190.00	87.10	46	60.00	11.40	19	430.00	142.20	33	1,433.00	1,087.60	76
2002	231.00	122.70	53	68.00	53.50	79	576.00	171.50	30	1,898.00	1,442.60	76

[2] This limit is currently $417,000.

2003	335.00	195.00	58	85.00	74.10	87	655.00	237.50	36	2,690.00	2,130.90	79
2004	540.00	362.63	67	200.00	158.60	79	515.00	233.40	45%	1,345.00	1,018.60	76
2005	625.00	465.00	74	380.00	332.30	87	570.00	280.70	49%	1,180.00	964.80	82
2006	600.00	448.60	75	400.00	365.70	91	480.00	219.00	46%	1,040.00	904.60	87

Source: Inside Mortgage Finance (2007).
Notes: Jumbo origination includes non-agency prime. Agency origination includes conventional/conforming and FHA/VA loans. Agency issuance GNMA, FHLMC, and FNMA. Figures are in billions of USD.

Interestingly, the increase in Subprime and Alt-A origination was associated with a significant increase in the ratio of issuance to origination, which is a reasonable proxy for the fraction of loans sold. In particular, the ratio of subprime MBS issuance to subprime mortgage origination was close to 75 percent in both 2005 and 2006. While there is typically a one-quarter lag between origination and issuance, the data document that a large and increasing fraction of both subprime and Alt-A loans are sold to investors, and very little is retained on the balance sheets of the institutions who originate them. The process through which loans are removed from the balance sheet of lenders and transformed into debt securities purchased by investors is called securitization.

2.1. The Seven Key Frictions

The securitization of mortgage loans is a complex process that involves a number of different players. Figure 1 provides an overview of the players, their responsibilities, the important frictions that exist between the players, and the mechanisms used in order to mitigate these frictions. An overarching friction which plagues every step in the process is asymmetric information: usually one party has more information about the asset than another. We think that understanding these frictions and evaluating the mechanisms designed to mitigate their importance is essential to understanding how the securitization of subprime loans could generate bad outcomes.[3]

2.1.1. Frictions Between the Mortgagor and Originator: Predatory Lending

The process starts with the mortgagor or borrower, who applies for a mortgage in order to purchase a property or to refinance and existing mortgage. The originator, possibly through a broker (yet another intermediary in this process), underwrites and initially funds and services the mortgage loans. Table 2 documents the top 10 subprime originators in 2006, which are a healthy mix of commercial banks and non-depository specialized monc-line lenders. The originator is compensated through fees paid by the borrower (points and closing costs), and by the proceeds of the sale of the mortgage loans. For example, the originator might sell a portfolio of loans with an initial principal balance of $100 million for $102 million, corresponding to a gain on sale of $2 million. The buyer is willing to pay this premium because of anticipated interest payments on the principal.

3 A recent piece in *The Economist* (September 20, 2007) provides a nice description of some of the frictions described here.

Table 1-2. Top Subprime Mortgage Originators

		2006		2005	
Rank	Lender	Volume ($b)	Share (%)	Volume ($b)	%Change
1	HSBC	$52.8	8.8%	$58.6	– 9.9%
2	New Century Financial	$51.6	8.6%	$52.7	– 2.1%
3	Countrywide	$40.6	6.8%	$44.6	– 9.1%
4	CitiGroup	$38.0	6.3%	$20.5	85.5%
5	WMC Mortgage	$33.2	5.5%	$31.8	4.3%
6	Fremont	$32.3	5.4%	$36.2	– 10.9%
7	Ameriquest Mortgage	$29.5	4.9%	$75.6	– 61.0%
8	Option One	$28.8	4.8%	$40.3	– 28.6%
9	Wells Fargo	$27.9	4.6%	$30.3	– 8.1%
10	First Franklin	$27.7	4.6%	$29.3	– 5.7%
	Top 25	$543.2	90.5%	$604.9	– 10.2%
	Total	$600.0	100.0%	$664.0	– 9.8%

Source: Inside Mortgage Finance (2007)

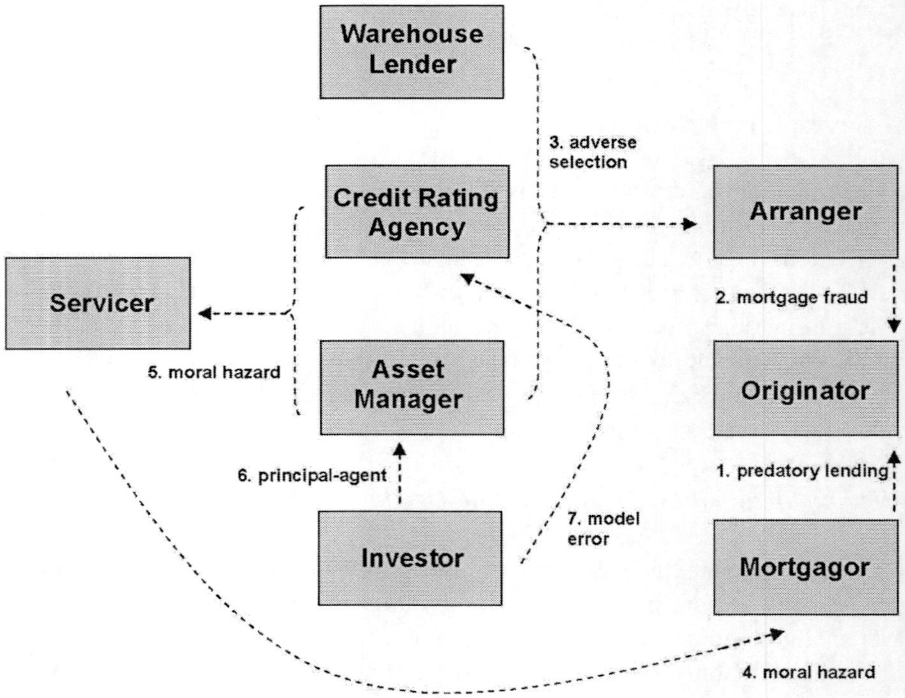

Figure 1: Key Players and Frictions in Subprime Mortgage Credit Securitization

The first friction in securitization is between the borrower and the originator. In particular, subprime borrowers can be financially unsophisticated. For example, a borrower might be unaware of all of the financial options available to him. Moreover, even if these options are known, the borrower might be unable to make a choice between different financial options that is in his own best interest. This friction leads to the possibility of predatory lending, defined by Morgan (2005) as the welfare-reducing provision of credit. The main safeguards against these practices are federal, state, and local laws prohibiting certain lending practices, as well as the recent regulatory guidance on subprime lending. See Appendix 1 for further discussion of these issues.

2.1.2. Frictions Between the Originator and the Arranger: Predatory Lending and Borrowing

The pool of mortgage loans is typically purchased from the originator by an institution known as the arranger or issuer. The first responsibility of the arranger is to conduct due diligence on the originator. This review includes but is not limited to financial statements, underwriting guidelines, discussions with senior management, and background checks. The arranger is responsible for bringing together all the elements for the deal to close. In particular, the arranger creates a bankruptcy-remote trust that will purchase the mortgage loans, consults with the credit rating agencies in order to finalize the details about deal structure, makes necessary filings with the SEC, and underwrites the issuance of securities by the trust to investors. Table 3 documents the list of the top 10 subprime MBS issuers in 2006. In addition to institutions which both originate and issue on their own, the list of issuers also includes investment banks that purchase mortgages from originators and issue their own securities. The arranger is typically compensated through fees charged to investors and through any premium that investors pay on the issued securities over their par value.

Table 1-3. Top Subprime MBS Issuers

		2006		2005	
Rank	**Lender**	**Volume ($b)**	**Share (%)**	**Volume ($b)**	**%Change**
1	Countrywide	$38.5	8.6%	$38.1	1.1%
2	New Century	$33.9	7.6%	$32.4	4.8%
3	Option One	$31.3	7.0%	$27.2	15.1%
4	Fremont	$29.8	6.6%	$19.4	53.9%
5	Washington Mutual	$28.8	6.4%	$18.5	65.1%
6	First Franklin	$28.3	6.3%	$19.4	45.7%
7	Residential Funding Corp	$25.9	5.8%	$28.7	– 9.5%
8	Lehman Brothers	$24.4	5.4%	$35.3	– 30.7%
9	WMC Mortgage	$21.6	4.8%	$19.6	10.5%
10	Ameriquest	$21.4	4.8%	$54.2	– 60.5%
	Top 25	$427.6	95.3%	$417.6	2.4%
	Total	$448.6	100.0%	$503.0	– 11.7%

Source: Inside Mortgage Finance (2007)

Table 1-4. Top Subprime Mortgage Servicers

		2006		2005	
Rank	Lender	Volume ($b)	Share (%)	Volume ($b)	%Change
1	Countrywide	$119.1	9.6%	$120.6	– 1.3%
2	JP MorganChase	$83.8	6.8%	$67.8	23.6%
3	CitiGroup	$80.1	6.5%	$47.3	39.8%
4	Option One	$69.0	5.6%	$79.5	– 13.2%
5	Ameriquest	$60.0	4.8%	$75.4	– 20.4%
6	Ocwen Financial Corp	$52.2	4.2%	$42.0	24.2%
7	Wells Fargo	$51.3	4.1%	$44.7	14.8%
8	Homecomings Financial	$49.5	4.0%	$55.2	– 10.4%
9	HSBC	$49..5	4.0%	$43.8	13.0%
10	Litton Loan Servicing	$47.0	4.0%	$42.0	16.7%
	Top 30	$1,105.7	89.2%	$1,057.8	4.5%
	Total	$1,240	100.0%	$1,200	3.3%

Source: Inside Mortgage Finance (2007)

The second friction in the process of securitization involves an information problem between the originator and arranger. In particular, the originator has an information advantage over the arranger with regard to the quality of the borrower. Without adequate safeguards in place, an originator can have the incentive to collaborate with a borrower in order to make significant misrepresentations on the loan application, which, depending on the situation, could be either construed as predatory lending (the lender convinces the borrower to borrow "too much) or predatory borrowing (the borrower convinces the lender to lend "too much"). See Appendix 2 on predatory borrowing for further discussion.

There are several important checks designed to prevent mortgage fraud, the first being the due diligence of the arranger. In addition, the originator typically makes a number of representations and warranties (R&W) about the borrower and the underwriting process. When these are violated, the originator generally must repurchase the problem loans. However, in order for these promises to have a meaningful impact on the friction, the originator must have adequate capital to buy back those problem loans. Moreover, when an arranger does not conduct or routinely ignores its own due diligence, as suggested in a recent Reuters piece by Rucker (1 Aug 2007), there is little to stop the originator from committing widespread mortgage fraud.

2.1.3. Frictions between the Arranger and Third-parties: Adverse Selection

There is an important information asymmetry between the arranger and third-parties concerning the quality of mortgage loans. In particular, the fact that the arranger has more information about the quality of the mortgage loans creates an adverse selection problem: the arranger can securitize bad loans (the lemons) and keep the good ones (or securitize them elsewhere). This third friction in the securitization of subprime loans affects the relationship that the arranger has with the warehouse lender, the credit rating agency (CRA), and the asset manager. We discuss how each of these parties responds to this classic lemons problem.

Adverse Selection and the Warehouse Lender

The arranger is responsible for funding the mortgage loans until all of the details of the securitization deal can be finalized. When the arranger is a depository institution, this can be done easily with internal funds. However, mono-line arrangers typically require funding from a third-party lender for loans kept in the "warehouse" until they can be sold. Since the lender is uncertain about the value of the mortgage loans, it must take steps to protect itself against overvaluing their worth as collateral. This is accomplished through due diligence by the lender, haircuts to the value of collateral, and credit spreads. The use of haircuts to the value of collateral imply that the bank loan is over-collateralized (o/c) – it might extend a $9 million loan against collateral of $10 million of underlying mortgages –, forcing the arranger to assume a funded equity position – in this case $1 million – in the loans while they remain on its balance sheet.

We emphasize this friction because an adverse change in the warehouse lender's views of the value of the underlying loans can bring an originator to its knees. The failure of dozens of mono-line originators in the first half of 2007 can be explained in large part by the inability of these firms to respond to increased demands for collateral by warehouse lenders (Wei, 2007; Sichelman, 2007).

Adverse Selection and the Asset Manager

The pool of mortgage loans is sold by the arranger to a bankruptcy-remote trust, which is a special-purpose vehicle that issues debt to investors. This trust is an essential component of credit risk transfer, as it protects investors from bankruptcy of the originator or arranger. Moreover, the sale of loans to the trust protects both the originator and arranger from losses on the mortgage loans, provided that there have been no breaches of representations and warranties made by the originator.

The arranger underwrites the sale of securities secured by the pool of subprime mortgage loans to an asset manager, who is an agent for the ultimate investor. However, the information advantage of the arranger creates a standard lemons problem. This problem is mitigated by the market through the following means: reputation of the arranger, the arranger providing a credit enhancement to the securities with its own funding, and any due diligence conducted by the portfolio manager on the arranger and originator.

Adverse Selection and Credit Rating Agencies

The rating agencies assign credit ratings on mortgage-backed securities issued by the trust. These opinions about credit quality are determined using publicly available rating criteria which map the characteristics of the pool of mortgage loans into an estimated loss distribution. From this loss distribution, the rating agencies calculate the amount of credit enhancement that a security requires in order for it to attain a given credit rating. The opinion of the rating agencies is vulnerable to the lemons problem (the arranger likely still knows more) because they only conduct limited due diligence on the arranger and originator.

2.1.4. Frictions between the Servicer and the Mortgagor: Moral Hazard

The trust employs a servicer who is responsible for collection and remittance of loan payments, making advances of unpaid interest by borrowers to the trust, accounting for principal and interest, customer service to the mortgagors, holding escrow or impounding funds related to payment of taxes and insurance, contacting delinquent borrowers, and supervising foreclosures and property dispositions. The servicer is compensated through a periodic fee by paid the trust. Table 4 documents the top 10 subprime servicers in 2006, which is a mix of depository institutions and specialty non-depository mono-line servicing companies.

Moral hazard refers to changes in behavior in response to redistribution of risk, e.g., insurance may induce risk-taking behavior if the insured does not bear the full consequences of bad outcomes. Here we have a problem where one party (the mortgagor) has unobserved costly effort that affects the distribution over cash flows which are shared with another party (the servicer), and the first party has limited liability (it does not share in downside risk). In managing delinquent loans, the servicer is faced with a standard moral hazard problem vis-à-vis the mortgagor. When a servicer has the incentive to work in investors' best interest, it will manage delinquent loans in a fashion to minimize losses. A mortgagor struggling to make a mortgage payment is also likely struggling to keep hazard insurance and property tax bills current, as well as conduct adequate maintenance on the property. The failure to pay property taxes could result in costly liens on the property that increase the costs to investors of ultimately foreclosing on the property. The failure to pay hazard insurance premiums could result in a lapse in coverage, exposing investors to the risk of significant loss. And the failure to maintain the property will increase expenses to investors in marketing the property after foreclosure and possibly reduce the sale price. The mortgagor has little incentive to expend effort or resources to maintain a property close to foreclosure.

In order to prevent these potential problems from surfacing, it is standard practice to require the mortgagor to regularly escrow funds for both insurance and property taxes. When the borrower fails to advance these funds, the servicer is typically required to make these payments on behalf of the investor. In order to prevent lapses in maintenance from creating losses, the servicer is encouraged to foreclose promptly on the property once it is deemed uncollectible. An important constraint in resolving this latter issue is that the ability of a servicer to collect on a delinquent debt is generally restricted under the Real Estate Settlement Procedures Act, Fair Debt Collection Practices Act and state deceptive trade practices statutes. In a recent court case, a plaintiff in Texas alleging unlawful collection activities against Ocwen Financial was awarded $12.5 million in actual and punitive damages.

2.1.5. Frictions between the Servicer and Third-parties: Moral Hazard

The servicer can have a significantly positive or negative effect on the losses realized from the mortgage pool. Moody's estimates that servicer quality can affect the realized level of losses by plus or minus 10 percent. This impact of servicer quality on losses has important implications for both investors and credit rating agencies. In particular, investors want to minimize losses while credit rating agencies want to minimize the uncertainty about losses in order to make accurate opinions. In each case articulated below we have a similar problem as in the fourth friction, namely where one party (here the servicer) has unobserved costly effort that affects the distribution over cash flows which are shared with other parties, and the first party has limited liability (it does not share in downside risk).

Moral Hazard between the Servicer and the Asset Manager[4]

The servicing fee is a flat percentage of the outstanding principal balance of mortgage loans. The servicer is paid first out of receipts each month before any funds are advanced to investors. Since mortgage payments are generally received at the beginning of the month and investors receive their distributions near the end of the month, the servicer benefits from being able to earn interest on float.[5]

There are two key points of tension between investors and the servicer: (a) reasonable reimbursable expenses, and (b) the decision to modify and foreclose. We discuss each of these in turn.

In the event of a delinquency, the servicer must advance unpaid interest (and sometimes principal) to the trust as long as it is deemed collectable, which typically means that the loan is less than 90 days delinquent. In addition to advancing unpaid interest, the servicer must also keep paying property taxes and insurance premiums as long as it has a mortgage on the property. In the event of foreclosure, the servicer must pay all expenses out of pocket until the property is liquidated, at which point it is reimbursed for advances and expenses. The servicer has a natural incentive to inflate expenses, especially in good times when recovery rates on foreclosed property are high.

Note that the un-reimbursable expenses of the servicer are largely fixed and front-loaded: registering the loan in the servicing system, getting the initial notices out, doing the initial escrow analysis and tax setups, etc. At the same time, the income of the servicer is increasing in the amount of time that the loan is serviced. It follows that the servicer would prefer to keep the loan on its books for as long as possible. This means it has a strong preference to modify the terms of a delinquent loan and to delay foreclosure.

Resolving each of these problems involves a delicate balance. On the one hand, one can put hard rules into the pooling and servicing agreement limiting loan modifications, and an investor can invest effort into actively monitoring the servicer's expenses. On the other hand, the investor wants to give the servicer flexibility to act in the investor's best interest and does not want to incur too much expense in monitoring. This latter point is especially true since other investors will free-ride off of any one investor's effort. It is not surprising that the credit rating agencies play an important role in resolving this collective action problem through servicer quality ratings.

In addition to monitoring effort by investors, servicer quality ratings, and rules about loan modifications, there are two other important ways to mitigate this friction: servicer reputation and the master servicer. As the servicing business is an important counter-cyclical source of income for banks, one would think that these institutions would work hard on their own to minimize this friction. The master servicer is responsible for monitoring the performance of

4 Several points raised in this section were first raised in a 20 February 2007 post on the blog http://calculatedrisk.blogspot.com/_entitled "Mortgage Servicing for Ubernerds."

5 In addition to the monthly fee, the servicer generally gets to keep late fees. This can tempt a servicer to post payments in a tardy fashion or not make collection calls until late fees are assessed.

the servicer under the pooling and servicing agreement. It validates data reported by the servicer, reviews the servicing of defaulted loans, and enforces remedies of servicer default on behalf of the trust.

Moral Hazard between the Servicer and the Credit Rating Agency

Given the impact of servicer quality on losses, the accuracy of the credit rating placed on securities issued by the trust is vulnerable to the use of a low quality servicer. In order to minimize the impact of this friction, the rating agencies conduct due diligence on the servicer, use the results of this analysis in the rating of mortgage-backed securities, and release their findings to the public for use by investors.

Servicer quality ratings are intended to be an unbiased benchmark of a loan servicer's ability to prevent or mitigate pool losses across changing market conditions. This evaluation includes an assessment of collections/customer service, loss mitigation, foreclosure timeline management, management, staffing & training, financial stability, technology and disaster recovery, legal compliance and oversight and financial strength. In constructing these quality ratings, the rating agency attempts to break out the actual historical loss experience of the servicer into an amount attributable to the underlying credit risk of the loans and an amount attributable to the servicer's collection and default management ability.

2.1.6. Frictions between the Asset Manager and Investor: Principal-Agent

The investor provides the funding for the purchase of the mortgage-backed security. As the investor is typically financially unsophisticated, an agent is employed to formulate an investment strategy, conduct due diligence on potential investments, and find the best price for trades. Given differences in the degree of financial sophistication between the investor and an asset manager, there is an obvious information problem between the investor and portfolio manger that gives rise to the sixth friction.

In particular, the investor will not fully understand the investment strategy of the manager, has uncertainty about the manager's ability, and does not observe any effort that the manager makes to conduct due diligence. This principal (investor)-agent (manager) problem is mitigated through the use of investment mandates, and the evaluation of manager performance relative to a peer benchmark or its peers.

As one example, a public pension might restrict the investments of an asset manager to debt securities with an investment grade credit rating and evaluate the performance of an asset manager relative to a benchmark index. However, there are other relevant examples. The FDIC, which is an implicit investor in commercial banks through the provision of deposit insurance, prevents insured banks from investing in speculative-grade securities or enforces risk-based capital requirements that use credit ratings to assess risk-weights. An actively-managed collateralized debt obligation (CDO) imposes covenants on the weighted average rating of securities in an actively-managed portfolio as well as the fraction of securities with a low credit rating.

As investment mandates typically involve credit ratings, it should be clear that this is another point where the credit rating agencies play an important role in the securitization process. By presenting an opinion on the riskiness of offered securities, the rating agencies help resolve the information frictions that exist between the investor and the portfolio manager. Credit ratings are intended to capture the expectations about the long-run or through-the-cycle performance of a debt security. A credit rating is fundamentally a statement about the suitability of an instrument to be included in a risk class, but importantly, it is an opinion only about credit risk; we discuss credit ratings in more detail in Section 5.1. It follows that the opinion of credit rating agencies is a crucial part of securitization, because in the end the rating is the means through which much of the funding by investors finds its way into the deal.

2.1.7. Frictions between the Investor and the Credit Rating Agencies: Model Error

The rating agencies are paid by the arranger and not investors for their opinion, which creates a potential conflict of interest. Since an investor is not able to assess the efficacy of rating agency models, they are susceptible to both honest and dishonest errors on the agencies' part. The information asymmetry between investors and the credit rating agencies is the seventh and final friction in the securitization process. Honest errors are a natural byproduct of rapid financial innovation and complexity. On the other hand, dishonest errors could be driven by the dependence of rating agencies on fees paid by the arranger (the conflict of interest).

Some critics claim that the rating agencies are unable to objectively rate structured products due to conflicts of interest created by issuer-paid fees. Moody's, for example, made 44 per cent of its revenue last year from structured finance deals (Tomlinson and Evans, 2007). Such assessments also command more than double the fee rates of simpler corporate ratings, helping keep Moody's operating margins above 50 per cent (Economist, 2007).

Beales, Scholtes and Tett (15 May 2007) write in the *Financial Times*:

The potential for conflicts of interest in the agencies' "issuer pays" model has drawn fire before, but the scale of their dependence on investment banks for structured finance business gives them a significant incentive to look kindly on the products they are rating, critics say. From his office in Paris, the head of the Autorité des Marchés Financiers, the main French financial regulator, is raising fresh questions over their role and objectivity. Mr Prada sees the possibility for conflicts of interest similar to those that emerged in the audit profession when it drifted into consulting. Here, the integrity of the auditing work was threatened by the demands of winning and retaining clients in the more lucrative consultancy business, a conflict that ultimately helped bring down accountants Arthur Andersen in the wake of Enron's collapse. "I do hope that it does not take another Enron for everyone to look at the issue of rating agencies," he says.

This friction is minimized through two devices: the reputation of the rating agencies and the public disclosure of ratings and downgrade criteria. For the rating agencies, their business is their reputation, so it is difficult – though not impossible – to imagine that they would risk deliberately inflating credit ratings in order to earn structuring fees, thus jeopardizing their franchise. Moreover, with public rating and downgrade criteria, any deviations in credit ratings from their models are easily observed by the public.[6]

---

[6] We think that there are two ways these errors could emerge. One, the rating agency builds its model honestly, but then applies judgment in a fashion consistent with its economic interest. The average deal is structured

2.2. Five Frictions that Caused the Subprime Crisis

We believe that five of the seven frictions discussed above help to explain the breakdown in the subprime mortgage market.

The problem starts with friction #1: many products offered to sub-prime borrowers are very complex and subject to mis-understanding and/or mis-representation. This opened the possibility of both excessive borrowing (predatory borrowing) and excessive lending (predatory lending.

At the other end of the process we have the principal-agent problem between the investor and asset manager (friction #6). In particular, it seems that investment mandates do not adequately distinguish between structured and corporate credit ratings. This is a problem because asset manager performance is evaluated relative to peers or relative to a benchmark index. It follows that asset managers have an incentive to reach for yield by purchasing structured debt issues with the same credit rating but higher coupons as corporate debt issues.[7]

Initially, this portfolio shift was likely led by asset managers with the ability to conduct their own due diligence, recognizing value in the wide pricing of subprime mortgage-backed securities. However, once the other asset managers started to under-perform their peers, they likely made similar portfolio shifts, but did not invest the same effort into due diligence of the arranger and originator.

This phenomenon worsened the friction between the arranger and the asset manager (friction #3). In particular, without due diligence by the asset manager, the arranger's incentives to conduct its own due diligence are reduced. Moreover, as the market for credit derivatives developed, including but not limited to the ABX, the arranger was able to limit its funded exposure to securitizations of risky loans. Together, these considerations worsened the friction between the originator and arranger, opening the door for predatory borrowing and provides incentives for predatory lending (friction #2). In the end, the only constraint on underwriting standards was the opinion of the rating agencies. With limited capital backing representations and warranties, an originator could easily arbitrage rating agency models, exploiting the weak historical relationship between aggressive underwriting and losses in the data used to calibrate required credit enhancement.

The inability of the rating agencies to recognize this arbitrage by originators and respond appropriately meant that credit ratings were assigned to subprime mortgage-backed securities with significant error. The friction between investors and the rating agencies is the final nail in the coffin (friction #7). Even though the rating agencies publicly disclosed their rating criteria for subprime, investors lacked the ability to evaluate the efficacy of these models.

While we have identified seven frictions in the mortgage securitization process, there are mechanisms in place to mitigate or even resolve each of these frictions, including for example anti-predatory lending laws and regulations. As we have seen, some of these mechanisms have failed to deliver as promised. Is it hard to fix this process? We believe not, and we think the solution might start with investment mandates. Investors should realize the incentives of asset managers to push for yield. Investments in structured products should be compared to a

appropriately, but the agency gives certain issuers better terms. Two, the model itself is knowingly aggressive. The average deal is structured inadequately.

benchmark index of investments in the same asset class. When investors or asset managers are forced to conduct their own due diligence in order to outperform the index, the incentives of the arranger and originator are restored. Moreover, investors should demand that either the arranger or originator – or even both – retain the first-loss or equity tranche of every securitization, and disclose all hedges of this position. At the end of the production chain, originators need to be adequately capitalized so that their representations and warranties have value. Finally, the rating agencies could evaluate originators with the same rigor that they evaluate servicers, including perhaps the designation of originator ratings.

It is not clear to us that any of these solutions require additional regulation, and note that the market is already taking steps in the right direction. For example, the credit rating agencies have already responded with greater transparency and have announced significant changes in the rating process. In addition, the demand for structured credit products generally and subprime mortgage securitizations in particular has declined significantly as investors have started to re-assess their own views of the risk in these products. Along these lines, it may be advisable for policymakers to give the market a chance to self-correct.

3. An Overview of Subprime Mortgage Credit

In this section, we shed some light on the subprime mortgagor, work through the details of a typical subprime mortgage loan, and review the historical performance of subprime mortgage credit.

The Motivating Example

In order to keep the discussion from becoming too abstract, we find it useful to frame many of these issues in the context of a real-life example which will be used throughout the paper. In particular, we focus on a securitization of 3,949 subprime loans with aggregate principal balance of $881 million originated by New Century Financial in the second quarter of 2006.[8]

Our view is that this particular securitization is interesting because illustrates how typical subprime loans from what proved to be the worst-performing vintage came to be originated, structured, and ultimately sold to investors. In each of the years 2004 to 2006, New Century Financial was the second largest subprime lender, originating $51.6 billion in mortgage loans during 2006 (Inside Mortgage Finance, 2007). Volume grew at a compound annual growth rate of 59% between 2000 and 2004. The backbone of this growth was an automated internet-based loan submission and pre-approval system called *FastQual*. The performance of New Century loans closely tracked that of the industry through the 2005 vintage (Moody's, 2005b). However, the company struggled with early payment defaults in early 2007, failed to meet a call for more collateral on its warehouse lines of credit on 2 March 2007 and

---

[7] The fact that the market demands a higher yield for similarly rated structured products than for straight corporate bonds ought to provide a clue to the potential of higher risk.

[8] The details of this transaction are taken from the prospectus filed with the SEC and with monthly remittance reports filed with the Trustee. The former is available on-line using the Edgar database at http://www.sec.gov/edgar/searchedgar/companysearch.html with the company name GSAMP Trust 2006-NC2 while the latter is available with free registration from http://www.absnet.net/.

ultimately filed for bankruptcy protection on 2 April 2007. The junior tranches of this securitization were part of the historical downgrade action by the rating agencies during the week of 9 July 2007 that affected almost half of first-lien home equity ABS deals issued in 2006.

As illustrated in Figure 2, these loans were initially purchased by a subsidiary of Goldman Sachs, who in turn sold the loans to a bankruptcy-remote special purpose vehicle named GSAMP TRUST 2006-NC2. The trust funded the purchase of these loans through the issue of asset-backed securities, which required the filing of a prospectus with the SEC detailing the transaction. New Century serviced the loans initially, but upon creation of the trust, this business was transferred to Ocwen Loan Servicing, LLC in August 2006, who receives a fee of 50 basis points (or $4.4 million) per year on a monthly basis. The master servicer and securities administrator is Wells Fargo, who receives a fee of 1 basis point (or $881K) per year on a monthly basis. The prospectus includes a list of 26 reps and warranties made by the originator. Some of the items include: the absence of any delinquencies or defaults in the pool; compliance of the mortgages with federal, state, and local laws; the presence of title and hazard insurance; disclosure of fees and points to the borrower; statement that the lender did not encourage or require the borrower to select a higher cost loan product intended for less creditworthy borrowers when they qualified for a more standard loan product.

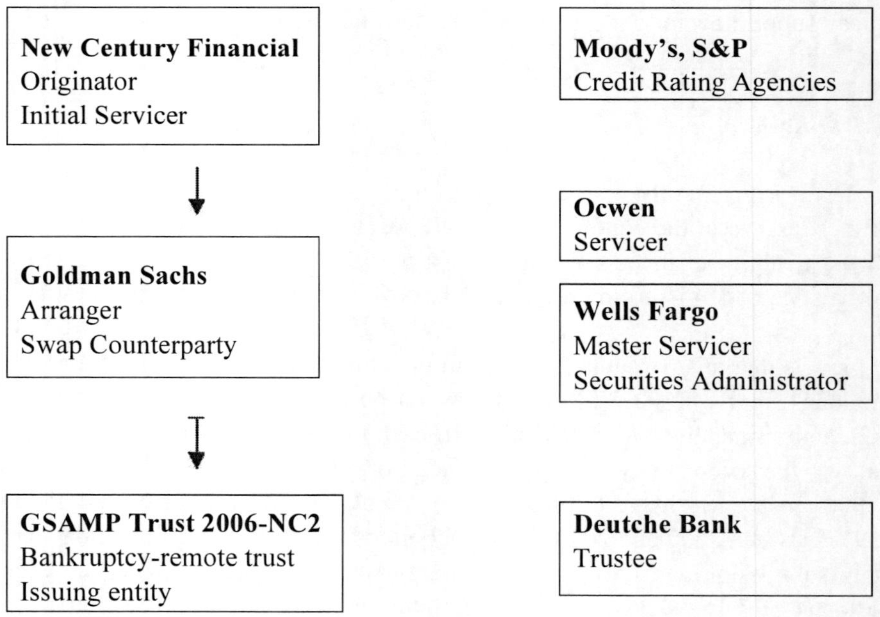

Figure 2: Key Institutions Surrounding GSAMP Trust 2006-NC2

Source: Prospectus filed with the SEC of GSAMP 2006-NC2

3.1. Who is the Subprime Mortgagor?

The 2001 *Interagency Expanded Guidance for Subprime Lending Programs* defines the subprime borrower as one who generally displays a range of credit risk characteristics, including one or more of the following:

- Two or more 30-day delinquencies in the last 12 months, or one or more 60-day delinquencies in the last 24 months;
- Judgment, foreclosure, repossession, or charge-off in the prior 24 months;
- Bankruptcy in the last 5 years;
- Relatively high default probability as evidenced by, for example, a credit bureau risk score (FICO) of 660 or below (depending on the product/collateral), or other bureau or proprietary scores with an equivalent default probability likelihood; and/or,
- Debt service-to-income ratio of 50 percent or greater; or, otherwise limited ability to cover family living expenses after deducting total debt-service requirements from monthly income.

The Motivating Example

The pool of mortgage loans used as collateral in the New Century securitization can be summarized as follows:

- 98.7% of the mortgage loans are first-lien. The rest are second-lien home equity loans.
- 43.3% are purchase loans, meaning that the mortgagor's stated purpose for the loan was to purchase a property. The remaining loans' stated purpose are cash-out refinance of existing mortgage loans.
- 90.7% of the mortgagors claim to occupy the property as their primary residence. The remaining mortgagors claim to be investors or purchasing second homes.
- 73.4% of the mortgaged properties are single-family homes. The remaining properties are split between multi-family dwellings or condos.
- 38.0% and 10.5% are secured by residences in California and Florida, respectively, the two dominant states in this securitization.
- The average borrower in the pool has a FICO score of 626. Note that 31.4% have a FICO score below 600, 51.9% between 600 and 660, and 16.7% above 660.
- The combined loan-to value ratio is sum of the original principal balance of all loans secured by the property to its appraised value. The average mortgage loan in the pool has a CLTV of 80.34%. However, 62.1% have a CLTV of 80% or lower, 28.6% between 80% and 90%, and 9.3% between 90% and 100%.
- The ratio of total debt service of the borrower (including the mortgage, property taxes and insurance, and other monthly debt payments) to gross income (income before taxes) is 41.78%.

It is worth pausing here to make a few observations. First, the stated purpose of the majority of these loans is not to purchase a home, but rather to refinance an existing mortgage loan. Second, 90 percent of the borrowers in this portfolio have at least 10 percent equity in their homes. Third, while it might be surprising to find borrowers with a FICO score above 660 in the pool, these loans are much more aggressively underwritten than the loans to the lower FICO-score borrowers. In particular, while not reported in the figures above, loans to borrowers with high FICO scores tend to be much larger, have a higher CLTV, are less likely to use full-documentation, and are less likely to be owner-occupied. The combination of good credit with aggressive underwriting suggests that many of these borrowers could be investors looking to take advantage of rapid home price appreciation in order to re-sell houses for profit. Finally, while the average loan size in the pool is $223,221, much of the aggregate principal balance of the pool is made up of large loans. In particular, 24% of the total number of loans are in excess of $300,000 and make up about 45% of the principal balance of the pool.

Industry trends

Table 5 documents average borrower characteristics for loans contained in Alt-A and Subprime MBS pools in panel (a) and (b), respectively, broken out by year of origination. The most dramatic difference between the two panels is the credit score, as the average Alt-A borrower has a FICO score that is 85 points higher than the average Subprime borrower in 2006 (703 versus 623). Subprime borrowers typically have a higher CLTV, but are more likely to document income and are less likely to purchase a home. Alt-A borrowers are more likely to be investors and are more likely to have silent 2nd liens on the property. Together, these summary statistics suggest that the example securitization discussed seems to be representative of the industry, at least with respect to stated borrower characteristics.

3.2. What is a Subprime Loan?

The motivating example

Table 6 documents that only 8.98% of the loans by dollar-value in the New Century pool are traditional 30-year fixed-rate mortgages (FRMs). The pool also includes a small fraction – 2.81% -- of fixed-rate mortgages which amortize over 40 years, but mature in 30 years, and consequently have a balloon payment after 30 years. Note that 88.2% of the mortgage loans by dollar value are adjustable-rate loans (ARMs), and that each of these loans is a variation on the 2/28 and 3/27 hybrid ARM. These loans are known as hybrids because they have both fixed- and adjustable-rate features to them. In particular, the initial monthly payment is based on a "teaser" interest rate that is fixed for the first two (for the 2/28) or three (for the 3/27) years, and is lower than what a borrower would pay for a 30-year fixed rate mortgage (FRM). The table documents that the average initial interest rate for a vanilla 2/28 loan in the first row is 8.64%. However, after this initial period, the monthly payment is based on a higher interest rate, equal to the value of an interest rate index (i.e. 6-month LIBOR) measured at the time of adjustment, plus a margin that is fixed for the life of the loan. Focusing again on the first 2/28, the margin is 6.22% and LIBOR at the time of origination is 5.31%. This interest rate is updated every six months for the life of the loan, and is subject to limits called adjustment caps on the amount that it can increase: the cap on the first adjustment is called the initial cap;

the cap on each subsequent adjustment is called the period cap; the cap on the interest rate over the life of the loan is called the lifetime cap; and the floor on the interest rate is called the floor. In our example of a simple 2/28 ARM, these caps are equal to 1.49%, 1.50%, 15.62%, and 8.62% for the average loan. More than half of the dollar value of the loans in this pool are a 2/28 ARM with a 40-year amortization schedule in order to calculate monthly payments. A substantial fraction are a 2/28 ARM with a five-year interest-only option. This loan permits the borrower to only pay interest for the first sixty months of the loan, but then must make payments in order to repay the loan in the final 25 years. While not noted in the table, the prospectus indicates that none of the mortgage loans carry mortgage insurance. Moreover, approximately 72.5% of the loans include prepayment penalties which expire after one to three years.

Table 1-5. Underwriting Characteristics of Loans in MBS Pools

	CLTV	Full Doc	Purchase	Investor	No Prepayment Penalty	FICO	Silent 2nd lien
A. Alt-A Loans							
1999	77.5	38.4	51.8	18.6	79.4	696	0.1
2000	80.2	35.4	68.0	13.8	79.0	697	0.2
2001	77.7	34.8	50.4	8.2	78.8	703	1.4
2002	76.5	36.0	47.4	12.5	70.1	708	2.4
2003	74.9	33.0	39.4	18.5	71.2	711	12.4
2004	79.5	32.4	53.9	17.0	64.8	708	28.6
2005	79.0	27.4	49.4	14.8	56.9	713	32.4
2006	80.6	16.4	45.7	12.9	47.9	708	38.9
B. Subprime Loans							
1999	78.8	68.7	30.1	5.3	28.7	605	0.5
2000	79.5	73.4	36.2	5.5	25.4	596	1.3
2001	80.3	71.5	31.3	5.3	21.0	605	2.8
2002	80.7	65.9	29.9	5.4	20.3	614	2.9
2003	82.4	63.9	30.2	5.6	23.2	624	7.3
2004	83.9	62.2	35.7	5.6	24.6	624	15.8
2005	85.3	58.3	40.5	5.5	26.8	627	24.6
2006	85.5	57.7	42.1	5.6	28.9	623	27.5

All entries are in percentage points except FICO.
Source: LoanPerformance (2007)

These ARMs are rather complex financial instruments with payout features often found in interest rate derivatives. In contrast to a FRM, the mortgagor retains most of the interest rate risk, subject to a collar (a floor and a cap). Note that most mortgagors are not in a position to easily hedge away this interest rate risk.

Table 1-6. Loan Type in the GSAMP 2006-NC2 Mortgage Loan Pool

Loan Type	Gross Rate	Margin	Initial Cap	Periodic Cap	Lifetime Cap	Floor	IO Period	Notional ($m)	% Total
FIXED	8.18	X	X	X	X	X	X	79.12	8.98
FIXED 40-year Balloon	7.58	X	X	X	X	X	X	24.80	2.81
2/28 ARM	8.64	6.22	1.49	1.49	15.62	8.62	X	221.09	25.08
2/28 ARM 40-year Balloon	8.31	6.24	1.5	1.5	15.31	8.31	X	452.15	51.29
2/28 ARM IO	7.75	6.13	1.5	1.5	14.75	7.75	60	101.18	11.48
3/27 ARM	7.48	6.06	1.5	1.5	14.48	7.48	X	1.71	0.19
3/27 ARM 40-year Balloon	7.61	6.11	1.5	1.5	14.61	7.61	X	1.46	0.17
Total	8.29	X	X	X	X	X	X	881.50	100.00

Note: LIBOR is 5.31% at the time of issue. Notional amount is reported in millions of dollars.
Source: SEC filings, Author's calculations

Table 7 illustrates the monthly payment across loan type, using the average terms for each loan type, a principal balance of $225,000, and making the assumption that six-month LIBOR remains constant. The payment for the 30-year mortgage amortized over 40 years is lower due to the longer amortization period and a lower average interest rate. The latter loan is more risky from a lender's point of view because the borrower's equity builds more slowly and the borrower will likely have to refinance after 30 years or have cash equal to 84 monthly payments. The monthly payment for the 2/28 ARM is documented in the third column. When the index interest rate remains constant, the payment increases by 14% in the month 25 at initial adjustment and by another 12% in month 31. When amortized over 40 years, as in the fourth column, the payment shock is more severe as the loan balance is much higher in every month compared to the 30-year amortization. In particular, the payment increases by 18% in month 25 and another 14% in month 31. However, when the 2/28 is combined with an interest-only option, the payment shock is even more severe since the principal balance does not decline at all over time when the borrower makes the minimum monthly payment. In this case, the payment increases by 19% in month 25, another 26% in month 31, and another 11% in month 61 when the interest-only option expires. The 3/27 ARMs exhibit similar patterns in monthly payments over time.

Table 7: Monthly Payment Across Mortgage Loan Type

Monthly Payment Across Mortgage Loan Type							
Month	30-year fixed	30-year fixed	2/28 ARM	2/28 ARM	2/28 ARM IO	3/27 ARM	3/27 ARM
1	$ 1,633.87	$ 1,546.04	$ 1,701.37	$ 1,566.17	$ 1,404.01	$ 1,533.12	$ 1,437.35
24	1.00	1.00	1.00	1.00	1.00	1.00	1.00
25	1.00	1.00	1.14	1.18	1.19	1.00	1.00
30	1.00	1.00	1.14	1.18	1.19	1.00	1.00
31	1.00	1.00	1.26	1.32	1.45	1.00	1.00
36	1.00	1.00	1.26	1.32	1.45	1.00	1.00
37	1.00	1.00	1.26	1.32	1.45	1.13	1.18
42	1.00	1.00	1.26	1.32	1.45	1.13	1.18

43	1.00	1.00	1.26	1.32	1.45	1.27	1.34
48	1.00	1.00	1.26	1.32	1.45	1.27	1.34
49	1.00	1.00	1.26	1.32	1.45	1.27	1.43
60	1.00	1.00	1.26	1.32	1.45	1.27	1.43
61	1.00	1.00	1.26	1.32	1.56	1.27	1.43
359	1.00	1.00	1.26	1.32	1.56	1.27	1.43
360	1.00	83.81	1.26	100.72	1.56	1.27	105.60
Amortization	30 years	40 years	30 years	40 years	30 years	30 years	40 years

Note: The first line documents the average initial monthly payment for each loan type. The subsequent rows document the ratio of the future to the initial monthly payment under an assumption that LIBOR remains at 5.31% through the life of the loan.

Source: SEC filing, Author's Calculations

In order to better understand the severity of payment shock, Table 8 illustrates the impact of changes in the mortgage payment on the ratio of debt (service) to gross income. The table is constructed under the assumption that the borrower has no other debt than mortgage debt, and imposes an initial debt-to-income ratio of 40 percent, similar to that found in the mortgage pool. The third column documents that the debt-to-income ratio increases in month 31 to 50.45% for the simple 2/28 ARM, to 52.86% for the 2/28 ARM amortized over 40 years, and to 58.14% for the 2/28 ARM with an interest-only option. Without significant income growth over the first two years of the loan, it seems reasonable to expect that borrowers will struggle to make these higher payments. It begs the question why such a loan was made in the first place.

Table 1-8. Ratio of Debt to Income Across Mortgage Loan Type

Ratio of Debt to Income Across Mortgage Loan Type							
Month	**30-year fixed**	**30-year fixed**	**2/28 ARM**	**2/28 ARM**	**2/28 ARM IO**	**3/27 ARM**	**3/27 ARM**
1	40.00%	40.00%	40.00%	40.00%	40.00%	40.00%	40.00%
24	40.00%	40.00%	40.00%	40.00%	40.00%	40.00%	40.00%
25	40.00%	40.00%	45.46%	47.28%	47.44%	40.00%	40.00%
30	40.00%	40.00%	45.46%	47.28%	47.44%	40.00%	40.00%
31	40.00%	40.00%	50.35%	52.86%	58.14%	40.00%	40.00%
36	40.00%	40.00%	50.35%	52.86%	58.14%	40.00%	40.00%
37	40.00%	40.00%	50.45%	52.86%	58.14%	45.36%	47.04%
42	40.00%	40.00%	50.45%	52.86%	58.14%	45.36%	47.04%
43	40.00%	40.00%	50.45%	52.86%	58.14%	50.83%	53.53%
48	40.00%	40.00%	50.45%	52.86%	58.14%	50.83%	53.53%
49	40.00%	40.00%	50.45%	52.86%	58.14%	50.83%	57.08%
60	40.00%	40.00%	50.45%	52.86%	58.14%	50.83%	57.08%
61	40.00%	40.00%	50.45%	52.86%	62.29%	50.83%	57.08%
359	40.00%	40.00%	50.45%	52.86%	62.29%	50.83%	57.08%
360	40.00%	3352.60%	50.45%	4028.64%	62.29%	50.83%	4223.92%
Amortization	30 years	40 years	30 years	40 years	30 years	30 ears	40 years

Note: The table documents the path of the debt-to-income ratio over the life of each loan type under an assumption that LIBOR remains at 5.31% through the life of the loan. The calculation assumes that all debt is mortgage debt.

Source: SEC filing, Author's Calculations

The likely answer is that lenders expected that the borrower would be able to refinance before payment reset.

Industry trends

Table 9 documents the average terms of loans securitized in the Alt-A and subprime markets over the last eight years. Subprime loans are more likely than Alt-A loans to be ARMs, and are largely dominated by the 2/28 and 3/27 hybrid ARMs. Subprime loans are less likely to have an interest-only option or permit negative amortization (i.e. option ARM), but are more likely to have a 40-year amortization instead of a 30-year amortization. The table also documents that hybrid ARMs have become more important over time for both Alt-A and subprime borrowers, as have interest only options and the 40-year amortization term. In the end, the mortgage pool referenced in our motivating example does not appear to be very different from the average loan securitized by the industry in 2006.

Table 1-9. Terms of Mortgage Loans in MBS Pools

Year	ARM	2/28 ARM	3/27 ARM	5/25 ARM	IO	Option ARM	40-year
A. Alt-A							
1999	6.3	2.6					
2000	12.8	4.7					
2001	20.0	4.9					
2002	28.0	3.7					
2003	34.0	4.8					
2004	68.7	8.9					
2005	69.7	4.0					
2006	69.8	1.8					
B. Subprime							
1999	51.0	31.0					
2000	64.5	45.5					
2001	66.0	52.1					
2002	71.6	57.4					
2003	67.2	54.5					
2004	78.0	61.3					
2005	83.5	66.7					
2006	81.7	68.7					

Source: Loan Performance (2007)

The immediate concern from the industry data is obviously the widespread dependency of subprime borrowers on what amounts to short-term funding, leaving them vulnerable to adverse shifts in the supply of subprime credit. Figure 3 documents the timing ARM resets over the next six years, as of January 2007. Given the dominance of the 2/28 ARM, it should not be surprising that the majority of loans that will be resetting over the next two years are subprime loans. The main source of uncertainty about the future performance of these loans is driven by uncertainty over the ability of these borrowers to refinance. This uncertainty has been highlighted by rapidly changing attitudes of investors towards subprime loans (see the box below on the ABX for the details). Regulators have released guidance on subprime loans that forces a lender to qualify a borrower on a fully-indexed and —amortizing interest rate and discourages the use of state-income loans. Moreover, recent changes in structuring criteria by the rating agencies have prompted several subprime lenders to stop originating hybrid ARMs. Finally, activity in the housing market has slowed down considerably, as the median price of existing homes has declined for the first time in decades while historical levels of inventory and vacant homes.

Exhibit 42: **Adjustable Rate Mortgage Reset Schedule**

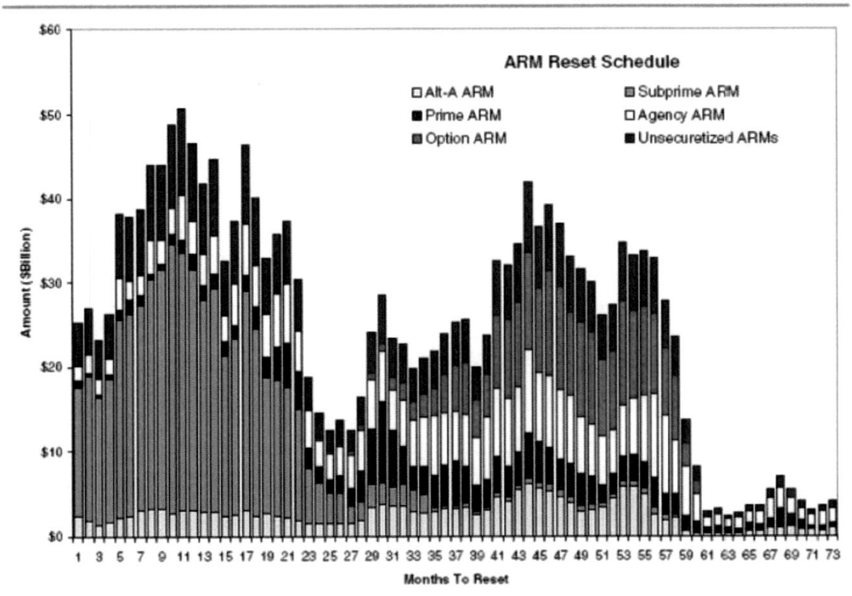

Note: Data as of January 2007.

Source: Credit Suisse Fixed Income U.S. Mortgage Strategy

Figure 3: ARM reset schedule

The Impact of Payment Reset on Foreclosure

The most important issue facing the sub-prime credit market is obviously the impact of payment reset on the ability of borrowers to continue making monthly payments. Given that over three-fourths of the subprime-loans underwritten over 2004 to 2006 were hybrid ARMS, it is not difficult to understand the magnitude of the problem. But what is the likely outcome? The answer depends on a number of factors, including but not limited to: the amount of equity that these borrowers have in their homes at the time of reset (which itself is a function of CLTV at origination and the severity of the decline in home prices), the severity of payment reset (which depends not only on the loan but also on the six-month LIBOR interest rate), and of course conditions in the labor market.

A recent study by Cagan (2007) of mortgage payment reset tries to estimate what fraction of resetting loans will end up in foreclosure. The author presents evidence suggesting that in an environment of zero home price appreciation and full employment, 12 percent of subprime loans will default due to reset. We review the key elements of this analysis.[9]

Table 10 documents the amount of loans issued over 2004-2006 that were still outstanding as of March 2007, broken out by initial interest rate group and payment reset size group. The data includes all outstanding securitized mortgage loans with a future payment reset date. Each row corresponds to a different initial interest rate bucket: RED corresponding to loans with initial rates between 1 and 3.9 percent; YELLOW corresponding to an initial interest rate of 4.0 to 6.49 percent; and ORANGE with an initial interest rate of 6.5 to 12 percent. Subprime loans can be easily identified by the high original interest rate in the third row (ORANGE). Each column corresponds to a different payment reset size group under an assumption of no change in the 6-month LIBOR interest rate: A to payments which increase between 0 and 25 percent; B to payments which increase between 26 and 50 percent; C to payments which increase between 51 and 99 percent; and D to payments which increase by at least 100 percent. Note that almost all of subprime payment reset is in either the 0-25% or the 26-50% groups, with a little more than $300 billion in loans sitting in each group. There is a clear correlation in the table between the initial interest rate and the average size of the payment reset. The most severe payment resets appear to be the problem of Alt-A and Jumbo borrowers.

Table 1-10. Distribution of Loans by First Reset Size

	Reset size ($ billions)				
Initial interest rate	**A (0-25%)**	**B (26-50%)**	**C (51-99%)**	**D (100%+)**	**Total**
RED (1.0-3.9%)	$0	$0	$61	$460	$521
YELLOW (4.0-6.49%)	$545	$477	$102	$0	$1,124
ORANGE (6.5-12%)	$366	$316	$49	$0	$631
Total	$811	$793	$212	$460	$2,276

Source: Cagan (2007); data refer to all ARMs originated 2004-2006.

Cagan helpfully provides estimates of the distribution of updated equity across the initial interest rate group in Table 11. The author uses an automated appraisal system in order to estimate the value of each property, and then constructs an updated value of the equity for each borrower. The table reports the cumulative distribution of equity for each initial interest rate bucket reported in the table above. Note that 22.4 percent of subprime borrowers (ORANGE) are estimated to have no equity in their homes, about half have no more than 10 percent, and two-thirds have less than 20 percent. Disturbingly, the table suggests that a national price decline of 10 percent could put half of all subprime borrowers underwater.

[9] The author is a PhD economist at First American, a credit union which owns LoanPerformance.

Table 1-11. Cumulative Distribution of Equity by Initial Interest Rate

	Initial Rate Group		
Equity	**Red**	**Yellow**	**Orange**
<-20%	2.2%	1.5%	2.7%
<-15%	3.2	2.0	4.0
<-10%	4.9	2.9	6.2
<-5%	8.2	4.8	11.6
<0%	14.1	8.6	22.4
<5%	23.9	15.5	36.0
<10%	36.7	24.5	47.7
<15%	49.7	34.7	57.9
<20%	62.4	45.4	67.3
<25%	73.3	56.8	76.8
<30%	81.3	67.5	84.6

Source: Cagan (2007); data refer to all ARMs originated 2004-2006.

In order to transform this raw data into estimates of foreclosure due to reset, the author makes assumptions in Table 12 about the amount of equity or the size of payment reset and the probability of foreclosures.[10] A borrower will only default given difficulty with payment reset and difficulty in refinancing. For example, 70% of borrowers with equity between -5% and 5% are assumed to face difficulty refinancing, while only 30% of borrowers with equity between 15% and 25% have difficulty. At the same time, the author assumes that only 10 percent of borrowers with payment reset 0-25% will face difficulty with the higher payment, while 70 percent with a payment reset of 51-99% will be unable to make the higher payment.

Table 1-12. Assumed Probability of Default by Reset Size and Equity Risk Group

		Reset Size Group			
		A	**B**	**C**	**D**
		25% or less	**26-50%**	**51-99%**	**100% or more**
Equity	**Pr(difficulty)**	10%	40%	70%	100%
>25%	10%	1%	4%	7%	10%
15–25%	30%	3	12	21	30
5–15%	50%	5	20	35	50
– 5–5%	70%	7	28	49	70
<– 5%	90%	9	36	63	90

Source: Cagan (2007).

Estimates of foreclosure due to reset in an environment of constant home prices are documented in Table 13. The author estimates that foreclosures due to reset will be 3.5% (= 106.2/3033.1) for the 0-25% reset group and 13.5% (= 446.4/3282.8) for the 26-50% group.

---

10 The author offers no rationale for these figures, but the analysis here should be transparent enough that one could use different inputs to construct their own alternative scenarios.

Given the greater equity risk of subprime mortgages documented in Table 11, a back-of-theenvelope calculation suggests that these numbers would be 4.5% and 18.6% for subprime mortgages.

Table 1-13. Summary of Foreclosure Estimates under 0% Home Price Appreciation

Reset Size	Reset Risk	Equity Risk	Pr(loss)	Loans (t)	Foreclosures (t)
A (25% or less)	10%	35%	3.5%	3033.1	106.2
B (26-50%)	40%	34%	13.6%	3282.8	446.4
C (51-99%)	70%	31%	21.7%	839.2	182.1
D (100% or more)	100%	36%	36.0%	1,216.7	438.0
			Total	8,371.9	1,172.7
			Percent foreclosures		14.0%

Source: Cagan (2007).

The author also investigates a scenario where home prices fall by 10 percent in Table 14, and estimates foreclosures due to reset for the two payment reset size groups to be 5.5% and 21.6%, respectively. Note that the revised July 2007 economic forecast for Moody's called for this exact scenario by the end of 2008.

Table 1-14. Summary of foreclosure estimates under 10% national home price decline

Reset Size	Reset Risk	Equity Risk	Pr (loss)	Loans (t)	Foreclosures (t)
A (25% or less)	10%	55%	5.5%	3033.1	166.8
B (26-50%)	40%	54%	21.6%	3282.8	709.1
C (51-99%)	70%	51%	35.7%	839.2	299.6
D (100% or more)	100%	56%	56.0%	1,216.7	681.3
			Total	8,371.9	1856.8
			Percent foreclosures		22.2%

Source: Cagan (2007).

Market conditions have deteriorated dramatically since this study was published, as the origination of both sub-prime and Alt-A mortgage loans has all but disappeared, making the author's assumptions about equity risk even in the stress scenario for home prices look optimistic. Moreover, the author's original assumption that reset risk is constant across the credit spectrum is likely to be optimistic. In particular, sub-prime borrowers are less likely to be able to handle payment reset, resulting with estimates of foreclosures that are quite modest relative to those in the research reports of investment banks.

3.3. How Have Subprime Loans Performed?

Motivating Example

Table 15 documents how the GSAMP 2006-NC2 deal has performed through August 2007. The first three columns report mortgage loans still in the pool that are 30-days, 60-days, and 90-days past due. The fourth column reports loans that are in foreclosure. The fifth column reports loans where the bank has title to the property. The sixth column reports actual cumulative losses. The last column documents the fraction of original loans that remain in the pool.

Table 1-15. Performance of GSAMP 2006-NC2

Date	30 day	60 day	90 day	Fore-closure	Bank-ruptcy	REO	Cum Loss	CPR	Principal
Aug-07	6.32%	3.39%	1.70%	7.60%	0.90%	3.66%	0.25%	20.35%	72.48%
Jul-07	5.77%	3.47%	1.31%	7.31%	1.03%	3.15%	0.20%	20.77%	73.90%
Jun-07	5.61%	3.09%	1.43%	6.92%	0.70%	2.63%	0.10%	25.26%	75.38%
May-07	4.91%	3.34%	1.38%	6.48%	0.78%	1.83%	0.08%	19.18%	77.26%
Apr-07	4.68%	3.38%	1.16%	6.77%	0.50%	0.72%	0.04%	15.71%	78.68%
Mar-07	4.74%	2.77%	1.12%	6.76%	0.38%	0.21%	0.02%	19.03%	79.84%
Feb-07	4.79%	2.59%	0.96%	6.00%	0.37%	0.03%	0.00%	23.08%	81.29%
Jan-07	4.58%	2.85%	0.88%	5.04%	0.36%	0.00%	0.00%	28.54%	83.12%

Source: ABSNet

What do these numbers imply for the expected performance of the mortgage pool. UBS (June 2007) outlines an approach to use actual deal performance in order to estimate lifetime losses. Using historical data on loans in an environment of low home price appreciation (less than 5 percent), the author documents that approximately 70 percent of loans in the 60-day, 90-day, and bankruptcy categories eventually default, defined as the event of foreclosure. Interestingly, only about 60-70 percent of loans in bankruptcy are actually delinquent. Moreover, these transitions into foreclosure take about 4 months.

The amount of default "in the pipeline" for remaining loans in the next four months is constructed as follows:

$$\text{Pipeline default} = 0.7 \times (\text{60-day} + \text{90-day} + \text{bankruptcy}) + (\text{foreclosure} + \text{real-estate owned})$$

For GSAMP 2006-NC2, the pipeline default from the August report is 15.45%, suggesting that this fraction of loans remaining in the pool are likely to default in the next four months.

Total default is constructed by combining this measure with the fraction of loans remaining in the pool, actual cumulative losses to date, and an assumption about the severity of loss. In the UBS study, the author assumes a loss given default of 37%.

$$\text{Total default} = \text{pipeline default} \times (\text{fraction of loans remaining}) + (\text{Cum loss})/(\text{loss severity})$$

For the GSAMP 2006-NC2, this number is 11.88%, which suggests that this fraction of the original pool will have defaulted in four months.

Finally, the paper uses historical data in order to estimate the fraction of total defaults over the life of deal. In particular, a mapping is constructed between weighted-average loan age and the fraction of lifetime default that a deal typically realizes. For example, the typical deal realizes 33% of its defaults by month 13, 59% by month 23, 75% by month 35, and 100% by month 60.

Projected cumulative default = Total default/Default timing factor

The New Century pool was originated in May 2006, implying that the average loan is about 16 months old at the end of August 2007. The default timing factor for 20 months, which must be used since defaults were predicted through four months in the future, is 51.2%, suggesting that projected cumulative default on this mortgage pool is 23.19%. Using a loss severity of 37% results in expected lifetime loss on this mortgage pool of 8.58%.

There are several potential weaknesses of this approach, the foremost being the fact that it is backward-looking and essentially ignores the elephant in the room, payment reset. In particular, in the fact of payment reset, losses are likely to be more back-loaded than the historical curve used above, implying the fraction of lifetime losses which have been observed to date is likely to be too small, resulting in lifetime loss estimates which are too low. In order to address this problem, UBS (23 October 2007) has developed a shut-down model to take into account the inability of borrowers to refinance their way out of payment resets. In that article, the authors estimate the lower prepayment speeds associate with refinancing stress will increase losses by an average of 50 percent. Moreover, the authors also speculate that loss severities will be higher than the 37 percent used above, and incorporate an assumption of 45 percent. Together, these assumptions imply that a more conservative view on losses would be to scale those from the loss projection model above by a factor of two, implying a lifetime loss rate of 17.16% on the example pool.

Industry

UBS (June 2007) applies this methodology to home equity ABS deals that constitute three vintages of the ABX: 06-1, 06-2, and 07-1. In order to understand the jargon, note that deals in 06-1 refer mortgages that were largely originated in the second half of 2005, while deals in 062 refer to mortgages that were largely underwritten in the first half of 2006.

Figure 4 illustrates estimates of the probability distribution of estimated losses as of the June remittance reports across the 20 different deals for each of the three vintages of loans. The mean loss rate of the 06-1 vintage is 5.6%, while the mean of the 06-2 and 07-1 vintages are 9.2% and 11.7%, respectively. From the figure, it is clear that not only the mean but also the variance of the distribution of losses at the deal level has increased considerably over the last year. Moreover, expected lifetime losses from the New Century securitization studied in the example are a little lower than the average deal in the ABX from 06-2.

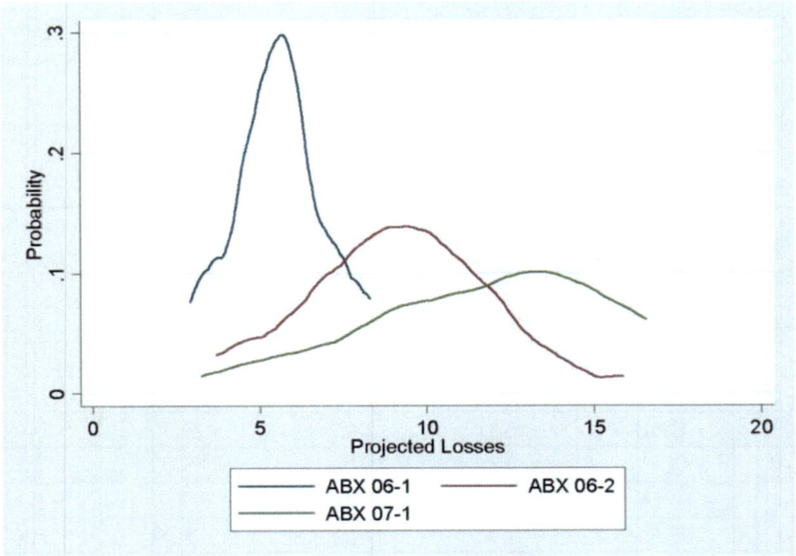

Figure 4: Subprime Projected Losses by Vintage

3.4. How are Subprime Loans Valued?

In January 2006, Markit launched the ABX, which is a series of indices that track the price of credit default insurance on a standardized basket of home equity ABS obligations.[11] The ABX actually has five indices, differentiated by credit rating: AAA, AA, A, BBB, and BBB-. Each of these indices is an equally-weighted average of the price of credit insurance at a maturity of 30-years across similarly-rated tranches from 20 different home equity ABS deals. For example, the BBB index tracks the average price of credit default insurance on the BBB-rated tranche.

Every six months, a new set of 20 home equity deals is chosen from the largest dealer shelves in the previous half year. In order to ensure proper diversification in the portfolio, the same originator is limited to no more than four deals and the same master servicer is limited to no more than six deals. Each reference obligation must be rated by both Moody's and S&P and have a weighted-average remaining life of 4-6 years.

In a typical transaction, a protection buyer pays the protection seller a fixed coupon at a monthly rate on an amount determined by the buyer. For example, Table 16 documents that the price of protection on the AAA tranche of the most recent vintage (07-2) is a coupon rate of 76 basis points per year. Note the significant increase in coupons on all tranches between 07-1 and 07-2, which reflects a significant change in investor sentiment from January to Jul 2007.

When a credit event occurs, the protection seller makes a payment to the protection buyer in an amount equal to the loss. Credit events include the shortfall of interest or principal (i.e.

[11] In the jargon, first-lien sub-prime mortgage loans as well as second- lien home equity loans and home equity lines of credit (HELCOs) are all part of what is called the Home Equity ABS sector. First- lien Alt-A and Jumbo loans are part of what is called the Residential Mortgage-backed Securities (RMBS) sector.

the servicer fails to forward a payment when it is due) as well as the write-down of the tranche due to losses on underlying mortgage loans. In the event that these losses are later reimbursed, the protection buyer must reimburse the protection seller.

Table 1-16. Overview of the ABX Index

Vintage	Credit Rating	Coupon Rate	Index Price	Estimated Duration	Implied Spread
07–2	AAA	76	98.04	5.19	114
07–2	AA	192	95.36	3.85	313
07–2	A	369	78.05	3.47	1002
07–2	BBB	500	54.43	3.31	1877
07–2	BBB-	500	47.31	3.30	2097
07–1	AAA	9	95.05	5.07	107
07–1	AA	15	88.36	3.7	330
07–1	A	64	65.5	3.44	1067
07–1	BBB	224	44.55	3.02	2060
07–1	BBB-	389	41.79	2.75	2506
06–2	AAA	11	96.45	4.68	87
06–2	AA	17	92.79	3.21	242
06-2	A	44	74.45	3.05	882
06–2	BBB	133	53.57	2.77	1809
06–2	BBB-	242	46.75	2.53	2347
06–1	AAA	18	99.04	4.27	40
06–1	AA	32	97.82	2.89	107
06–1	A	54	85.04	2.74	600
06–1	BBB	154	74.79	2.57	1135
06–1	BBB-	267	66.93	2.42	1634

Source: Coupon and Price: Markit (24 July 2007); duration: UBS; Implied spread is author's calculation as follows: implied spread = 100*[100-price]/duration + coupon rate.

For example, if one tranche of a securitization referenced in the index is written down by an amount of 1%, and the current balance of the tranche is 70% of its original balance, an institution which has sold $10 million in protection must make a payment of $583,333 [= $10m × 70% × (1/20)] to the protection buyer. Moreover, the future protection fee will be based on a principal balance that is 0.20% [= 1% × (1/20)] lower than before the write-down of the tranche.

Changes in investor views about the risk of the mortgage loans over time will affect the price at which investors are willing to buy or sell credit protection. However, the terms of the insurance contract (i.e. coupon, maturity, pool of deals) are fixed. The ABX tracks the amount that one party has to pay the other at the onset of the contract in order for both parties to accept the terms. For example, when investors think the underlying loans have become more risky since the index was created, a protection buyer will have to pay an up-front fee to the protection seller in order to only pay a coupon of 76 basis points per year. On 24 July, the ABX.AAA.07 was at 98.04, suggesting that a protection buyer would have to pay the seller a fee of 1.96% up-front. Using an estimate of 5.19 from UBS of this tranche's estimated duration, it is possible to write the implied spread on the tranche as 114 basis points per year [= 100 × (100 - 98.04)/5.19 + 76].

Figure 5 documents the behavior of the BBB-rated 06-2 vintage of the ABX over the first six and a half months of 2007. Note from Table 16 that the initial coupon on this tranche was 133 basis points. However, the first two months of the year marked a significant adverse change in investor sentiment against the home equity sector. In particular, the BBB-rated index fell from 95 to below 75 by the end of February. Using an estimated duration of 3.3, the implied spread increased from just under 300 basis points to almost 900 basis points. Through the end of May, this index fluctuated between 80 and 85, consistent with an implied spread of about 650 basis points. However, the market responded adversely to a further deterioration in performance following the May remittance report, and at the time of this writing, the index has dropped to about 54, consistent with an implied spread of approximately 1800 basis points.

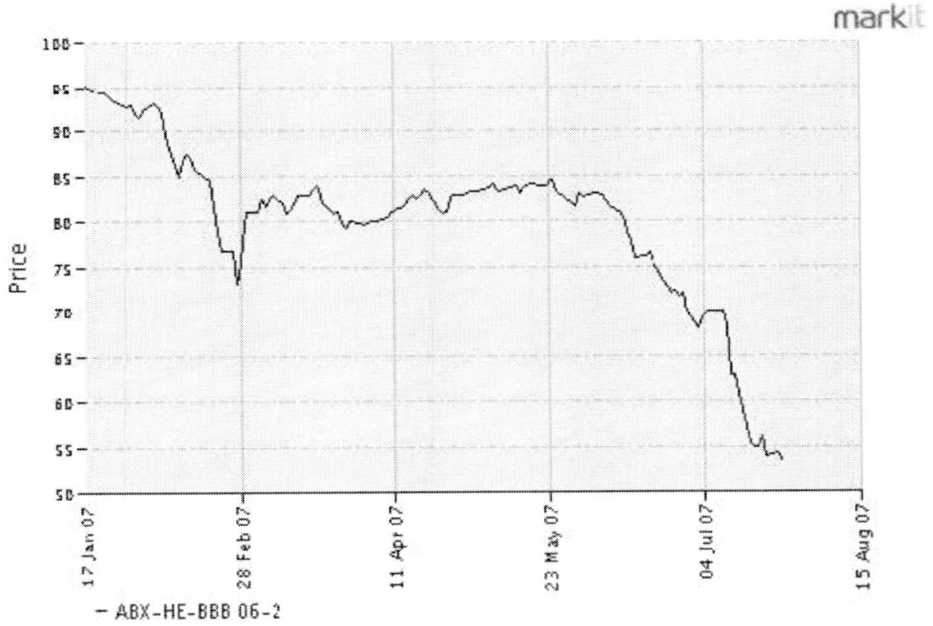

Figure 5: ABX.BBB 06-2

Source: Markit

While it is not clear what exactly triggered the sell-off in the first two months of January, there were some notable events that occurred over this period. There were early concerns about the vintage in the form of early payment defaults resulting in originators being forced to repurchase loans from securitizations. These repurchase requests put pressure on the liquidity of originators. Moreover, warehouse lenders began to ask for more collateral, putting further liquidity pressure on originators.

4. OVERVIEW OF SUBPRIME MBS

The typical subprime trust has the following structural features designed to protect investors from losses on the underlying mortgage loans:

- Subordination
- Excess spread
- Shifting interest
- Performance triggers
- Interest rate swap

We discuss each of these forms of credit enhancement in turn.

4.1. Subordination

The distribution of losses on the mortgage pool is typically tranched into different classes. In particular, losses on the mortgage loan pool are applied first to the most junior class of investors until the principal balance of that class is completely exhausted. At that point, losses are allocated to the most junior class remaining, and so on.

The most junior class of a securitization is referred to as the equity tranche. In the case of subprime mortgage loans, the equity tranche is typically created through over-collateralization (o/c), which means that the principal balance of the mortgage loans exceeds the principal balance of all the debt issued by the trust. This is an important form of credit enhancement that is funded by the arranger in part through the premium it receives on offered securities. O/C is used to reduce the exposure of debt investors to loss on the pool mortgage loans.

A small part of the capital structure of the trust is made up of the mezzanine class of debt securities, which are next in line to absorb losses once the o/c is exhausted. This class of securities typically has several tranches with credit ratings that vary between AA and B. With greater risk comes greater return, as these securities pay the highest interest rates to investors. The lion's share of the capital structure is always funded by the senior class of debt securities, which are last in line to absorb losses. Senior securities are protected not only by o/c, but also by the width of the mezzanine class. In general, the sum of o/c and the width of all tranches junior is referred to as subordination. Senior securities generally have the highest rating, and since they are last in line (to absorb losses), pay the lowest interest rates to investors.

The capital structure of GSAMP 2006-NC1 is illustrated in Table 17. First, note that the o/c is the class X, which represents 1.4% of the principal balance of the mortgages. There are two B classes of securities not offered in the prospectus. The mezzanine class benefits from a total of 3.10% of subordination created by the o/c and the class B securities. However, note that the mezzanine class is split up into 9 different classes, M-1 to M-10, which class M-2 being junior to class M-1, etc. For example, the M-8 class tranche, which has an investment grade-rating of BBB, has subordination of 3.9% and pays a coupon of 100 basis points. Investors receive 1/12 of this amount on the distribution date, which is the 25th of each month.

The senior class benefits from 20.65% of total subordination, including the width of the mezzanine class (19.25%).

Table 1-17. Capital Structure of GSAMP Trust 2006-NC2

Tranche description				Credit Ratings		Coupon Rate	
Class	**Notional**	**Width**	**Subordination**	**S&P**	**Moody's**	**(1)**	**(2)**
A-1	$239,618,000	27.18%	72.82%	AAA	Aaa	0.15%	0.30%
A-2A	$214,090,000	24.29%	48.53%	AAA	Aaa	0.07%	0.14%
A-2B	$102,864,000	11.67%	36.86%	AAA	Aaa	0.09%	0.18%
A-2C	$99,900,000	11.33%	25.53%	AAA	Aaa	0.15%	0.30%
A-2D	$42,998,000	4.88%	20.65%	AAA	Aaa	0.24%	0.48%
M-1	$35,700,000	4.05%	16.60%	AA+	Aa1	0.30%	0.45%
M-2	$28,649,000	3.25%	13.35%	AA	Aa2	0.31%	0.47%
M-3	$16,748,000	1.90%	11.45%	AA-	Aa3	0.32%	0.48%
M-4	$14,986,000	1.70%	9.75%	A+	A1	0.35%	0.53%
M-5	$14,545,000	1.65%	8.10%	A	A2	0.37%	0.56%
M-6	$13,663,000	1.55%	6.55%	A-	A3	0.46%	0.69%
M-7	$12,341,000	1.40%	5.15%	BBB+	Baa1	0.90%	1.35%
M-8	$11,019,000	1.25%	3.90%	BBB	Baa2	1.00%	1.50%
M-9	$7,052,000	0.80%	3.10%	BBB-	Baa3	2.05%	3.08%
B-1	$6,170,000	0.70%	2.40%	BB+	Ba1	2.50%	3.75%
B-2	$8,815,000	1.00%	1.40%	BB	Ba2	2.50%	3.75%
X	$12,340,995	1.40%	0.00%	NR	NR	N/A	N/A

Source: Prospectus filed with the SEC of GSAMP 2006-NC2

Note that the New Century structure is broken into two groups of Class A securities, corresponding to two sub-pools of the mortgage loans. In Group I loans, every mortgage has original principal balance lower than the GSE-conforming loan limits. This feature permits the GSEs to purchase these Class A-1 securities. However, in the Group II loans, there is a mixture of mortgage loans with original principal balance above and below the GSE-conforming loan limit.

The table does not mention either the class P or class C certificates, which have no face value and are not entitled to distributions of principal or interest. The class P securities are the sole beneficiary of all future prepayment penalties. Since the arranger will be paid for these rights, it reduces the premium needed on other offered securities for the deal to work. The class C securities contain a clean-up option which permits the trust to call the offered securities should the principal balance of the mortgage pool fall to a sufficiently low level.[12] In our example deal, the offered debt securities are rated by both S&P and Moody's. Note that Table 17 documents that there is no disagreement between the agencies in their opinion of the appropriate credit rating for each tranche.

[12] The figure also omits discussion of certain "residual certificates" that are not entitled to distributions of interest but appear to be related to residual ownership interests in assets of the trust.

4.2. Excess Spread

Subordination is not the only protection that senior and mezzanine tranche investors have against loss. As an example, the weighted average coupon from the mortgage loan will typically be larger than fees to the servicers, net payments to the swap counterparty, and the weighted average coupon on debt securities issued by the trust. This difference is referred to as excess spread, which is used to absorb credit losses on the mortgage loans, with the remainder distributed each month to the owners of the Class X securities. Note that this is the first line of defense for investors for credit losses, as the principal of no tranche is reduced by any amount until credit losses reduce excess spread to a negative number. The amount of credit enhancement provided by excess spread depends on both the severity as well as the timing of losses.

In the New Century deal, the weighted average coupon on the tranches at origination is LIBOR plus 23 basis points. With LIBOR at 5.32% at the time of issue, this implies an interest cost of 5.55%. In addition to this cost, the trust pays 51 basis points in servicing fees and initially pays 13 basis points to the swap counterparty (see below). As the weighted average interest rate on collateral at the time of issue is 8.30%, the initial excess spread on this mortgage pool is 2.11%.

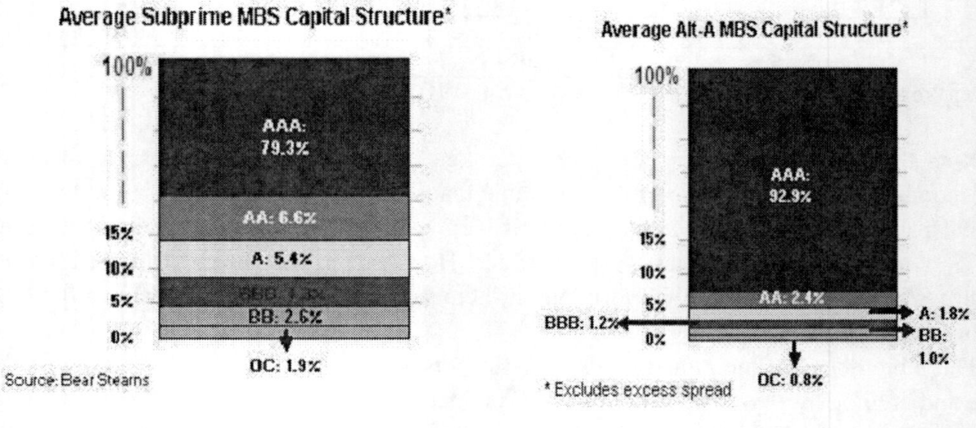

Figure 6: Typical Capital Structure of Subprime and Alt-A MBS

More generally, the amount of excess spread varies by deal, but averaged about 2.5 percent during 2006. Dealers estimate that loss rates must reach 9 percent before the average BBB minus bond sustains its first dollar of principal loss, about twice its initial subordination of 4.5 percent in Figure 6 above.

4.3. Shifting Interest

Senior investors are also protected by the practice of shifting interest, which requires that all principal payments to be applied to senior notes over a specified period of time (usually the first 36 months) before being paid to mezzanine bondholders. During this time, known as the "lockout period," mezzanine bondholders receive only the coupon on their notes. As the principal of senior notes is paid down, the ratio of the senior class to the balance of the entire deal (senior interest) decreases during the first couple years, hence the term "shifting interest". The amount of subordination (alternatively, credit enhancement) for the senior class increases over time because the amount of senior bonds outstanding is smaller relative to the amount outstanding for mezzanine bonds.

4.4. Performance Triggers

After the lockout period, subject to passing performance tests,[13] the o/c is released and principal is applied to mezzanine notes from the bottom of the capital structure up until target levels of subordination are reached (usually twice the initial subordination, as a percent of current balance). In addition to protecting senior note holders, the purpose of the shifting interest mechanism is to adjust subordination across the capital structure after sufficient seasoning. Also, the release of o/c and pay-down of mezzanine notes reduces the average life of these bonds and the interest costs of the securitization.

In our example securitization, o/c is specified to be 1.4% of the principal balance of the mortgage loans as of the cutoff-date, at least until the step-down date. The step-down date is the earlier of the date on which the principal balance of the senior class has been reduced to zero and the later to occur of 36 months or subordination of the senior class being greater than or equal to 41.3% of the aggregate principal balance of remaining mortgage loans. The trigger event is defined as a distribution date when one of the following two conditions is met:

- The rolling three-month average of 60-days or more delinquent (including those in foreclosure, REO properties, or mortgage loans in bankruptcy) divided by the remaining principal balance of the mortgage loans is larger than 38.70% of the subordination of the senior class from the previous month; or,
- The amount of cumulative realized losses incurred over the life of the deal as a fraction of the original principal balance of the mortgage loans exceeds the thresholds in Figure 7.

If the trigger event does not occur, the deal is 36 months old, and the subordination of the senior class is larger than 41.3%, then the deal will step-down. In this case, o/c is specified to be 2.8 percent of the principal balance of the mortgage loans in the previous month, subject to a floor equal to 0.5% of the principal balance of the mortgage loans as of the cut-off date. At this time, any excess o/c is released to holders of the Class X tranche. Note that the trigger event only affects whether or not o/c is released.

---

[13] There are two types of performance tests in subprime deals, one testing the deal's cumulative losses against a loss schedule, and another test for 60+ day delinquencies.

4.5. Interest Rate Swap

While most of the loans are ARMs, as discussed above, the interest rates will not adjust for two to three years following origination. It follows that the trust is exposed to the risk that interest rates increase, so that the cost of funding increases faster than interest payments received on the mortgages. In order to mitigate this risk, the trust engages in an interest rate swap with a third-party named the swap counterparty. In particular, the third-party has agreed to accept a sequence of fixed payments in return for promising to send a sequence of adjustable-rate payments.

In our example, Goldman Sachs is the Swap counterparty, which has agreed to pay 1-month LIBOR and accept a fixed interest rate of 5.45% on a notional amount described in Figure 8 over a term of 60 months. Note that the notional amount hedged decreases over time, as the trust expects pre-payments of principal on the pool of mortgage loans to reduce the amount of debt securities outstanding.

4.6 Remittance Reports

The trustee makes monthly reports to investors known as remittance reports. In this section, we use data from these reports in order to document the performance of the New Century deal through August 2007.

Table 18 documents cash receipts of the trust. Scheduled principal and interest are collected from a borrower's monthly payment. Unscheduled principal is collected from borrowers who pay more than their required monthly payment, as well as borrowers who either pre-pay or default on their loans. The first three columns of the table report the remittance of scheduled and unscheduled principal as well as interest and pre-payment penalties. The fourth column reports advances of principal and interest made to the trust by the servicer to cover the nonpayment of these items by certain borrowers. The fifth column documents the repurchase of loans by New Century which have been determined to violate the originator's representations and warranties. Note that only one loan has been repurchased with a principal balance of $184,956 as of this writing. Finally, realized losses are reported in the sixth column.

Table 1-18. GSAMP Trust 2006-NC2 Cash Receipts

Date	Remittances of principal		Remittances of interest and prepayment penalties	Servicer Advances	Loan Repurchases	Realized losses	Deposits
	Scheduled	Unscheduled					
Jul-06	$329,304	$9,067,656	$5,860,567	$233,039	$0	$0	$15,561,090
Aug-06	$328,927	$11,818,842	$5,772,726	$483,778	$0	$0	$18,492,964
Sep-06	$328,005	$18,872,868	$5,099,068	$1,317,531	$0	$0	$25,783,064
Oct-06	$324,632	$21,123,948	$5,874,901	$1,230,848	$0	$0	$28,870,206
Nov-06	$320,165	$21,913,838	$5,669,909	$1,191,300	$0	$0	$29,496,641
Dec-06	$315,176	$42,949,370	$5,496,644	$1,174,086	$0	$0	$50,229,238
Jan-06	$303,981	$20,805,981	$4,992,533	$1,342,346	$0	$0	$27,717,274
Feb-06	$298,715	$15,842,586	$4,874,742	$1,293,706	$184,956	– $1,162	$22,738,857

Mar-06	$294,018	$12,488,956	$4,845,576	$1,346,264	$0	– $179,720	$18,945,495
Apr-06	$292,054	$9,947,596	$4,781,758	$1,369,108	$0	– $166,703	$16,351,873
May-06	$290,315	$12,190,508	$4,605,848	$1,493,314	$0	– $323,425	$18,459,415
Jun-06	$285,113	$16,320,384	$4,554,347	$1,577,756	$0	– $233,174	$22,742,178
Jul-06	$279,953	$12,764,719	$4,386,611	$1,712,117	$0	– $835,539	$18,504,802
Aug-06	$275,885	$12,226,786	$4,425,290	$1,720,552	$0	– $459,357	$18,380,129

Source: remittance reports through ABSNet

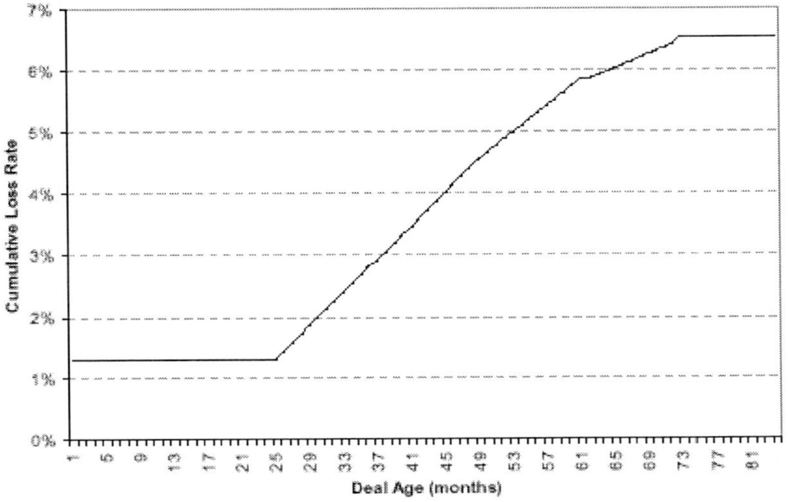

Figure 7: Cumulative Loss Thresholds for GSAMP Trust 2006-NC2 Trigger Event

Source: SEC Prospectus for GSAMP Trust 2006-NC2

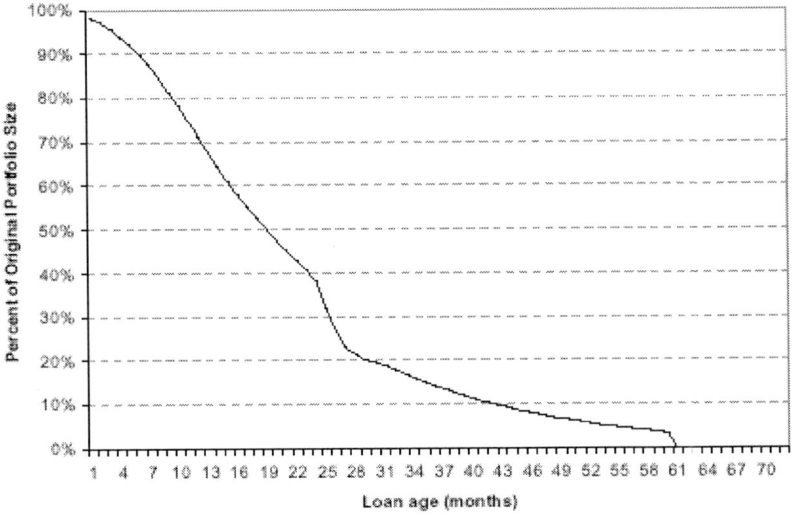

Figure 8: Schedule of Interest Swap Notional for GSAMP Trust 2006-NC2

Source: SEC Prospectus for GSAMP Trust 2006-NC2

Table 19 documents the cash expenses of the trust. The net swap payments are reported in the first column. Recall that the trust pays Goldman Sachs a fixed interest rate of 5.45 percent and receives an amount equal to one-month LIBOR, each on the amount referenced by Table 18 above. The servicer fees are based on the outstanding principal balance of the mortgage loans at the end of the last month, with 50 basis points paid to the servicer (Owcen) and just under 1 basis point paid to the master servicer (Wells Fargo). All principal paid by the borrower is advanced to the holders of Class A certificates. Each tranche is paid the stated coupon from Table 18 above based on the amount outstanding at the end of the previous month. Prepayment penalties are paid to the owners of the Class P tranche. The residual is denoted excess spread, and is paid to the owners of the Class X tranche each month.

Table 1-19. Trust Cash Outlays

Date	Net Swap payments	Servicing fees	Servicer advance reimburesements	LIBOR certificate		Prepayment penalties	Excess Spread
				Principal	Interest		
Jul-06	$62,518	$374,270	$0	$9,396,455	$3,503,784	$70,524	$2,153,539
Aug-06	$47,927	$370,280	$233,039	$12,147,768	$4,159,454	$88,691	$1,445,805
Sep-06	$91,323	$365,123	$483,778	$19,200,881	$4,058,029	$165,593	$1,418,337
Oct-06	$82,957	$356,970	$1,317,531	$21,448,581	$3,844,241	$315,875	$1,504,051
Nov-06	$96,794	$347,863	$1,230,848	$22,234,002	$4,114,629	$401,429	$1,071,070
Dec-06	$82,988	$338,423	$1,191,300	$43,264,545	$3,518,752	$293,963	$1,539,266
Jan-06	$64,178	$320,054	$1,174,086	$21,109,962	$3,463,517	$272,433	$1,313,044
Feb-06	$86,137	$311,091	$1,342,346	$16,141,301	$3,573,069	$245,315	$1,039,598
Mar-06	$72,641	$304,238	$1,293,706	$12,782,974	$3,058,328	$150,401	$1,283,208
Apr-06	$74,677	$298,810	$1,346,264	$10,239,650	$3,219,019	$128,060	$1,045,393
May-06	$71,316	$294,463	$1,369,108	$12,480,823	$3,172,768	$202,855	$868,082
Jun-06	$70,108	$289,163	$1,493,314	$16,605,497	$3,220,305	$237,753	$826,037
Jul-06	$64,543	$282,113	$1,577,756	$13,044,672	$3,041,335	$196,941	$297,443
Aug-06	$67,536	$276,574	$1,712,117	$12,502,671	$3,280,603	$190,972	$349,654

Source: remittance reports from ABSNet

The face value of the Class X tranche is $12.3 million. To date, this tranche has been paid excess spread in the amount of $16.1 million. Note that the amount paid to this tranche has decreased over time as credit losses have reduced excess spread. Interestingly, even if the owners of this class are not paid another dollar of interest, they will have received an amount equal to 130.9% of par.[14]

There are two trigger events which prevent the release of over-collateralization at the step-down date, as shown in Table 20. The trigger amount in the third column for the 3-month moving average of 60-day delinquencies is 38.7 percent of the previous month's senior enhancement percentage reported in the fourth column. Recall that the trigger amount for the cumulative losses is constant at 1.3 percent over the first two years of the deal. While losses to date remain lower than the loss trigger amount, the 3-month moving average of 60-day delinquencies has been larger than the threshold amount since the April 2007 remittance report.

[14] Note given the amount of cash being paid out to equity tranche investors in such a bad state of nature, it is likely that these investors have paid a premium over par for these securities, so this should not be interpreted as a return.

Table 1-20. Key Triggers

Date	LIBOR	Moving Average 60d Delinquency		Senior Enhancement		Cumulative Loss	
	1-month	Amount	Trigger	Amount	Specified	Amount	Trigger
Jul-06	5.35%	0.04%	7.99%	20.87%	41.30%	0.00%	1.30%
Aug-06	5.38%	0.02%	8.08%	21.17%	41.30%	0.00%	1.30%
Sep-06	5.32%	0.78%	8.19%	21.65%	41.30%	0.00%	1.30%
Oct-06	5.33%	2.32%	8.38%	22.22%	41.30%	0.00%	1.30%
Nov-06	5.32%	4.84%	8.60%	22.84%	41.30%	0.00%	1.30%
Dec-06	5.32%	6.42%	8.84%	24.18%	41.30%	0.00%	1.30%
Jan-06	5.35%	7.97%	9.35%	24.84%	41.30%	0.00%	1.30%
Feb-06	5.32%	9.12%	9.61%	25.40%	41.30%	0.00%	1.30%
Mar-06	5.32%	4.47%	9.83%	25.86%	41.30%	0.02%	1.30%
Apr-06	5.32%	12.62%	10.10%	26.25%	41.30%	0.04%	1.30%
May-06	5.32%	14.32%	10.16%	26.73%	41.30%	0.08%	1.30%
Jun-06	5.32%	16.07%	10.34%	27.40%	41.30%	0.10%	1.30%
Jul-06	5.32%	17.83%	10.60%	27.94%	41.30%	0.19%	1.30%
Aug-06	5.32%	19.66%	10.81%	28.49%	41.30%	0.24%	1.30%

Source: remittance reports from ABSnet

The remittance report also discloses loan modifications performed by the servicer each month. Note that through the August remittance report, there have been no modifications of any mortgage loan in the pool. This is not surprising as the first payment reset date for these 2/28 ARMs will not be until spring 2008.

Finally, the remittance report also discloses information that permits a calculation of loss severity. At the time of this writing, the trust has incurred a loss of $2.199 million on 44 mortgage loans with principal balance of $5.042 million, for a loss severity of 43.6 percent. This number is only modestly higher than the assumption used in forecasting the lifetime performance of the deal using the UBS methodology.

5. An Overview of Subprime MBS Ratings

This section is intended to provide an overview of how the rating agencies assign credit ratings on tranches of a securitization. We start with a general discussion of credit ratings before moving into the details on the rating process. We continue with an overview of the process through which the credit rating agencies monitor performance of securitization deals over time, and review performance of credit ratings on securities secured by subprime mortgages. In this section there are a number of asides to complement the analysis: conceptual differences between corporate and structured credit ratings; a note on how through-the-cycle structured credit ratings can amplify the housing cycle; an explanation of the timing of recent downgrades.

5.1. What is a Credit Rating?

A credit rating by a CRA represents an overall assessment and opinion of a debt obligor's creditworthiness and is thus meant to reflect only credit or default risk. To be sure, it is not the obligor but the instrument issued by the obligor which receives a credit rating. The distinction is not that relevant for corporate bonds, where the obligor rating is commensurate with the rating on a senior unsecured instrument, but is quite relevant for structured credit products such as asset-backed securities (ABS). Nonetheless, in the words of a Moody's presentation (Moody's 2004), "[t]he comparability of these opinions holds regardless of the country of the issuer, is industry, asset class, or type of fixed-income debt." A recent S&P document states "[o]ur ratings represent a uniform measure of credit quality globally and across all types of debt instruments. In other words, an 'AAA' rated corporate bond should exhibit the same degree of credit quality as an 'AAA' rated securitized issue." (S&P 2007, p.4).

This stated intent implies that an investor can assume that, say, a double-A rated instrument is the same in the U.S. as in Belgium or Singapore, regardless whether that instrument is a standard corporate bond or a structured product such as a tranche on a collateralized debt obligation (CDO); see also Mason and Rosner (2007). The actual behavior of rated obligors or instruments may turn out to have more heterogeneity across countries, industries, and product types, and there is substantial supporting evidence. See Nickell, Perraudin, and Varvotto (2000) for evidence across countries of domicile and industries for corporate bond ratings, and CGFS (2005) for differences between corporate bonds and structured products.

The rating agencies differ about what exactly is assessed. Whereas Fitch and S&P evaluate an obligor's overall capacity to meet its financial obligation, and hence is best through of as an estimate of probability of default, Moody's assessment incorporates some judgment of recovery in the event of loss. In the argot of credit risk management, S&P measures PD (probability of default) while Moody's measure is somewhat closer to EL (expected loss) (BCBS, 2000).[15] Interestingly, these differences seem to remain for structured products. In describing their ratings criteria and methodology for structured products, S&P states: "[w]e base our ratings framework on the likelihood of default rather than expected loss or loss given default. In other words, our ratings at the rated instrument level don't incorporate any analysis or opinion on post-default recovery prospects." (S&P, 2007, p. 3) By contrast, Fitch incorporates some measure of expected recovery into their structured product ratings.[16]

Credit ratings issued by the agencies typically represent an unconditional view, sometimes called "cycle-neutral" or "through-the-cycle:" the rating agency's own description of their rating methodology broadly supports this view.

> (Moody's 1999, p. 6-7) "...[O]ne of Moody's goals is to achieve stable *expected* [italics in original] default rates across rating categories and time ... Moody's

---

[15] Specifically, EL = PD×LGD, where LGD is loss given default. However, given the paucity of LGD data, little variation in EL exists at the obligor (as opposed to instrument) level can be attributed to variation in LGD making the distinction between the agencies modest at best.

[16] See http://www.fitchratings.com/corporate/fitchResources.cfm?detail=1&rd_file=intro#rtng_actn.

believes that giving only modest weight to cyclical conditions serves the interests of the bulk of investors."

(S&P 2001, p. 41): "Standard & Poor's credit ratings are meant to be forward-looking; ... Accordingly, the anticipated ups and downs of business cycles – whether industry specific or related to the general economy – should be factored into the credit rating all along ... The ideal is to rate 'through the cycle'".

This unconditional or firm-specific view of credit risk stands in contrast to risk measures such as EDFs (expected default frequency) from Moody's KMV. An EDF has two principal inputs: firm leverage and asset volatility, where the latter is derived from equity (stock price) volatility. As a result EDFs can change frequently and significantly since they reflect the stock market's view of risk for that firm at a given point in time, a view which incorporates both systematic and idiosyncratic risk.

Unfortunately there is substantial evidence that credit rating changes, including changes to default, exhibit pro-cyclical or systematic variation (Nickell, Perraudin, and Varotto, 2000; Bangia et. al, 2002; Lando and Skodeberg, 2002), especially for speculative grades (Hanson and Schuermann, 2006).

5.2. How Does One Become a Rating Agency?[17]

Credit ratings have a long history of playing a role in the regulatory process going back to the 1930s in the U.S. (Sylla, 2002). Asset managers such as pension funds and insurers often have strict asset allocation guidelines which are ratings driven, such as, for instance, a ceiling on the amount that can be invested in speculative grade debt.[18] With the introduction of the Basel 2 standards, ratings have entered bank capital regulation. But whose ratings can be used is left up to the host country supervisor.[19] In the U.S. we use the SEC designation of a "Nationally Recognized Statistical Rating Organization," NRSRO, introduced in 1975. All three main rating agencies at the time – Moody's, S&P and Fitch – received this designation (White, 2002). It was not until 1997 that the SEC laid out formal criteria for becoming an NRSRO (Levich, Majnoni and Reinhart, 2002). Only with the Credit Rating Agency Reform Act of 2006 did the SEC officially obtain authority to regulate and supervise CRAs that have been designated NRSROs.[20]

Under the Reform Act, in order to qualify as an NRSRO, a credit agency must register with the SEC and it must have been in business as a credit rating agency for at least three consecutive years proceeding the date of its application.[21] The application must contain, among other things, information regarding the applicant's credit ratings performance measurement statistics over short-term, mid-term, and long-term periods; the procedures and

---

[17] We are indebted to Michelle Meertens for help with this section.

[18] ERISA, the Employee Retirement Income Security Act of 1974, is one such example.

[19] European guidelines can be found in "Committee of European Banking Supervisors, Guidelines on the Recognition of External Credit Assessment Institutions (Jan 20, 2006); available at http://www.bundesbank.de/download/bankenaufsicht/pdf/cebs/GL07.pdf.

[20] The final rule did not come out until June 2007 (http://www.sec.gov/rules/final/2007/34-55857fr.pdf).

[21] 15 U.S.C. 78c(a)(62).

methodologies that the applicant uses in determining credit ratings; policies or procedures adopted and implemented to prevent misuse of material, nonpublic information; and any conflict of interest relating to the issuance of credit ratings by the applicant.[22] All documentation submitted by the applicant must be made publicly available on its website,[23] and the information must be kept up to date and current.[24]

Since the early 1970s (1970 for Moody's and Fitch, S&P a few years later), issuers rather than investors are charged for obtaining a rating. These ratings are costly: $25,000 for issues up to $500 million, ½ bp for issues greater than $500 million (Kliger and Sarig, 2000). Treacy and Carey (2000) report that the usual fee charged by S&P is 3.25 bp of the face amount, though it may be up to 4.25 bp (Tomlinson and Evans, 2007); Fitch charges 3-7 bp (Tomlinson and Evans, 2007). The fees charged for rating structured credit products are higher: up to 12 bp by S&P and 7-8 bp by Fitch (Tomlinson and Evans, 2007). Moody's does not publish its pricing schedule.

5.3. When is A Credit Rating Wrong? How Could We Tell?

Highly rated firms default quite rarely. For example, Moody's reports that the one-year investment grade default rate over the period 1983-2006 was 0.073% or 7.3 bp. This is an average over four letter grade ratings: Aaa through Baa. Thus in a pool of 10,000 investment grade obligors or instruments we would expect seven to default over the course of one year. What if only three default? What about eleven? Higher than expect default could be the result of either a bad draw (bad luck) or an indicator that the rating is wrong, and it is very hard to distinguish between the two, especially for small probabilities (see also Lopez and Saidenberg, 2000). Indeed the use of the regulatory color scheme, which is behind the 1996 Market Risk Amendment to the Basel I, was motivated precisely by this recognition, and in that case the probability to be validated is comparatively large 1% (for 99% VaR) (BCBS, 1996) with daily data.

There are other approaches. Although rating agencies insist that their ratings scale reflects an ordinal ranking of credit risk, they also publish default rates for different horizons by rating. Thus we would expect default rates or probabilities to be monotonically increasing as one descends the credit spectrum. Using ratings histories from S&P, Hanson and Schuermann (2006) show formally that monotonicity is violated frequently for most notch-level investment grade one-year estimated default probabilities. The precision of the probability of default (PD) point estimates is quite low; see Appendix 3 for further discussion. Indeed there have been no defaults over one year for triple-A or AA+ (Aa1) rated firms, yet surely we do not believe that the one-year probability of default is identically equal to zero.

Although the one-year horizon is typical in credit analysis (and is also the horizon used in Basel 2), most traded credit instruments have longer maturity. For example, the typical CDS contract is five years, and over that horizon there are positive empirical default rates for Aaa and Aa1 which Moody's reports to be 7.8bp and 14.9bp respectively (Moody's, 2007c).

[22] 15 U.S.C. 78o-7(a)(1)(B).

[23] 15 U.S.C. 78o-7(a)(3).

[24] 15 U.S.C. 78o-7(b)(1).

"We perform a very significant but extremely limited role in the credit markets. We issue reasoned, forward-looking opinions about credit risk," says Fran Laserson, vice president of corporate communications at Moody's. "Our opinions are objective and not tied to any recommendations to buy and sell."

5.4. The Subprime Credit Rating Process

The rating process can be split into two steps: (1) estimation of a loss distribution, and (2) simulation of the cash flows. With a loss distribution in hand, it is straightforward to measure the amount of credit enhancement necessary for a tranche to attain a given credit rating. Credit enhancement (CE) is simply the amount of loss on underlying collateral that can be absorbed before the tranche absorbs any loss. When a credit rating is associated with the probability of default, the amount of credit enhancement is simply the level of loss CE such that the probability that loss is higher than CE is equal to the probability of default.

Figure 9 below illustrates how one can use the portfolio loss distribution in order map the PD associated with a credit rating on a particular tranche to a level of credit enhancement required for that tranche. For example, given a PD associated with a AAA credit rating, the credit enhancement is quite high at CE(AAA). However, given a higher PD associated with a BBB credit rating, the required credit enhancement is much lower at CE(BBB). A better credit rating is achieved through greater credit enhancement.

In a typical subprime structure, credit enhancement comes from two sources: subordination and excess spread. Subordination refers to the par value of tranches with claims junior to the tranche in question relative to the par value of collateral. It represents the maximum level of loss that could occur immediately without investors in the tranche losing one dollar of interest or principal. Excess spread refers to the difference between the income and expenses of the structure. On the income side, the trust receives interest payments and prepayment penalties from borrowers. On the expense side, the trust pays interest on tranches to investors, pays a fee to the servicer, and might have other payments to make related to derivatives like interest rate swaps. In most structures, excess spread is captured for the first three to five years of the life of the deal, which increases the amount of subordination for each rated tranche over time. Determining how much credit excess spread can be given to meet the required credit enhancement is a dynamic problem that involves simulating cash flows over time, and is the second step of the rating process. We now discuss each of these two steps in greater detail.

5.4.1. Credit Enhancement

In the first step of the rating process, the rating agency estimates the loss distribution associated with a given pool of collateral. The mean of the loss distribution is measured through the construction of a baseline frequency of foreclosure and loss severity for each loan that depends on the characteristics of the loan and local area economic conditions. The distribution of losses is constructed by estimating the sensitivity of losses to local area economic conditions for each mortgage loan, and then simulating future paths of local area economic conditions.

In order to construct the baseline, the rating agency uses historical data in order to estimate the likely sensitivity of the frequency of foreclosure and severity of loss to underwriting characteristics of the loan, the experience of the originator and servicer, and local area and national economic conditions. Most of the agencies claim to rely in part on loan-level data from *LoanPerformance* over 1992-2000 in order to estimate these relationships.

The key loan underwriting characteristics include:

- cumulative loan-to-value ratio (CLTV)
- consumer credit score (FICO)
- loan maturity (15 years, 30 years, 40 years, etc)
- interest rate
- fixed-rate (FRM) vs. adjustable-rate (ARM)
- property type (single-family, townhouse, condo, multi-family)
- home value
- documentation of income and assets
- loan purpose (purchase, term refinance, cash-out refinance)
- owner occupancy (owner-occupied, investor)
- mortgage insurance
- asset class (Jumbo, Alt-A, Subprime)

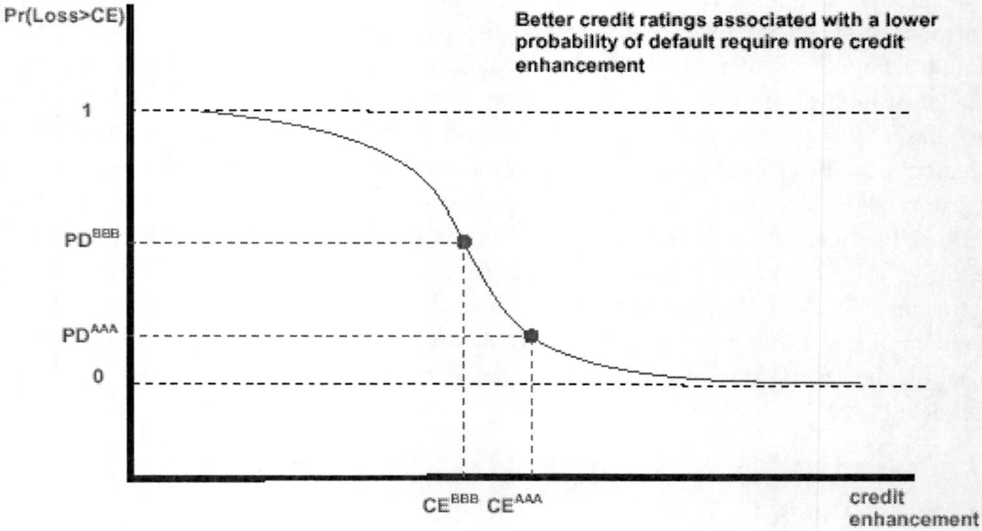

Figure 9: Mapping the Loss Distribution to Required Credit Enhancement

The key originator and servicer adjustments include:

- past performance of the originator's loans
- underwriting guidelines of the mortgage loans and adherence to them
- loan marketing practices

- credit checks made on borrowers
- appraisal standards
- experience in origination of mortgages
- collection practices
- loan modification and liquidation practices

Table 21 documents how the credit support (the product of the frequency of foreclosure and loss severity) for a pool of mortgage loans is sensitive to changes in loan attributes.

Table 1-21. Sensitivity of Aaa Credit Enhancement Levels to Loan Attributes

	Sample Pool A		Sample Pool B	
	Aaa credit support	Change from Base	Aaa credit support	Change from Base
Base Pool	3.17		2.57	
LTV+5%	4.28	35%	3.52	37%
LTV–5%	2.32	– 27%	1.85	– 28%
FICO+20	3.02	– 5%	2.49	– 3%
FICO-20	3.42	8%	2.75	7%
All Cashout				
Appraisal Quality	4.68	48%	3.91	52%
All Purchase	2.62	– 17%	2.15	– 16%
All Investor	3.69	16%	2.99	16%
All 15-year term	2.42	– 24%	1.93	– 25%
All ARM	3.47	9%	2.81	9%
All Condo	3.31	4%	2.68	4%
All Alt Doc	3.35	6%	2.78	8%
Price > $300k, LTV constant	3.8	20%	3.10	21%

Source: *Moody's Mortgage Metrics*

Pool A: LTV 67, FICO 732, CashOut 19%, Purch 21%, Single Fam 89%, Owner 98%, Fulldoc 75%, 30-year 98%, Fixed Rate 100% Pool B: LTV 65, FICO 744, CashOut 17%, Purch 21%, Single Fam 89%, Owner 96%, Fulldoc 95%, 30-year 98%, Fixed Rate 100%

The Aaa credit enhancement for the base pools are illustrated in the first row. As Pool A has a higher LTV, lower FICO, and lower percentage of full documentation than Pool B, it has a higher level of credit support (3.17 percent versus 2.57 percent). Table 21 also illustrates the impact of changing one characteristic of the pool for all loans in the pool, holding all other characteristics constant. For example, if all loans in the pool were underwritten under an Alternative Documentation program, the credit support of Pool A would increase by 6 percent to 3.35 percent and Pool B would increase by 8 percent to 2.78 percent. Note that the change in support depends on both the sensitivity of support to the loan characteristic as well as the size of the change in the characteristic. Changes in leverage appear to have significant effects on credit support, as an increase of five percentage points is associated with an increase in credit support by more than one-third.[25]

The rating agency will typically adjust this baseline for current local area economic conditions like the unemployment rate, interest rates, and home price appreciation. The agencies are quite opaque about this relationship, and for some reason do not illustrate the impact of changes in local area economic conditions on credit enhancement in their public rating criteria. For example, Fitch employs scaling factors developed by University Financial Associates which control for four different components of regional factors: macro factors like employment rates and construction activity, demographic factors like population growth; political/legal factors; and even topographic factors that might constrain the growth of housing markets. The multipliers typically range from 0.5 to 1.7 and are updated quarterly.

In order to simulate the loss distribution, the rating agency needs to estimate the sensitivity of losses to local area economic conditions. Fitch tackles this problem by breaking out actual losses on mortgage loans into independent national and state components for each quarter. The sensitivity of losses to each factor is equal to one by construction. The final step is to fix a distribution for each of these components, and then simulate the loss distribution of the mortgage pool using random draws from the distribution of state and national components of unexpected loss.[26]

5.5. Conceptual Differences Between Corporate and ABS Credit Ratings

Subprime ABS ratings differ from corporate debt ratings in a number of different dimensions:

- Corporate bond (obligor) ratings are largely based on firm-specific risk characteristics. Since ABS structures represent claims on cash flows from a portfolio of underlying assets, the rating of a structured credit product must take into account systematic risk. It is correlated losses which matter especially for the more senior (higher rated) tranches, and loss correlation arises through dependence on shared or common (or systematic) risk factors.[27] For ABS deals which have a large number of underlying assets, for instance MBS, the portfolio is large enough such that all idiosyncratic risk is diversified away leaving only systematic exposure to the risk factors particular to that product class (here, mortgages). By contrast, a substantial amount of idiosyncratic risk may remain in ABS transactions with smaller asset pools, for instance CDOs (CGFS, 2005; Amato and Remolona, 2005).

[25] Note that Moody's have increased subordination levels in subprime RMBS by 30 percent over last three years, and this can be largely attributed to an increase in support required by a decline in underwriting standards.

[26] Note that Fitch actually simulates the frequency of foreclosure and loss severity separately, but the discussion here focuses on the product (expected loss) for simplicity. Each of the national and state components is likely transformed by subtracting the mean and dividing by the standard deviation, so that the distribution converges to a standard normal distribution. This permits the agency to use a two-factor copula model in order to simulate the loss distribution. Note that the sensitivity of losses to the normalized component would be equal to the inverse of the standard deviation of the actual component.

[27] Note that correlation includes more than just economic conditions, as it includes (a) model risk by the agencies (b) originator and arranger effects (c) servicer effects.

Because these deals are portfolios, the effect of correlation is not the same for all tranches: equity tranches prefer higher correlation, senior tranches prefer lower correlation (tail losses are driven by loss correlation). As correlation increases, so does portfolio loss volatility. The payoff function for the equity tranche is, true to its name, like a call option. Indeed equity itself is a call option on the assets of the underlying firm, and the value of a call option is increasing in volatility. If the equity tranche is long a call option, the senior tranche is short a call option, so that their payoffs behave in an opposite manner. The impact of increased correlation on the value of mezzanine tranches is ambiguous and depends on the structure of a particular deal (Duffie, 2007). By contrast, correlation with systematic risk factors should not matter for corporate ratings.

As a result of the portfolio nature of the rated products, the ratings migration behavior may also be different than for ordinary obligor ratings. Moody's (2007a) reports that rating changes are much more common for corporate bond than for structured product ratings, but the magnitude of changes (number of notches up- or downgraded) was nearly double for the structured products.

- Subprime ABS ratings refer to the performance of a static pool instead of a dynamic corporation. When a firm becomes distressed, it has the option to change its investment strategy and inject more capital. As long as a firm is deemed to be creditworthy during neutral economic conditions, it is reasonable to expect that the firm could take prompt corrective action in order to avoid defaulting on its debt during a transitory decline in aggregate or industry conditions. However, the pool of mortgages underlying subprime ABS is fixed, and investors do not expect an issuer to support a weakly-performing deal.
- Subprime ABS ratings rely heavily on quantitative models while corporate debt ratings rely heavily on analyst judgment. In particular, corporate credit ratings require the separation of a firm's long-run condition and competitiveness from the business cycle, the assessment of whether or not an industry downturn is cyclical or permanent, and determination about whether or not a firm could actually survive a pro-longed transitory downturn.
- Unlike corporate credit ratings, ABS ratings rely heavily on a forecast of economic conditions. Note that a corporate credit rating is based on the agency's assessment that a firm will default during neutral economic conditions (i.e. full employment at the national and industry level). However, the rating agency is unable to focus on neutral economic conditions when assigning subprime ABS ratings, because in the model, uncertainty about the level of loss in the mortgage pool is driven completely by changes in economic conditions. If one were to fix the level of economic activity – for example at full employment – the level of losses is determined, and according to the model, the probability of default is either zero or one. It follows that the credit rating on an ABS tranche is the agency's assessment that economic conditions will deteriorate to the point where losses on the underlying mortgage pool will exceed the tranche's credit enhancement. In other words, it is largely based on a forecast of economic conditions combined with the agency's estimated sensitivity of losses to that forecast.

- Finally, while an ABS credit rating for a particular rating grade should have similar expected loss to corporate credit rating of the same grade, the volatility of loss can be quite different across asset classes.

5.6. How Through-the-Cycle Rating Could Amplify the Housing Cycle

Like corporate credit ratings, the agencies seek to make subprime ABS credit ratings through the housing cycle. Stability means that one should not see upgrades concentrated during a housing boom and downgrades concentrated during a housing bust.

It is not difficult to understand that changes in economic conditions affect the distribution of losses on a mortgage pool. The unemployment rate and home price appreciation have obvious effects on the ability of a borrower to avoid default and the severity of loss in the event of default.

Consider a AAA-rated tranche issued during an environment of high home price appreciation (HPA). Figure 10 illustrates that the level of credit enhancement is determined using the probability associated with a AAA credit rating and the rating agency's estimate of the loss distribution (blue) in this economic environment. However, as the housing market slows down, the loss distribution shifts to the right, as any level of probability is now associated with a higher level of loss. If the rating agency does not respond to this new loss distribution and uses the same level of credit enhancement to structure new deals in a tough economic environment, the probability of default associated with these AAA-rated tranche will actually be closer to a AA than a AAA. It follows that keeping enhancement constant through the cycle will result in ratings instability, with upgrades during a boom and downgrades during a bust.

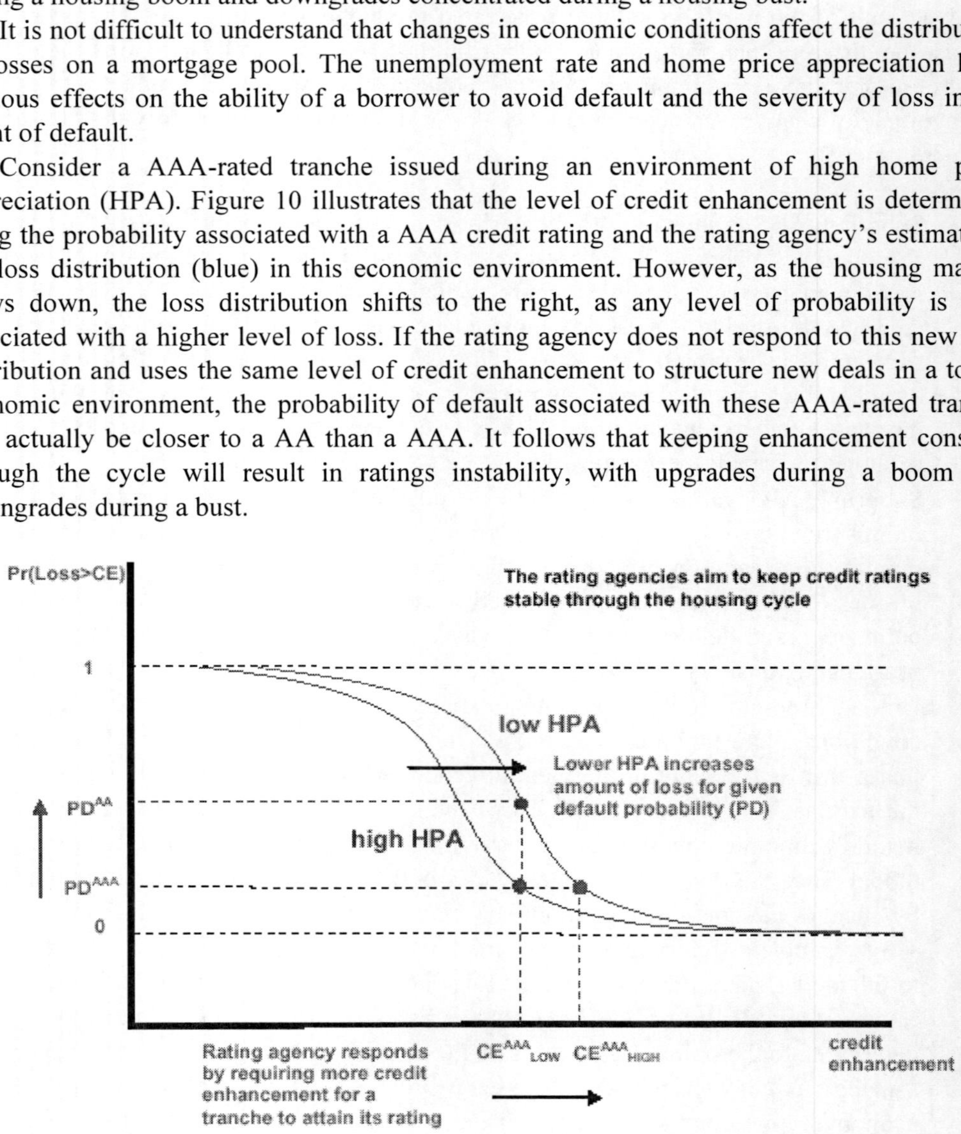

Figure 10: Credit enhancement and economic conditions

Rating agency must respond to shifts in the loss distribution by increasing the amount of needed credit enhancement to keep ratings stable as economic conditions deteriorate, as illustrated in the Figure. It follows that the stabilizing of ratings through the cycle is associated with pro-cyclical credit enhancement: as the housing market improves, credit enhancement falls; as the housing market slows down, credit enhancement increases.

This phenomenon has two important implications:

- Pro-cyclical credit enhancement has the potential to amplify the housing cycle, creating credit and asset price bubbles on the upside and contributing to severe credit crunches and on the downside. In order to understand this point, consider the hypothetical example in Figure 11. On the left is an aggressive structure based on strong housing market conditions. The AAA tranche is 80 percent of the funding, and the weighted-average cost of funds is LIBOR+92 bp. However, as the housing market slows down, the rating agency removes leverage from the structure, and increases the subordination of the AAA-rated tranche from 20 to 25 percent. By requiring a larger fraction of the deal to be financed by BBB-rated debt, the weighted-average cost of funds increases to LIBOR+100 bp. This higher cost of funds will require higher interest rates on subprime mortgage loans, or will require a significant tightening in underwriting standards on the underlying mortgage loans. Note that the de-leveraging the structure has a knock-on effect on economic activity by reducing the supply of credit. It is difficult at this point to assess the importance of this phenomenon to what appeared to be a bubble in housing credit and prices on the upside. One source of concern is that the ratio of upgrades to downgrades appeared to be fairly stable for home equity ABS over 2001-2006 (see the discussion on rating performance below). However, the impact on the downside is fairly certain. One week after a historical downgrade action by the agencies, leading subprime lenders discontinued offering the 2/28 and 3/27 hybrid ARM (see the discussion of ratings performance below).

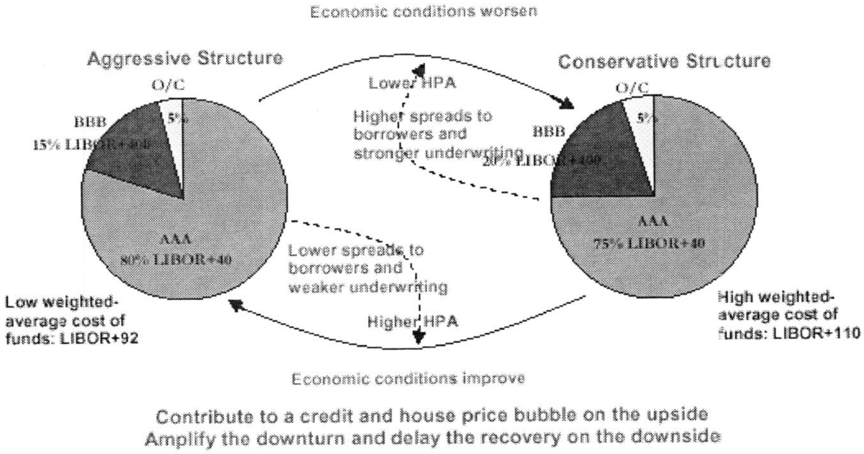

Figure 11: Procyclic credit enhancement

- Investors in subprime ABS are vulnerable to the ability of the rating agency to predict turning points in the housing cycle and respond appropriately. One must be fair to note that the downturn in housing did not surprise the rating agencies, who had been warning investors about the possibility and the impact on performance for quite some time. However, it does not appear that the agencies appropriately measured the sensitivity of losses to economic activity or anticipated the severity of the downturn.

5.7. Cash Flow Analytics for Excess Spread

The second part of the rating process involves simulating the cash flows of the structure in order to determine how much credit excess spread will receive towards meeting the required credit enhancement. As an example, in Table 22 we consider the credit enhancement corresponding to a hypothetical pool of subprime mortgage loans. In this example, the required credit enhancement for the Aaa tranche is 22.50%. A simulation of cash flows suggests that excess spread can contribute 9.25% to meet this requirement, suggesting that the amount of subordination for this tranche must be 13.25%. In this section, we briefly describe how the rating agencies measure this credit attributed to excess spread, focusing on subprime RMBS.

Table 1-22. Cash Flow Analytics

Tranche Rating	Required Credit Enhancement	Spread Credit	Subordination	Class Size
Aaa	22.50%	9.25%	13.25%	86.75%
Aa2	16.75%	9.25%	7.50%	5.75%
A2	12.25%	8.75%	3.50%	4.00%
Baa2	8.50%	8.50%	0.00%	3.50%
Total				100%

Source: Moody's

The key inputs into the cash flow analysis involve:

- the credit enhancement for given credit rating
- the timing of these losses
- prepayment rates
- interest rates and index mismatches
- trigger events
- weighted average loan rate decrease
- prepayment penalties
- pre-funding accounts
- swaps, caps, and other derivatives.

The first input to the analysis is amount of losses on collateral that a tranche with a given rating would be able to withstand without sustaining a loss, which corresponds to the required credit enhancement implied from the loss distribution. Note that better credit ratings are associated with higher levels credit enhancement, and thus are associated with a higher level of expected loss on the underlying collateral.

The Timing of Losses

Table 23 illustrates Moody's assumption about the timing of losses, which is based on historical performance over 1993-1999. Note there are slight differences in the timing between fixed-rate and ARMs. Except for the first year, losses are assumed to be distributed evenly throughout the year. In the first year, losses are distributed evenly throughout the last six months. Adjustments to this assumption need to be made if the pool contains seasoned or delinquent loans.

Table 1-23. First-Lien Loss Curve (As % of Original Pool Balance)

Year	FRMs	ARMs
1	3%	3%
2	12%	17%
3	20%	25%
4	25%	25%
5	20%	20%
6	15%	10%
7	5%	0%
8	0%	0%
Total	100%	0%

Source: Moody's; based on historical performance over 1993-1999

Note that an acceleration in the timing of losses implies a lower level of excess spread in later periods, which reduces the contribution that excess spread can make to meet the required credit enhancement. It follows that a conservative approach to rating involves front-loading the timing of losses. Moreover, given the importance of the timing, it is possible to understand how the existence of elevated early payment defaults observed in the 2006 vintages of RMBS will correspond to significant adverse effects on the ratings performance.

Prepayment Risk

Prepayments of principal include both the voluntary and involuntary (i.e. default) varieties. Note that the path of the dollar value of involuntary prepayments over time has been tied down by assumptions about the level and timing of losses. It follows that assumptions about the prepayment curve really just pin down the severity of loss on defaulted mortgages (in order to identify the number of involuntary prepayments) and the number of voluntary prepayments. Table 24 documents Moody's assumptions about prepayment rates for a Baa2-rated tranche secured by a portfolio of subprime loans. The standard measure of prepayment frequency is the Constant Prepayment Rate (CPR), defined as the annualized one-month prepayment rate of loans that remain in the pool.

Table 1-24. Pre-payment Assumption for Baa2-Rated Tranches

Loan age (months)	FRMs	ARMs	2/28s	3/27s
1	6%	5.5%	5.5%	5.5%
2-18	↑ by 1.33%/mth	↑ by 1.639%/mth	↑ by 1.639%/mth	↑ by 1.639%/mth
19-24	30%	35%	33%	33%
25-30	30%	35%	55%	33%
31-36	30%	35%	33%	33%
37-42	30%	35%	33%	55%
43+	30%	35%	33%	33%

Source: Moody's

Table 1-25. Adjustments by Tranche Credit Rating to Baa2 Pre-payment Curves

Rating	FRM	ARM
Aaa	133%	115%
Aa1	126%	112.5%
Aa2	120%	110%
Aa3	117%	108.5%
A1	113%	106.5%
A2	110%	105%
A3	107%	103.5%
Baa1	103%	101.5%
Baa2	100%	100%
Baa3	97%	98.5%
Ba1	93%	96.5%
Ba2	90%	95%
Ba3	87%	93.5%
B1	83%	91.5%
B2	80%	90%
B3	77%	88.5%

Source: Moody's

For both fixed-rate (FRMs) and adjustable-rate mortgages (ARMs), the CPR increases every month until the 19th month, where it stays constant through the remaining life of the deal. However, for hybrid ARMs, which have a fixed interest rate for either 2 or 3 years and then revert to an ARM, there is a spike in the CPR in the six months following payment reset. Note that since prepayments include defaults, it is necessary to adjust the prepayment curve for the credit rating of the tranche under analysis. Recall that a better credit rating is associated with a higher level of loss on collateral, which means a higher frequency of involuntary prepayments. Table 25 documents adjustments that Moody's makes to the CPR by rating category. For example, the prepayment rate is 15 percent higher for a Aaa-rated tranche than a Baa2-rated tranche in order to capture the higher frequency of involuntary prepayment (i.e. default) associated with the Aaa level of loss.

The assumptions made above identify the dollar value of involuntary prepayments and the total number of prepayments. In order to identify the number of involuntary prepayments (and consequently the number of voluntary prepayments), it is necessary to make an assumption about loss severity. Note that this assumption about severity is different from the one used in the determination of credit enhancement in the first step outlined above. Moody's makes the assumption that the fraction of involuntary prepayments in total prepayments increases with the severity of loss (i.e. as the credit rating improves). This phenomenon is described in Table 26.

Table 1-26. Loss Severity Assumptions for 1st Lien Subprime Mortgages

Aaa	60%
Aa	55%
A	50%
Baa	45%
Ba	42.5%
B	40%

Source: Moody's

In the end, voluntary prepayments reduce principal and thus the benefit of excess spread. It follows that a conservative view toward rating will typically make high and front-loaded assumptions about the path of voluntary prepayments, as this reduces the contribution that excess spread makes towards credit enhancement.

Interest Rate Risk

The key remaining source of uncertainty in the analysis of cash flows is the behavior of interest rates. Note that the coupons on tranches typically have floating interest rates tied to the one-month LIBOR. Moreover, note that interest rates on some of the underlying loans are adjustable, which makes receipts from collateral vary with the level of interest rates. Interest rate risk is created by mis-matches between the sensitivity of collateral and tranches to interest rates. Some examples include:

- Fixed rate loans funded with floating rate certificates
- Prime rate index funded with LIBOR based certificates
- six-month LIBOR loans funded with one-month LIBOR certificates

Based on a number of factors, including the state of the economy, the forward-rate curve, and the current level of interest rates, interest rate stresses are determined.

Interest rate risk had an adverse impact on the performance of RMBS structures issued during the 2002 to 2004. In particular, throughout 2002 to mid-2004, the one-month LIBOR maintained a level to 1% - 1.8%. However, in June 2004, the one-month LIBOR began to increase quickly, reaching 5.3% in 2006. This increase in interest rates has an adverse impact through three channels. First, the coupons on ARM collateral adjust less quickly than the coupons on floating-rate certificates. Second, while rising rates will reduce the prepayment of fixed-rate loans, they also encourage a deterioration in the coupons on adjustable-rate loans as these obligors refinance out of high interest-rate loans, leaving a higher fraction of low- and fixed-interest rates in the pool. Finally, the increase in prepayment rates leads to quick return of principal to investors in senior tranches, where credit spreads are the smallest. Each of these factors leads to a compression of excess spread.

Many structures enter into an interest rate swap agreement which replaces the flexible-rate coupon paid to the tranches with a fixed-rate coupon in order to avoid this type of problem. However, note that this swap does not completely remove interest rate risk. For example, when pools contain ARM mortgages, the structure is vulnerable to a decline in interest rates which reduces the cash flows from collateral.

Table 1-27. Interest Rate Stresses

	Decreases from LIBOR				**Increases from LIBOR**			
Month	**BBB**	**A**	**AA**	**AAA**	**BBB**	**A**	**AA**	**AAA**
6	– 1.06%	– 1.24%	– 1.42%	– 1.68%	0.88%	1.40%	2.07%	3.10%
12	– 1.81%	– 2.09%	– 2.37%	– 2.76%	1.22%	2.02%	3.06%	4.66%
24	– 2.28%	– 2.68%	– 3.08%	– 3.64%	2.01%	3.15%	4.63%	6.90%
36	– 2.52%	– 2.95%	– 3.39%	– 4.00%	2.18%	3.43%	5.05%	7.53%
48	– 2.52%	– 2.97%	– 3.43%	– 4.09%	2.52%	3.85%	5.58%	8.24%
60	– 2.52%	– 2.98%	– 3.45%	– 4.12%	2.65%	4.02%	5.79%	8.52%

Source: Fitch (August 2007)

The approach of the rating agencies to interest rate risk is to construct a path of interest rate stresses in order to capture the worst likely movement in interest rates. Table 24 illustrates the interest rate stresses used by Fitch.

Note that these are changes (in percentage points) relative to the one-month LIBOR. The magnitude of the interest rate shocks is larger for better credit ratings and longer maturities.

Other Details

Cash flow analysis is performed incorporating step-down triggers. For each rating level, the triggers are analyzed for the probability that they will be breached. As the triggers are set at levels which protect the rated tranches, they typically will be breached in stress scenarios. It follows that one typically assumes that the transaction does not step down (i.e. credit enhancement is not released) and that all tranches are paid sequentially for its life. Finally, mortgage loans with higher interest rates tend to prepay first, which reduces excess spread of the transaction over time. In order to capture this, Moody's assumes that the weighted average coupon (WAC) of the loans decreases by one basis point each month over the first three years of the deal.

Motivating Example

In order to better understand the cash flow analysis, we will illustrate using a structure similar to GSAMP Trust 2006-NC2. In particular, we focus on a hypothetical pool of 2/28 ARM mortgage loans with an initial interest rate of 8 percent, a margin of 6 percent, and interest rate caps of 1.5%. The servicer receives a fee of 50 bp and master servicer receives a fee of 1 bp, each per annum and senior to any distributions to investors. The trust enters into an interest rate swap with a counterparty paying a fixed rate of 5.45% and receiving LIBOR – initially at 5.32% --according to a swap notional schedule described in Figure 8. Each month, the net payment to the swap counterparty is senior to any distributions to investors. Table 28 documents that the capital structure is similar to that of the New Century deal, but with fewer tranches in order to simplify the analysis.

Table 1-28. Capital Structure

Tranche	Width	Spread
AAA	79.35%	0.25%
AA	9.20%	0.31%
A	4.90%	0.37%
BBB	3.45%	1.00%
BB	1.70%	2.50%
O/C	1.40%	

Note: spread over 1-month LIBOR

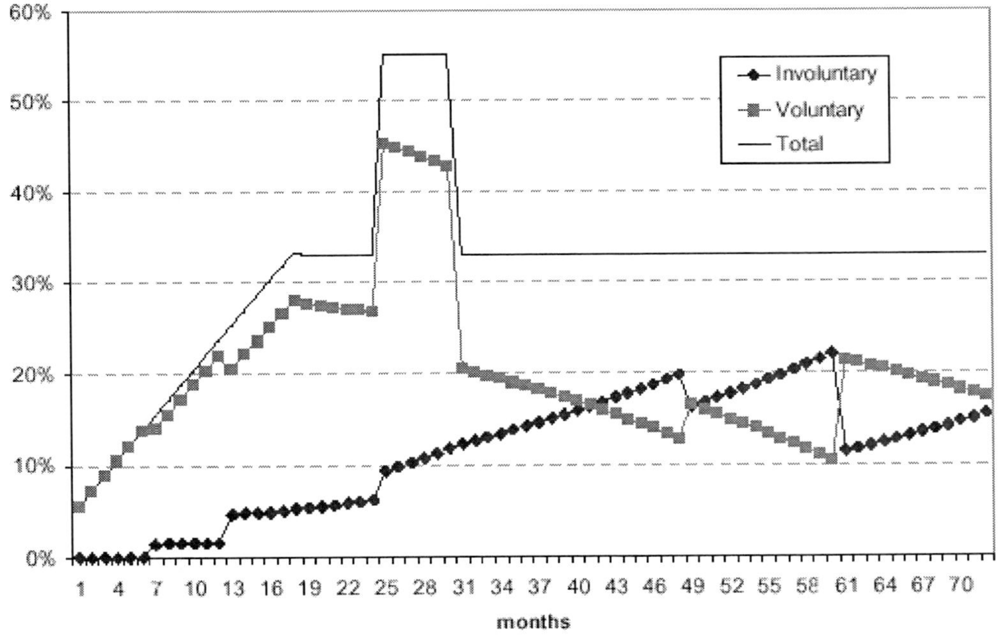

Figure 12: Decomposing Constant Prepayment Rates (CPRs)

We focus our analysis on the BBB-rated tranche. Our analysis starts with prepayment rates, which are illustrated in Figure 12. The total CPR is the fraction of remaining loans which prepay each month at an annualized rate, and is taken from Table 24 above for 2/28 ARMs. Notice the spike in prepayment rates shortly following payment rest at 24 months. The involuntary CPR is tied down by (a) the level of losses, assumed in this case to be 10% given the BBB rating; (b) the timing of losses documented in Table 23; (c) and the severity of losses from Table 26 in order to convert dollars of principal loss into an involuntary prepayment rate. Since the timing assumption precludes losses after 72 months, we only focus on the first six years of the deal life. As the capital structure of the deal is fixed, this exercise is essentially a test of whether or not the BBB-rated tranche as structured can receive a 6.9% credit (= 10% - 3.1%) from excess spread to meet the required credit enhancement.

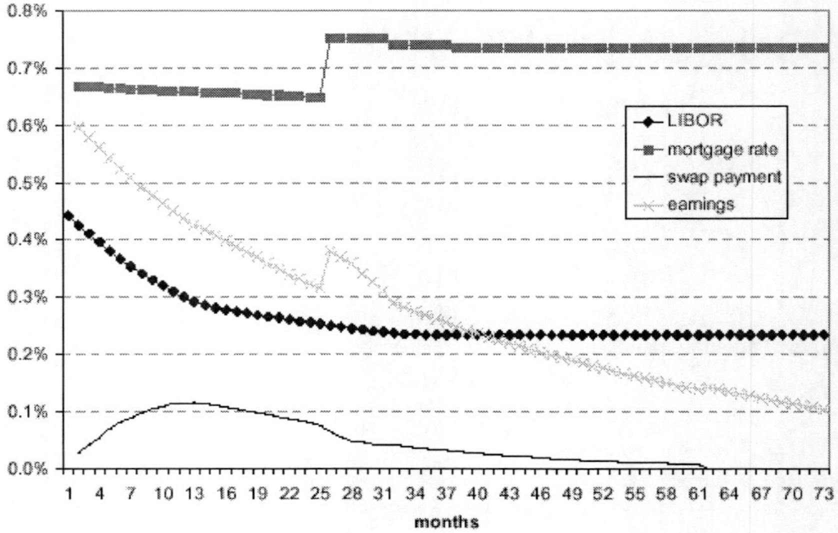

Figure 13: LIBOR stress, trust earnings, and the net swap payment
Note: the swap payment and earnings are each measured at a monthly rate and relative to original portfolio par. Earnings is defined as the difference between mortgage interest income, the net swap payment, and servicer fees of 51 basis points per annum.

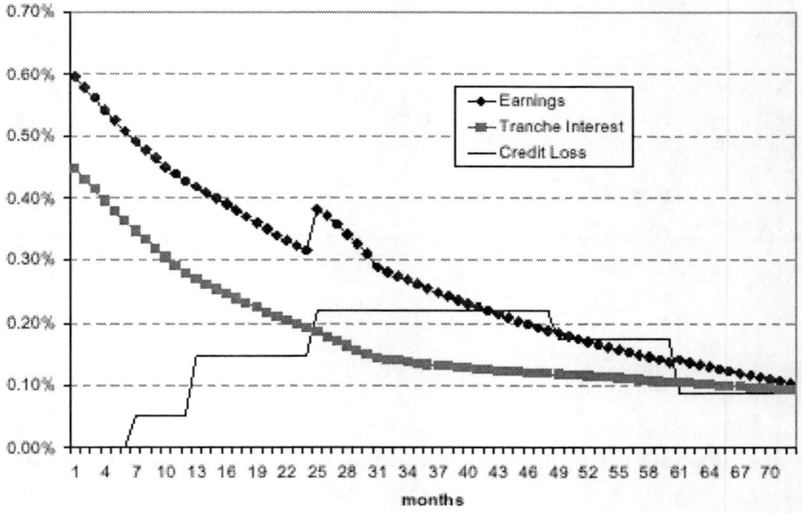

Figure 14: Earnings, Tranche Interest, and Credit Loss
Note: Earnings, tranche interest, and credit loss are measured each at a monthly rate and relative to original portfolio par

Given the path of pre-payments, one needs to use the interest rate stresses in order to simulate future cash flows. Since the structure is hedged, the most severe interest rate shock is a decline in interest rates. When the interest rate on mortgages declines but the interest rate on tranches is fixed there is pressure on earnings. Figure 13 documents that assumed path of LIBOR, taken from Table 27 above, but converted into a monthly interest rate. The slow decrease over the first 24 months in the mortgage income reflects adverse selection in prepayment (high interest rates pre-paying first). There is an obvious spike in the mortgage interest rate at 24 months once payments reset. As LIBOR is falling, there is a net payment made to the swap counterparty, but this declines over time as the amount of swap notional goes to zero over the five-year life of the contract. The earnings of the trust before distributions and loss falls over time as mortgages prepay and the interest rate on remaining mortgages falls.

Figure 14 documents the path of trust earnings, tranche interest, and credit losses over time, each measured at a monthly rate and relative to portfolio par. Tranche interest declines over time as interest rates fall and as pre-payments reduce the principal value of the senior tranche. While earnings are adequate to cover tranche interest initially, after the first year credit losses are eating into over-collateralization. After 42 months, earnings no longer cover losses, and the structure is struggling greatly.

Figure 15 documents that these losses reduce the subordination available to each tranche over time. At 56 months, over-collateralization has been exhausted and the BB-rated tranche defaults. However, the BBB-rate tranche is able to survive until 72 months, suggesting that this tranche could withstand a loss rate of 10 percent. It follows that the deal is structured adequately.

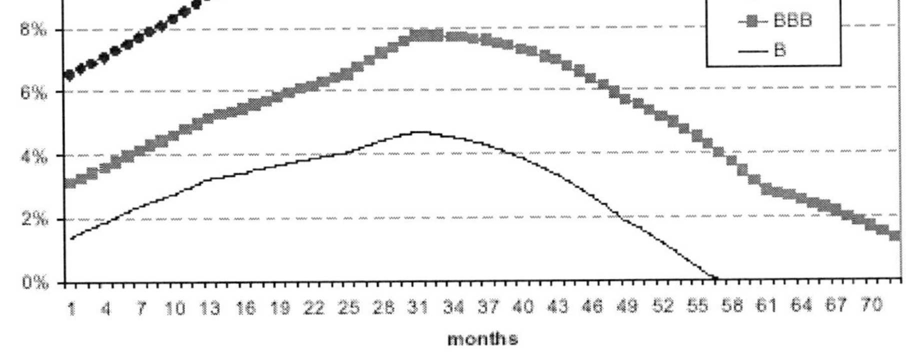

Figure 15: Dynamic subordination of mezzanine tranches (10% required enhancement)

Figure 16 documents the dynamic subordination of the same capital structure in the event that losses are only 50 basis points higher. In this case, the BBB rated tranche defaults in month 70. The actual losses to investors in this tranche would be quite low because there are no losses after 72 months. However, when losses on the pool increase to 14%, the investors in the BBB-rated tranche are completely wiped out and the A-rated tranche defaults.

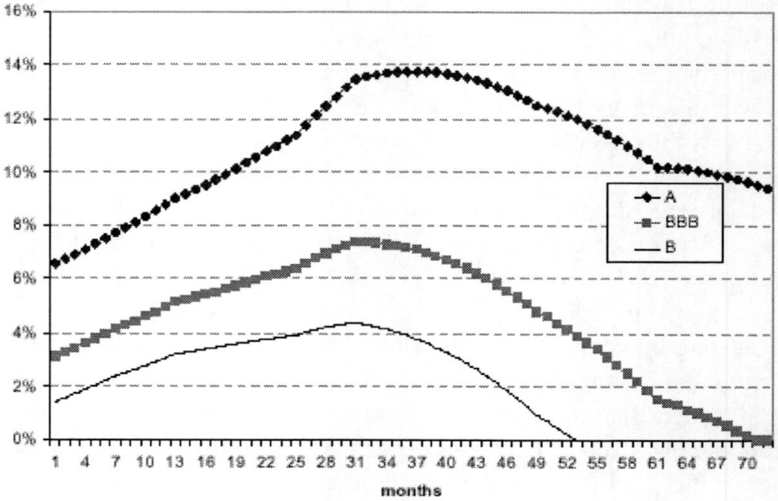

Figure 16: Dynamic subordination of mezzanine tranches (10.5% required enhancement)

5.8. Performance Monitoring

The rating agencies currently monitor the performance of approximately 10,000 pools of mortgage loan collateral. Deal performance is tracked using monthly remittance from Intex Solutions, Inc. Since there is no uniform reporting methodology, the first step is to ensure the integrity of the data.

The agencies use this performance data in order to identify which deals merit a detailed review, but do complete such a review for every deal at least once a year. The key performance metric is the loss coverage ratio (LCR), which is defined as the ratio of the current credit enhancement for a tranche relative to estimated unrealized losses. Note that losses are estimated using underwriting characteristics for unseasoned loans (less than 12 months), and actual performance for seasoned loans. When the loss coverage ratio falls below an acceptable level given the rating of the tranche, the agency will perform a detailed review of the transaction, and consider ratings action.

In the example subprime deal described in Table 29, which is taken from a Fitch (2007) and does not correspond to the New Century deal, the pipeline measure of loss is constructed by applying historical default rates to the fraction of loans in each delinquency status bucket, and applying a projected loss severity. For example, the rating agency assumes that 68 percent of loans 90 days past due will default, while only 11 percent of current loans will default.

Table 1-29. Example of Projected Loss as a Percentage of Current Pool Balance

Status	Delinquency Status Distribution	Projected Default As % of Bucket	Projected Default As % of Pool	Projected Loss Severity	Expected Loss As % of Pool
Current	83	11	9.1	35	3.2
30 Days	4.0	37	1.5	35	0.5
60 Days	2.6	54	1.4	35	0.5
90 Days	2.5	68	1.7	35	0.6
Bankruptcies	1.7	54	0.9	35	0.3
Foreclosure	3.8	76	2.9	35	1.0
REO	2.6	100	2.6	35	0.9
Total	100.0		20.0	35	7.1

Notes: The example transaction is 18 months seasoned, has 63% of the original pool remaining (called the pool factor), incurred 0.77% loss to date, and reports a 60+ day of 13.15% (=2.6+2.5+1.7+3.8+2.6). The delinquency bucket figures (with the exception of REO) have a 98% home price appreciation adjustment applied. The example deal's current three-month loss severity is 25%, and the projected lifetime loss severity is approximately 35%. The expected loss figures are as a percentage of the remaining pool balance. The expected loss as a percentage of original pool balance is 5.25% = (7.1%*63%+0.77%)

The current subordination of a tranche reflects excess spread that has been retained as well as any losses to date. In this example in Table 30 the M-1 tranche rated AA currently has subordination of 20.61 percent. However, due to expected future accumulation of excess spread, this class can withstand losses of 26.90 percent, corresponding to a loss coverage ratio of 3.8 (= 26.9/7.1). Note that the target loss coverage ratio for the AA rating is 2.82, suggesting that the original rating is sound. However, the B-2 class rated BBB- currently has subordination of 3 percent and a break-loss rate of 10.41 percent. Note that the target break-loss for this rating is 11.04 percent, and the target break-loss of 9.95 for the BB+ rating (not reported). In this case, the rating agency is using tolerance to prevent this tranche from being downgraded at this time. A conversation with a ratings analyst suggested that a tranche would not be downgraded until it failed the target break-loss level for one full rating-grade below the current level.

It is worth taking the time to highlight how changes in rating criteria affect the ratings monitoring process. In particular, if the rating agencies become more conservative in structuring new deals, it is not clear that anything should change when it comes to making a decision to downgrade securities secured by seasoned loans. The numerator of the loss coverage ratio is the current subordination of the tranche, which is unaffected by any change in criteria. The denominator is the estimated unrealized loss. Unless the rating agency also changes its mapping from current loan performance to the probability of default, or updates its view on loss severity, the key input into the ratings monitoring process is unchanged. In this sense, there is no need to change the way the agency monitors existing transactions. If an existing transaction was structured with inadequate initial subordination, the normal ratings monitoring process will pick this up and downgrade appropriately. In this sense, there is no need to update existing transactions.

Table 1-30. Example of Ratings Analysis Using Break-Loss Figures

Class	Current Rating	Current Subordi-nation (%)	Current Break-Loss (%)	Current Loss Coverage Ratio (%)	Target Break-Loss (%)	Target Loss Coverage Ratio (%)	Model Proposed After Tolerances
A	**AAA**	31.59	39.71	5.61	27.18	3.84	AAA
M-1	**AA**	20.61	26.90	3.80	19.95	2.82	AA
M-2	**A**	12.08	18.25	2.58	15.79	2.23	A
M-3	**BBB+**	7.50	15.62	2.21	13.32	1.88	BBB+
B-1	**BBB**	5.92	13.14	1.86	12.09	1.71	BBB
B-2	**BBB–**	3.00	10.41	1.47	11.04	1.56	BBB–

Notes: The example transaction is 18 months seasoned and has a projected loss as a percent of current balance of 7.1%. Based on the projected delinquency, the triggers will pass at the step-down date and toggle thereafter. The current annualized excess spread available to cover losses is 3.10% (including interest rate derivatives). Current break-loss: the amount of collateral loss that would call the class to default. This figure includes excess spread and triggers. Current loss coverage ratio (LCR): determined by dividing the bond's current break-loss amount by the current base-case projected loss of 7.1%. Model proposed: Considers the difference between the current LCR and the target LCR

5.9. Home Equity ABS Rating Performance

Table 31 documents the performance of Moody's Subprime RMBS over the last five years. The table documents downgrades in the top panel and upgrades in the bottom panel, broken out across first- and second-lien mortgage loans, as well as by origination year. Rating actions are measured by fraction of origination volume affected, the fraction of tranches affected, and the fraction of deals affected. The first observation to note is that by any measure, the rating agencies have appeared to struggle rating subprime deals throughout the period, as the ratio of downgrades to upgrades is larger than one. That being said, the recent performance of subprime RMBS ratings has been historically bad. The table documents that 92 percent of 1st lien subprime deals originated in 2006 as well as 84.5 percent of 2nd-lien deals originated in 2005 and 91.8 percent of 2nd-lien deals originated in 2006 have been downgraded.

Note that half of all downgrades of tranches in the history of Home Equity ABS were made in the first seven months of 2007. About half of these were made during the week of 9 July, when Moody's downgraded 399 tranches. About two-thirds of these downgrades involved securitizations by four issuers who accounted for about one-third of 2006 issuance: New Century, WMC, Long Beach, and Fremont. Note that 86% of the downgraded tranches were originally rated Baa2 or worse, which meant that the notional amount downgraded was only about $9 billion. However, the ratings action affected just under 50 percent of 2006 1st-lien deals and almost two-thirds of 2005 2nd-lien deals, and the mean downgrade severity was 3.2 notches. Table 32 documents the ratings transition matrices for the 2005 and 2006 vintages across 1st and 2nd-lien status as of October 2007. It is clear from the table that ratings action has been concentrated in the mezzanine tranches, but there are some notable downgrades of Aaarated tranches in the 2006 vintage of 2nd-lien loans.

In addition to the ratings action, the rating agencies announced significant changes to rating criteria, and took a more pessimistic view on the housing market. At the time of the downgrade action, Moody's announced that it expected median existing family home prices to fall by 10 percent from the peak in 2005 to a trough at the end of 2008. The rating agency also significantly increased its loss expectations for certain flavors of sub-prime mortgages (hybrid ARMs, stated-income, high CLTV, first-time home-buyer), reduced the credit for excess spread, and adjusted its cash flow analysis to incorporate the likely impact of loan modifications.

In response to the historic rating action on subprime ABS during the week of 9 July 2007, the rating agencies were heavily criticized in the press about the timing. In particular, investors pointed to the fact that the ABX had been trading at very high implied spreads since February. Some examples of recent business press:

> "A lot of these should be downgraded sooner rather than later," said Jeff Given at John Hancock Advisors LLC in Boston, who oversees $3.5 billion of mortgage bonds. The ratings companies may be embarrassed to downgrade the bonds, he said. "It's easier to say two years from now that you were wrong on a rating than it is to say you were wrong five months after you rated it." [*Bloomberg*, 29 June 2007]
>
> "Standard & Poor's, Moody's Investors Service and Fitch Ratings are masking burgeoning losses in the market for subprime mortgage bonds by failing to cut the credit ratings on about $200 billion of securities backed by home loans...Almost 65 percent of the bonds in indexes that track subprime mortgage debt don't meet the ratings criteria in place when they were sold, according to data compiled by Bloomberg." [ibid]
>
> In response, the rating agencies counter that their actions are justified.
>
> "People are surprised there haven't been more downgrades," Claire Robinson, a managing director at Moody's, said during an investor conference sponsored by the firm in New York on June 5. "What they don't understand about the rating process is that we don't change our ratings on speculation about what's going to happen." Bloomberg, 10 July 2007]

From the description of the ratings monitoring process above, it is clear that for unseasoned loans, the rating agencies weight their initial expectations of loss heavily in computing lifetime expected loss on the vintage. While the 2006 vintage did show some early signs of trouble with early payment defaults (EPDs), it was not clear if this just reflected the impact of lower home price appreciation on investors using subprime loans to flip properties, or foreshadowed more serious problems.

Figure 17 documents that the increase in serious delinquencies on a month-over-month basis on the ABX 06-1 and 06-2 vintages was actually slowing down through the remittance report released at the end of April. Figure 18 documents that implied spreads on the ABX tranches retreated from their February highs through the end of May. However, the remittance report at the end of May suggested a reversal of this trend, as serious delinquency accelerated.

This pattern was confirmed with the report at the end of June, and the ratings action came approximately two weeks after the June 25 report.

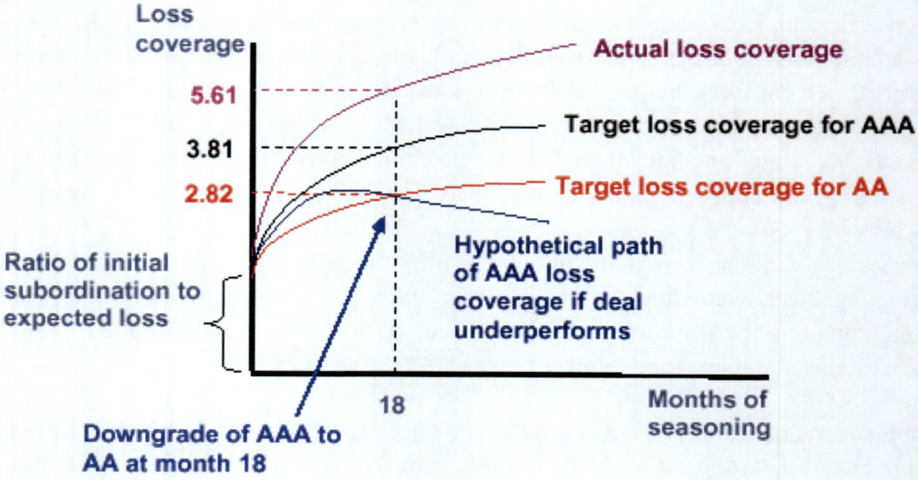

Figure 17A: Anatomy of a downgrade

While the aggregated data helps the rating agencies tell a reasonable story, it is certainly possible that aggregation hides a number of deals that were long overdue for downgrade. Given the public rating downgrade criteria, this is a quantitative question that we intend to address with future empirical work.[28]

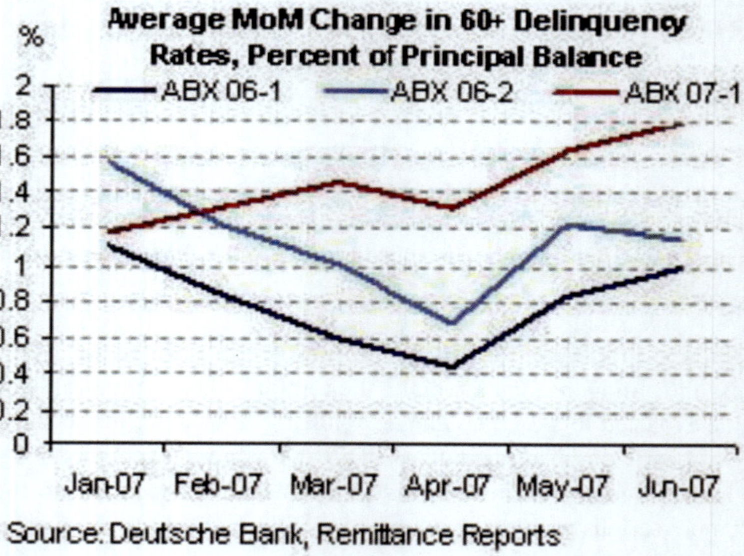

Figure 17B: Change in Serious Delinquency on Mortgages Referenced by the ABX

[28] Note that the rating agencies took another wave of rating actions on RMBS in October.

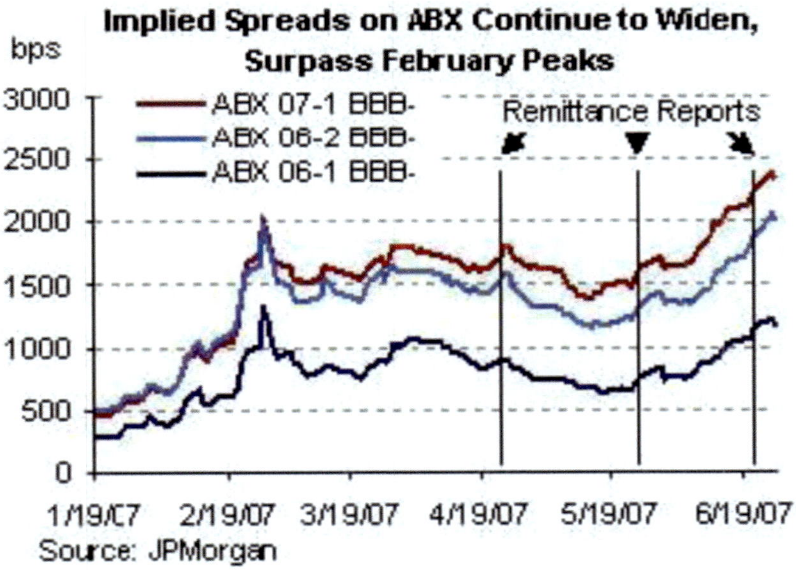

Figure 18: ABX Implied Spreads and Remittance Reporting Dates

Table 1-31. Rating Changes in RMBS and Home Equity ABS, by Year

Negative rating action									
	Subprime 1st lein			**Subprime 2nd lein**			**Subprime all Lein**		
Vintage	**$**	**# tranche**	**# deals**	**$**	**# tranche**	**# deals**	**$**	**# tranche**	**# deals**
2002	2.90%	13.80%	48.80%	1.50%	4.00%	9.10%	2.90%	13.20%	46.40%
2003	1.70%	10.10%	38.50%	0.70%	2.90%	11.10%	10.60%	9.60%	36.50%
2004	0.90%	6.20%	34.30%	1.70%	5.90%	44.00%	0.90%	6.20%	35.00%
2005	0.60%	3.60%	20.90%	3.30%	18.50%	85.40%	0.70%	4.90%	28.00%
2006	13.40%	48.00%	92.10%	60.00%	84.50%	91.80%	16.70%	52.30%	92.00%
Positive rating action									
	Subprime 1st lein			**Subprime 2nd lein**			**Subprime all Lein**		
Vintage	**$**	**# tranche**	**# deals**	**$**	**# tranche**	**# deals**	**$**	**# tranche**	**# deals**
2002	2.10%	6.40%	20.80%	6.70%	17.30%	63.60%	2.30%	7.00%	23.50%
2003	2.80%	8.60%	26.40%	9.20%	30.10%	83.30%	2.90%	10.00%	30.50%
2004	1.20%	3.30%	15.00%	7.20%	22.30%	56.00%	1.40%	4.30%	17.90%
2005	0.00%	0.00%	0.00%	5.30%	9.60%	39.60%	0.20%	0.90%	4.40%
2006	0.00%	0.00%	0.00%	0.00%	0.00%	0.00%	0.00%	0.00%	0.00%

Source: Moodys (26 October 2007)

Table 1-32. Rating Transition Matrices

Current Rating/Last Rating (1st lein)												
2005	**Aaa**	**Aa**	**A**	**Baa**	**Ba**	**B**	**Caa**	**Ca**	**C**	**Total**	**Down**	**Up**
Aaa	100.00%									2,058	0	0
Aa		100.00%								983	0	0
A			99.40%	0.60%						1,003	6	0
Baa				94.90%	3.50%	1.40%	0.20%			1,066	54	0
Ba					81.10%	14.50%	4.40%			318	60	0
Current Rating/Last Rating (2nd lein)												
2005	**Aaa**	**Aa**	**A**	**Baa**	**Ba**	**B**	**Caa**	**Ca**	**C**	**Total**	**Down**	**Up**
Aaa	100.00%									113	0	0
Aa	22.00%	78.00%								100	0	22
A	0.90%	14.70%	81.90%	1.70%	0.90%					116	3	18
Baa				81.50%	9.60%	6.80%	1.40%	0.007		146	27	0
Ba					21.20%	34.80%	0.30%	0.273	0.136	66	52	0
Current Rating/Last Rating (1st lein)												
2006	**Aaa**	**Aa**	**A**	**Baa**	**Ba**	**B**	**Caa**	**Ca**	**C**	**Total**	**Down**	**Up**
Aaa	100.00%									2,121	0	0
Aa		100.00%								1,265	0	0
A			43.90%	27.90%	17.80%	10.10%	0.20%	0.001		1,295	726	0
Baa				17.30%	18.80%	32.40%	13.50%	0.111	0.07	1,301	1,076	0
Ba					6.20%	18.40%	8.20%	0.14	0.531	450	422	0
Current Rating/Last Rating (2nd lein)												
2006	**Aaa**	**Aa**	**A**	**Baa**	**Ba**	**B**	**Caa**	**Ca**	**C**	**Total**	**Down**	**Up**
Aaa	53.80%	34.90%	7.00%	4.30%						186	0	86
Aa		23.50%	38.80%	27.90%	6.60%	1.60%	0.50%	0.011		183	0	140
A			7.00%	32.60%	35.80%	11.80%	0.50%	0.064	0.059	187	0	174
Baa				5.60%	13.60%	17.80%	6.10%	0.145	0.425	214	0	202
Ba					1.00%	6.10%		0.051	0.879	99	0	98

Source: Moodys (26 October 2007)

6. The Reliance of Investors on Credit Ratings: A Case Study

A recent New York Times Editorial (08/07/2007) writes:

> Protecting pensioners from bad investments will not be easy. A good place to start would be to make rating agencies more accountable, perhaps by asking regulators to monitor their quality. Many pension plans lack the analytical skills needed to evaluate these investments, relying on outside advisers and rating agencies. But the stellar triple-A rating assigned to many of these bonds proved to be misleading -- with the agencies now rushing to downgrade them.

In a recent Fortune article by Benner and Lachinsky (5 July 2007), Ohio Attorney General Marc Dann claims that the Ohio state pension funds have been defrauded by the rating agencies. "The ratings agencies cashed a check every time one of these subprime pools was created and an offering was made. [They] continued to rate these things AAA. [So they are] among the people who aided and abetted this continuing fraud." The authors note that Ohio has the third-largest group of public pensions in the United States, and that The Ohio Police & Fire Pension Fund has nearly 7 percent of its portfolio in mortgage- and asset-backed obligations:

> Dann and a growing legion of critics contend that the agencies dropped the ball by issuing investment-grade ratings on securities backed by subprime mortgages they should have known were shaky. To his mind, the seemingly cozy relationship between ratings agencies and investment banks like Bear Stearns only heightens the appearance of impropriety.

In this section, we review the extent to which investors rely on rating agencies, focusing on the case of this Ohio pension fund, drawing upon on public disclosures of the fund.

- Overview of the fund
- Fixed-income investment guidelines
- Conclusions

6.1. Overview of the Fund

The Ohio Police & Fire Pension Fund (http://www.op-f.org/) is a cost sharing multiple-employer public employee retirement system. The fund provides pension and disability benefits to qualified participants, survivor and death benefits as well as access to health care coverage for qualified spouses children, and dependent parents. In 2006, the fund had 912 participating employers from police and fire departments in Ohio municipalities, townships, and villages. Membership in the plan at the end of 2006 included 24,766 retired employees and 28,026 active employees. At the end of 2006, the fund had an investment portfolio of $11.2 billion. The fund's total rate of return was 16.15 percent in 2006 and 9.07 percent in 2005, each relative to an assumed actuarial rate of return of 8.25 percent.

Fund Adequacy

The current actuarial analysis performed on the pension benefits reflects an "infinite" amortization period and a funding level of 78.3 percent. While the fund believes that the current funding status is strong, Ohio law requires that a 30-year amortization period is achieved.[29] A plan was approved by the Board and submitted to ORSC that included major changes to health care funding and benefits, and a recommendation that the legislature amend the law to provide for member contribution increases and employer contribution increases. However, the legislature has not taken action on the recommended contribution increases.

---

29 Page ix in the 2006 Comprehensive Annual Financial Report, available at http://www.op-f.org/downloads/reports/CAFR2006.pdf.

Portfolio Composition

Table 33 documents the exposure of the total fund to different asset classes. At the end of 2006, about 6.7% of total assets are invested in mortgages and mortgage-backed securities.

Table 1-33. Investment Portfolio

	2006		2005	
	($ m)	%	($ m)	%
Commercial Paper	594.6	5.03%	425.1	3.97
US Government Bonds	596.2	5.04	574.3	5.36
Corporate Bonds and Obligations	783.7	6.62	709.5	6.62
Mortgage & Asset Backed Obligations	799.4	6.76	734.6	6.85
Municipal Bonds		0.00	3.8	0.04
Domestic Stocks	2209.4	18.67	1967.7	18.36
Domestic Pooled Stocks	3181.9	26.89	2957.3	27.59
International Securities	2642.9	22.34	2328.2	21.72
Real Estate	658.	5.56	606.6	5.66
Commercial Mortgage Funds	73.3	0.62	80.4	0.75
Private Equity	291.9	2.47	230.2	2.15
Grand Total	11832.3	100.0	10717.9	100.0

Source: 2006 Comprehensive Annual Financial Report, Ohio Police & Fire Pension Fund

Table 34 documents the composition of the investment-grade fixed-income portfolio in 2006 and 2005. Non-agency MBS are likely included in the first four columns of the second row, which report the amount of mortgage and MBS broken out by credit rating. At the end of 2006, it appears that the fund held $740 million in non-agency MBS which had a credit rating of A- or better. Moreover, note that the share of non-agency MBS in the total fixed-income portfolio increased from 12% (245/2022) in 2005 to 34% (740/2179) in 2006. In other words, the pension fund almost tripled its exposure to non-agency MBS. Further, note that this increase in exposure to risky MBS was at the expense of exposure to MBS backed by full faith and credit of the United States government, or an agency or instrumentality thereof, which dropped from $489.6 million to $58.9 million.

Table 1-34. Fixed Income Investment Portfolio for 2006 [2005]

Rating of at least	A-	BBB-	B-	C-	Full Faith & Credit	Unrated	Total
Corporate Bond Obligations	$179.9 [$187.6]	$73.9 [$67.1]	$458.2 [$416.2]	$69.5 [$35.8]		$2.1 [$2.9]	$783.7 [$709.5]
Mortgage and ABS	$740.4 [$245.0]				$58.9 [$489.6]		$799.4 [$734.6]
Agency ABS	$37.7 [$3.8]						$37.7 [$3.8]
Munis	– [$36.4]						– [$36.4]

Treasury Strips					$62.3 [$29.4]		$62.3 [$29.4]
Treasury Notes					$496.1 [$508.5]		$496.1 [$508.5]
Total	$958.1	$73.9	$458.2	$69.5	$617.4	$2.1	$2179.3
	[$472.8]	[$67.1]	[$416.2]	[$35.8]	[$1027.5]	[$2.9]	[$2022.3]

Source: 2006 Comprehensive Annual Financial Report, Ohio Police & Fire Pension Fund

In order to better understand the motivation for such a shift, consider Table 35, which illustrates spreads on the ABX and credit derivatives (CDS) by credit rating during 2006. While MBS backed by full faith and credit trade at close to zero credit spreads, securities secured by subprime loans pay significantly higher spreads.

Table 1-35. Subprime ABS vs. Corporate CDS Spreads

	June 2006		December 2006	
	ABX	**CDS**	**ABX**	**CDS**
AAA	18	11	11	9
AA	32	16	17	12
A	54	24	44	20
BBB	154	48	133	43

Source: ABX from Markit tranche coupon; CDS spread from Markit, average across US firms for 5-year contract with modified restructuring documentation clause.

6.2. Fixed-income asset management

From the investment guidelines in the 2006 annual report:

- The fixed-income portfolio has a target allocation of 18% of total fund assets, with a range of 13% to 23%. The portfolio includes investment grade securities (target of 12%), global inflation-protected securities (target of 6%), and commercial real estate (target of 0% and maximum of 2%).
- The investment grade fixed income allocation will be managed solely on an active basis in order to exploit the perceived inefficiencies in the investment grade fixed income markets.
- The return should exceed the return on the Lehman Aggregate Index over a three-year period on an annual basis.
- The total return of each manager's portfolio should rank above the median when compared to their peer group over a three-year period on an annualized basis and should exceed their benchmark return as specified in each manager's guidelines.

Mandates (from ORC Sec 742.11)

1. The main focus of investing will be on dollar denominated fixed income securities. Non-US dollar denominated securities are prohibited.
2. The composite portfolio as well as each manager's portfolio shall have similar portfolio characteristics as that of the Lehman Aggregate Index.
3. Issues must have a minimum credit rating of BBB- or equivalent at the time of purchase.
4. Each manager's portfolio has a specified effective duration band.
5. For diversification purposes, sector exposure limits exist for each manager's portfolio. In addition, each manager's portfolio will have a minimum number of issues.
6. Each manager's portfolio has a maximum threshold for the amount of cash that may be held at any one time.
7. Each manager's portfolio must have a dollar-weighted average quality of A or above.

Note that the Lehman Aggregate Index has a weight of less than one percent on non-agency MBS.

Asset Management

In 2006, the fund's assets were 100% managed by external investment managers. The fixed-income group is comprised of eight asset managers who collectively have over $2.2 trillion in assets under management (AUM). They are (with AUM in parentheses):

- JPMorgan Investment Advisors, Inc. ($1.1 trillion, 2006)
- Lehman Brothers Asset Management ($225 billion, 2006)
- Bridgewater Associates ($165 billion, 2006)
- Loomis Sayles & Company, LP ($115 billion, 2006)
- MacKay Shields LLC ($40 billion, 2006)
- Prima Capital Advisors, LLC ($1.8 billion, 2006)
- Quadrant Real Estate Advisors LLC ($2.7 billion, 2006)
- Western Asset Management ($598 billion, 2007)

The 2005 performance audit of this fund suggested that investment managers in the core fixed income portfolio are compensated 16.3 basis points. The fund paid these investment managers approximately $1.304 million in 2006 in order to manage an $800 million portfolio of investment-grade fixed-income securities. While the 2006 financial statement reports that these managers out-performed the benchmark index by 26 basis points (= 459 - 433), this was accomplished in part through a significant reallocation of the portfolio from relatively safe to relatively risk non-agency mortgage-backed securities. One might note that after adjusting for the compensation of asset managers, this aggressive strategy netted the pension fund only 10 basis points of extra yield relative to the benchmark index, for about $2.1 million.

7. CONCLUSIONS

While this paper focuses on the securitization of subprime mortgages, many of the basic issues—intermediation and the frictions it introduces—are generic to the securitization process, regardless of the underlying pool of assets. The credit rating agencies play an important role in resolving or at least mitigating several of these frictions.

Our view is that the rating of securities secured by subprime mortgage loans by credit rating agencies has been flawed. There is no question that there will be some painful consequences, but we think that the rating process can be fixed along the lines suggested in the text above.

However, it is important to understand that repairing the securitization process does not end with the rating agencies. The incentives of investors and investment managers need to be aligned. The structured investments of investment managers should be evaluated relative to an index of structured products in order to give the manager appropriate incentives to conduct his own due diligence. Either the originator or the arranger needs to retain unhedged equity tranche exposure to every securitization deal. And finally, originators should have adequate capital so that warranties and representations can be taken seriously.

REFERENCES

Aguesse, P. (2007). "Is Rating an Efficient Response to the Challenges of the Structured Finance Markets?" Risk and Trend Mapping No.2, Autorité des Marchés Financiers; available at http://www.amf-france.org/documents/general/7693_1.pdf.

Altman, E. I. & Rijken, H. A. (2004). "How Rating Agencies Achieve Rating Stability." *Journal of Banking & Finance, 28*, 2679-2714.

Amato, J. D. & Remolona, E. M. (2005). "*The Pricing of Unexpected Credit Losses*." BIS Working Paper No. 190.

Bangia, A., Diebold, F. X., Kronimus, A., Schagen, C., & Schuermann, T. (2002). "Ratings Migration and the Business Cycle, With Applications to Credit Portfolio Stress Testing." *Journal of Banking & Finance, 26*: 2/3, 445-474.

Basel Committee on Banking Supervision (1996). "*Amendment to the Capital Accord to Incorporate Market Risks*." Basel Committee Publication No. 24. Available: www.bis.org/publ/bcbs24.pdf.

———. (2000). "Credit Ratings and Complementary Sources of Credit Quality Information." BCBS Working Paper No. 3, available at http://www.bis.org/publ/bcbs_wp3.htm, August.

———. (2005). "International Convergence of Capital Measurement and Capital Standards: A Revised Framework." Available at http://www.bis.org/publ/bcbs118.htm, November.

Cagan, Christopher (2007): "Mortgage Payment Reset," unpublished mimeo, May; available at http://www.facorelogic.com/landingpages/caganform.jsp?id=8037.

Cantor, R. & Packer, F. (1995). "The Credit Rating Industry", *Journal of Fixed Income, 5*:3 (December), 10-34.

Cantor, R. & Mann, C. (2007). "Analyzing the Tradeoff between Ratings Accuracy and Stability." *Journal of Fixed Income, 16*:4 (Spring), 60-68.

Committee on the Global Financial System (2005). "The Role of Ratings in Structured Finance: Issues and Implications." Available at http://www.bis.org/publ/cgfs23.htm, January.

Duffie, Darrell (2007), "Innovations in Credit Risk Transfer: Implications for Financial Stability," Stanford University GSB Working Paper, available at http://www.stanford.edu/~duffie/BIS.pdf.

The Economist (2007). "Measuring the Measurers." May 31.

———. (2007). "Securitisation: When it goes wrong..." September 20.

Federal Reserve Board (2003). "Supervisory Guidance on Internal Ratings-Based Systems for Corporate Credit," Attachment 2 in http://www.federalreserve.gov/boarddocs/meetings/2003/20030711/attachment.pdf.

Fitch Ratings (2007): "U.S. Subprime RMBS/HEL Upgrade/Downgrade Criteria," Residential Mortgage Criteria Report, 12 July 2007.

Gourse, Alexander (2007): "The Subprime Bait and Switch," In These Times, July 16.

Hagerty, James & Hudson (2006): "Town's Residents Say They Were Targets of Big Mortgage Fraud," *Wall Street Journal*, September 27.

Hanson, S.G. & Schuermann, T. (2006). "Confidence Intervals for Probabilities of Default." *Journal of Banking & Finance, 30*:8, 2281-2301.

Inside Mortgage Finance (2007): "The 2007 Mortgage Market Statistical Annual."

Knox, Noelle (2006): "Ten mistakes that I made flipping a flop," USA Today, 22 October.

Kliger, D. & Sarig, O. (2000). "The Information Value of Bond Ratings." *Journal of Finance, 55*:6, 2879-2902.

Lando, D. & Skødeberg, T. (2002). "Analyzing Ratings Transitions and Rating Drift with Continuous Observations." *Journal of Banking & Finance, 26*: 2/3, 423-444.

Levich, R.M., Majnoni, G., & Reinhart, C.M. (2002). "Introduction: Ratings, Ratings Agencies and the Global Financial System: Summary and Policy Implications." In R.M. Levich, C. Reinhart, and G. Majnoni, eds. *Ratings, Rating Agencies and the Global Financial System*, Amsterdam, NL: Kluwer. 1-15.

Lopez, J.A. & Saidenberg, M. (2000). "Evaluating Credit Risk Models." *Journal of Banking & Finance, 24*, 151-165.

Mason, J.R. & Rosner, J. (2007). "Where Did the Risk Go? How Misapplied Bond Ratings Cause Mortgage Backed Securities and Collateralized Debt Obligation Market Disruptions." Hudson Institute Working Paper.

Moody's Investors Services (1996). "Avoiding the 'F' Word: The Risk of Fraud in Securitized Transaction," Moody's Special Report, New York,

———. (1999). "Rating Methodology: The Evolving Meanings of Moody's Bond Ratings." Moody's Global Credit Research, New York, August.

———. (2003). "Impact of Predatory Lending an RMBS Securitizations," Moody's Special Report, New York, May.

———. (2004). "Introduction to Moody's Structured Finance Analysis and Modelling." Presentation given by Frederic Drevon, May 13.

———. (2005a). "The Importance of Representations and Warranties in RMBS Transactions," Moody's Special Report, New York, January.

———. (2005b). "Spotlight on New Century Financial Corporation," Moody's Special Report, New York, July.

———. (2007a). "Structured Finance Rating Transitions: 1983-2006." Special Comment, Moody's Global Credit Research, New York, January.

———. (2007b) "Early Defaults Rise in Mortgage Securitization," Moody's Special Report, New York, January.

———. (2007c). "Corporate Default and Recovery Rates: 1920-2006." Special Comment, Moody's Global Credit Research, New York, February.

———. (2007d). "Update on 2005 and 2006 Vintage U.S. Subprime RMBS Rating Actions: October 2007," Moodys Special Report, New York, October 26.

Morgan, Don (2007): "Defining and Detecting Predatory Lending," Staff Report #273, Federal Reserve Bank of New York.

New York Times (2007): "Pensions and the Mortgage Mess," Editorial, 7 August.

Nickell, P, Perraudin, W. & Varotto, S. (2000). "Stability of Rating Transitions", *Journal of Banking & Finance*, *24*, 203-227.

Scholtes, Saskia (2007). "Moody's alters its subprime rating model." *Financial Times*, September 25.

Sichelman, L. (2007). "Tighter Underwriting Stymies Refinancing of Subprime Loans." *Mortgage Servicing News*, May 1.

Smith, R.C. & Walter, I. (2002). "Rating Agencies: Is there an Agency Issue?" in R.M. Levich, C. Reinhart, and G. Majnoni, eds. *Ratings, Rating Agencies and the Global Financial System*, Amsterdam, NL: Kluwer. 290-318.

Standard & Poor's (2001). "Rating Methodology: Evaluating the Issuer." Standard & Poor's Credit Ratings, New York, September.

———. (2007). "Principles-Based Rating Methodology for Global Structured Finance Securities." Standard & Poor's RatingsDirect Research, New York, May.

Sylla, R. (2002). "An Historical Primer on the Business of Credit Rating." In R.M. Levich, C. Reinhart, and G. Majnoni, eds. *Ratings, Rating Agencies and the Global Financial System*, Amsterdam, NL: Kluwer. 19-40.

Thompson, Chris (2006): "Dirty Deeds," East Bay Express, July 23, 2007.

Tomlinson, R. & Evans, D. (2007). "CDO Boom Masks Subprime Losses, Abetted by S&P, Moody's, Fitch." Bloomberg News, May 31.

Treacy, W.F. & Carey, M. (2000). "Credit Risk Rating Systems at Large U.S. Banks." *Journal of Banking & Finance, 24*, 167-201.

UBS Investment Research (26 June 2007): "Mortgage Strategist."

UBS Investment Research (23 October 2007): "Mortgage Strategist."

Wei, L (2007). "Subprime Lenders May Face Funding Crisis." *Wall Street Journal*, 10 January.

White, L. (2002). "The Credit Rating Industry: An Industrial Organization Analysis." in R.M. Levich, C. Reinhart, and G. Majnoni, eds. *Ratings, Rating Agencies and the Global Financial System*, Amsterdam, NL: Kluwer. 41-64.

APPENDIX 1: PREDATORY LENDING

Predatory lending is defined by Morgan (2007) as the welfare-reducing provision of credit. In other words, the borrower would have been better off without the loan. While this practice includes the willful misrepresentation of material facts about a real estate transaction by an insider without the knowledge of a borrower, it has been defined much more broadly. For example, the New Jersey Division of Banking and Insurance (2007) defines predatory lending as an activity that involves at least one, and perhaps all three, of the following elements:

- Making unaffordable loans based on the assets of the borrower rather than on the borrower's ability to repay an obligation;
- Inducing a borrower to refinance a loan repeatedly in order to charge high points and fees each time the loan is refinanced ("loan flipping"); or
- Engaging in fraud or deception to conceal the true nature of the loan obligation, or ancillary products, from an unsuspecting or unsophisticated borrower.

Loans to borrowers who do not demonstrate the capacity to repay the loan, as structured, from sources other than the collateral pledged are generally considered unsafe and unsound. Some anecdotal examples of predatory lending:

> Ira and Hazel purchased their home in 1983, shortly after getting married, financing their purchase with a loan from the Veterans' Administration. By 2002, they had nearly paid off their first mortgage. The elderly couple got a call from a lender, urging them to consolidate all of their debt into a single mortgage. The lender assured the husband who had excellent credit that the couple would receive an interest rate between 5-6% which would reduce their monthly mortgage payments. However, according to the couple, when the lender came to their house to have them sign the paperwork for their new mortgage, the lender failed to mention that the loan did not contain the low interest rate which they had been promised. Instead, it contained an interest rate of 9.9% and an annual percentage rate of 11.8%. Moreover, the loan contained 10 "discount points" ($15,289.00) which were financed into the loan, inflating the loan amount and stripping away the elderly couple's equity. Under the new loan, the monthly mortgage payments increased to $1,655.00, amounting to roughly 57% of the couple's monthly income. Moreover, the loan contained a substantial prepayment penalty, forcing them to pay approximately $7,500 to escape this predatory loan.

Source: Center for Responsible Lending (2007)

> In 2005, Betty and Tyrone, a couple living on the south side of Chicago, took out a refinance loan with a lender in order to refurnish their basement. "We just kept asking them whether we were going to remain on a fixed rate, and they just kept lying to us, telling us we'd get a fixed rate," Betty alleges in a lawsuit against lender. As they later discovered, however, the terms of the loan were not as they expected. Not only did the loan have an adjustable rate that can go as high as 13.4 percent, but the couple allege that the lender falsely told them that their home had doubled in value since they had bought it a few years earlier, thus qualifying them for a larger

loan amount. As the lender didn't give them copies of their loan documents at closing, and the couple did not realize that the terms had been changed until well after the three-day period during which they could legally cancel the loan. They have since tried to refinance, but have been unable to find another lender willing to lend them the amount currently owed, as the artificially-inflated appraisal value has in effect trapped them in a loan with a rising interest rate.

Source: Gourse (2007)

One scheme targets distressed borrowers at risk of foreclosure. The predator claims to the borrower that it is necessary to add someone else with good credit to the title, and their good credit will help secure a new loan on good terms. After the title holder uses the loan to make payments for a year, predator claims that the title would be transferred back to the original borrower. However, predator cashes most of the remaining equity out of the house with a larger loan, and leaves the distressed borrower in a worse situation.

Source: Thompson (2006)

The center for responsible lending has identified seven signs of a predatory loan:

- Excessive fees, defined as points and other fees of five percent or more of the loan
- Abusive prepayment penalties, defined as a penalty for more than three years or in an amount larger than six months interest
- Kickbacks to brokers, defined as compensation to a broker for selling a loan to a borrower at a higher interest rate than the minimum rate that the lender would be willing to charge
- Loan flipping, defined as the repeated refinancing of loans in order to generate fee income without any tangible benefit to the borrower
- Unnecessary products
- Mandatory arbitration requires a borrower to waive legal remedies in the event that loan terms are later determined to be abusive
- Steering and targeting borrowers into subprime products when they would qualify for prime products. Fannie Mae has estimated that up to half of borrowers with subprime mortgages could have qualified for loans with better terms

The Role of the Rating Agencies

The rating agencies care about predatory lending to the extent that federal, state, and local laws might affect the amount of cash available to pay investors in residential mortgage-backed securitizations (RMBS) in the event of violations. Moody's analysis of RMBS transactions "includes an assessment of the likelihood that a lender might have violated predatory lending laws, and the extent to which violations by the lender would reduce the proceeds available to repay securitization investors" (Moody's, 2003).

In particular, Moody's requires that loans included in a securitization subject to predatory lending statutes satisfy certain conditions: (1) the statue must be sufficiently clear so that the lender can effectively comply; (2) the penalty to the trust for non-compliance is limited; (3) the lender demonstrates effective compliance procedures, which include a third-party review; (4) the lender represents that the loans comply with statutory requirements and agrees to repurchase loans that do not comply; (5) the lender indemnifies the trust for damages resulting from a particular statute; (6) the lender's financial resources and commitment to the business are sufficient to make these representations meaningful; and (7) concentration limits manage the risk to investors when penalties are high or statues are ambiguous.

APPENDIX 2: PREDATORY BORROWING:

While mortgage fraud has been around as long as the mortgage loan, it is important to understand that fraud becomes more prevalent in an environment of high and increasing home prices. In particular, when home prices are high relative to income, borrowers unwilling to accept a low standard of living can be tempted into lying on a mortgage loan application. When prices are high and rapidly increasing, there is an even greater incentive to commit fraud given that the cost of waiting is an even lower standard of living. Rapid home price appreciation also increases the return to speculative and criminal activity. Moreover, while benefits of fraud are increasing, the costs of fraud decline as expectations of higher future prices create equity that reduces the probability of default and severity of loss in the event of default.

In support of this claim, the IRS reports that the number of real-estate fraud investigations doubled between 2001 and 2003. Recent statistics from the FBI and Financial Crimes Network (FINCEN) document that suspicious activity reports (SARs) filed by federally-regulated institutions related to mortgage fraud have increased from 3,500 in 2000 to 28,000 in 2006. The Mortgage Asset Research Institute (2007) estimates that direct losses from mortgage fraud exceeded $1 billion in 2006, more than double the amount from 2005. The rapid slowdown in home price appreciation has made it more difficult to buy and sell houses quickly for profit, is quickly revealing the extent to which fraud permeated mortgage markets. For example, subprime and Alt-A loans originated in 2006 have experienced historical levels of serious early payment default (EPD), defined as being 90 days delinquent only three months after origination. Moody's (2007) notes that EPDs appear to be driven by borrowers using the loan to purchase for investment purposes, as opposed to borrowers refinancing an existing loan or purchasing a home for occupancy.

Predatory borrowing is defined as the willful misrepresentation of material facts about a real estate transaction by a borrower to the ultimate purchaser of the loan. This financial fraud might also involve cooperation of other insiders – realtors, mortgage brokers, appraisers, notaries, attorneys. The victims of this fraud include the ultimate purchaser of the loan (for example a public pension), but also include honest borrowers who have to pay higher interest rates for mortgage loans and prices for residential real estate. Below, I summarize the most common forms of predatory borrowing.

Fraud for Housing

Fraud for housing constitutes illegal actions perpetrated solely by the borrower in order to acquire and maintain ownership of a home. This type of fraud is typified by a borrower who makes misrepresentations regarding income, employment, credit history, or the source of down payment. A recent example from Dollar (2006):

A real estate agent would tell potential home buyers that they could receive substantial funds at closing under the guise of repair costs that they would be able to use for their personal benefit so long as they agreed to purchase certain "hard to sell" homes at an inflated price. Brokers would facilitate the submission of fraudulent loan applications for the potential homeowners that could not qualify for the loans. In some cases temporary loans were provided to buyers for down payments with the understanding they would be reimbursed at closing from the purported remodeling or repair costs, marketing services fees and other undisclosed disbursements. The buyers in those cases would falsely represent the sources of the down payments.

Fraud for Profit

Fraud for profit refers to illegal actions taken jointly by a borrower and insiders to inflate the price of a property with no motivation to maintain ownership. The FBI generally focuses its effort on fraud perpetrated by industry insiders, as historically it involves an estimated 80 percent of all reported fraud losses. A recent example from Hagerty and Hudson (2006):

> The borrowers, who include truck drivers, factory workers, a pastor and a hair stylist, say they were duped by acquaintances into signing stacks of documents and didn't know they were applying for loans. Instead, they thought they were joining a risk-free "investment group." Now, many of the loans are in default, the borrowers' credit ratings are in ruins, and lenders are pursuing the organizers of the purported investment group in court. Companies stuck with the defaulting loans include Countrywide Financial Corp., the nation's largest home lender, and Argent Mortgage Co., another big lender. A lawsuit filed by Countrywide accuses the organizers of acquiring homes and then fraudulently selling them for a quick profit to the Virginia borrowers. Representatives of the borrowers put the total value of loans involved at about $80 million, which would make it one of the largest mortgage-fraud cases ever.

A Summary by the Federal Bureau of Investigation of Some Popular Fraud-for-Profit Schemes:

- Property flipping involves repeatedly selling a property to an associate at an artificially inflated price through false appraisals.
- A silent second the non-disclosure of a loaned down-payment to a first lien lender.
- Nominee loans involve concealing the true identify of the true borrower, who use the name and credit history of the of the nominee's name to qualify for a loan. The nominee could be a fictitious or stolen identity.
- Inflated appraisals involve an appraiser acts in collusion with a borrower and provides a misleading appraisal report to the lender.
- Foreclosure schemes involve convincing homeowners who are at risk of defaulting on loans or whose houses are already in foreclosure to transfer their deed and pay up-front fees. The perpetrator profits from these schemes by re-mortgaging the property or pocketing fees paid by the homeowner.

- Equity skimming involves the purchase of a property by an investor through a nominee, who does not make any mortgage payments and rents the property until foreclosure takes place several months later.
- Air Loans involve a non-existent property loan where a broker invents borrowers and properties, establishes accounts for payments, and maintains custodial accounts for escrows.

Source: Federal Bureau of Investigation

The Role of the Rating Agencies

(Moody's, 1996) claim that the vast majority of all securitizations are tightly structured to eliminate virtually all fraud risk. The risk of fraud is greatest when structures and technology developed for large, established issuers are mis-applied to smaller, less experienced issuers. Moreover, the lack of third-party monitors or involvement of entities with little or no track record increases the risk of fraud. The authors identify three potential types of fraud in a securitization:

- borrower fraud: the misrepresentation of key information during the application process by the borrower
- fraud in origination: misrepresentation of assets by the originator before securitization occurs, resulting in assets which do not conform with transaction's underwriting standards
- servicer fraud: the deliberate diversion, commingling, or retention of funds that are otherwise due to investors; the risk most significant among unrated, closely-held servicers that operate without third-party monitoring.

ComFed is a historical example of fraud in a mortgage securitization:

> The parties involved at ComFed exaggerated property values to increase the volume-oriented commissions that they received for originating loans. To increase underwriting volumes still more, ComFed employees granted loans to unqualified borrowers by concealing the fact that these obligors had financed down payments with second-lien mortgages.

To prevent such instances of lower-level fraud, the originator's entire underwriting process should be reviewed to ensure that marketing and underwriting capacities remain entirely separate. Personnel involved in credit decisions should report to executives who are not responsible for marketing or sales. Underwriters' compensation should not be tied to volume; rather, if an incentive program is in place, the performance of the originated loans should be factored into the level of compensation.

(Moody's, 1996) claim that exposure to fraud can be minimized by the following:

- determine the integrity and competence of the management of the seller/servicer of a transaction through due diligence and background checks
- complete a thorough review of the underwriting process, including lines of reporting and employee compensation, to eliminate interests conflicting with those of investors

- establish independent third part monitoring of closely held entities with little external accountability that originate or service assets
- consider internal and external factors that could influence a servicer's conduct during the life of a securitization

This statement makes it clear that it is largely the responsibility of investors to conduct their own due diligence in order to avoid becoming victims of fraud.

Investors do receive a small but important amount of protection against fraud from representations and warranties made by the originator. Standard provisions protect investors from misinformation regarding loan characteristics, as well as guard against risks such as fraud, previous liens, and/or regulatory noncompliance.

(Moody's, 2005a) documents that an originator's ability to honor it obligation is the crucial component in evaluating the importance of these warranties. An investment grade credit rating often suffices to meet this standard. Otherwise, the rating agency claims that it will review established practices and procedures in order to ensure compliance and adequate tangible net worth relative to the liability created by the representations and warranties.

APPENDIX 3: SOME ESTIMATES OF PD BY RATING

A credit rating at a minimum provides an ordinal risk ranking: an AAA rating is better (in the sense of lower likelihood of default and loss) than an AA rating which is better than a BBB rating, and so on. More useful, however, is a cardinal ranking which would assign a numerical value such as a PD to each rating. Roughly speaking obligor PDs increase exponentially as one descends the credit spectrum.

The three major rating agencies have seven broad rating categories as well as rating modifiers, bringing the total to 19 rating classes, plus 'D' (default, an absorbing state[30]) and 'NR' (not rated – S&P, Fitch) or 'WR' (withdrawn rating – Moody's).[31] Typically ratings below 'CCC', e.g. 'CC' and 'C', are collapsed into 'CCC', reducing the total ratings to 17.[32] Although the rating modifiers provide a finer differentiation between issuers within one letter rating category, an investor may suffer a false sense of accuracy. Empirical estimates of *PD*s using credit rating histories can be quite noisy, even with over twenty-five year years of data. Under the new Basel Capital Accord (Basel 2), U.S. regulators would require banks to have a minimum of seven non-default rating categories (FRB, 2003).

A detailed discussion of PD accuracy is given in Hanson and Schuermann (2006), but in Table 36 we provide smoothed one-year PD estimates using S&P ratings histories from 1981-2006 for their global corporate obligor base. We present estimates at both the grade and notch level. Guided by the results Hanson and Schuermann (2006), we assign color codes to the PD estimates reflecting their estimation accuracy, with green being accurate, yellow moderately

---

30 One consequence of default being an absorbing state arises when a firm re-emerges from bankruptcy. They are classified as a new firm.

31 The CCC (S&P) and Caa (Moody's) ratings contain all ratings below as well – except default, of course. Fitch uses the same labeling or ratings nomenclature as S&P.

32 Sometimes a C rating constitutes a default in which case it is included in the 'D' category. For no reason other than convenience and expediency, we will make use of the S&P nomenclature for the remainder of the paper.

and red not accurate.[33] Hanson and Schuermann, using a shorter sample period (1981-2002), show that 95% confidence intervals of notch-level PD estimates are highly overlapping for investment grades (AAA through BBB-) but not so for speculative grades (BB through CCC). Since the point estimates for investment grade ratings are very small, a few basis points or less, it is effectively impossible to statistically distinguish the PD for an AA-rated obligor from an A-rated one. Indeed the new Basel Capital Accord, perhaps with this in mind, has set a lower bound of 3bp for any PD estimate (BCBS 2005, §285), commensurate with about a single-A rating.

Rating Categories	Smoothed PD estimates (notch level)	Smoothed PD estimates (grade level)[34]
AAA	0.02	0.02
AA+	0.06	
AA	0.6	0.8
AA–	1.3	
A+	1.8	
A	1.9	2.1
A–	2.1	
BBB+	4.4	
BBB	8.0	8.5
BBB–	12.6	
BB+	22.5	
BB	40.1	51.9
BB–	71.3	
B+	145	
B	540	368
B–	964	
CCC[35]	3,633	3,633

Table 36: S&P one-year PDs in basis points (1981 – 2006), global obligor base. Each entry is the average of two approaches: cohort based on monthly migration matrices and duration or intensity based.

33 Accurate (green) means that adjacent notch-level PDs are statistically distinguishable, moderately accurate (yellow) means that PDs two notches apart are distinguishable, and not accurate (red) means that PDs two notches apart are not distinguishable (but may be so three or more notches apart).

34 Note that grade level PD estimates for a given grade, say AA, need not be the same as the mid-point of the notch evel PD estimate because a) PDs increase non-linearly (in fact approximately exponentially) as one descends the atings spectrum, and b) the obligor distribution is uneven across (notch-level) ratings.

35 Includes all grades below CCC.

In: Securitization of Subprime Mortages
Editor: Milton R. Spotgeste
ISBN: 978-1-60692-200-2

Chapter 2

UNDERSTANDING THE SUBPRIME MORTGAGE CRISIS*

***Yuliya Demyanyk and Otto Van Hemert*†**

ABSTRACT

Using loan-level data, we analyze the quality of subprime mortgage loans by adjusting their performance for differences in borrower characteristics, loan characteristics, and house price appreciation since origination. We find that the quality of loans deteriorated for six consecutive years before the crisis and that securitizers were, to some extent, aware of it. We provide evidence that the rise and fall of the subprime mortgage market follows a classic lending boom-bust scenario, in which unsustainable growth leads to the collapse of the market. Problems could have been detected long before the crisis, but they were masked by high house price appreciation between 2003 and 2005.

1 INTRODUCTION

The subprime mortgage crisis of 2007 was characterized by an unusually large fraction of subprime mortgages originated in 2006 being delinquent or in foreclosure only

---

* This website information has been edited, reformatted and augmented from http:/papers.ssrn.com/sol3/papers.cfm?abstract_id=1020396, dated 09 October 2007. This version is dated 29 February 2008.

† Demyanyk: Banking Supervision and Regulation, Federal Reserve Bank of St. Louis, P.O. Box 442, St. Louis, MO 63166, Yuliya.Demyanyk@stls.frb.org. Van Hemert: Department of Finance, Stern School of Business, New York University, 44 W. 4th Street, New York, NY 10012, ovanheme@stern.nyu.edu. The authors would like to thank Joost Driessen, William Emmons, Scott Frame, Xavier Gabaix, Ralph Koijen, Andreas Lehnert, Chris Mayer, Andrew Meyer, Matt Richardson, Stefano Risa, Bent Sorensen, Stijn Van Nieuwerburgh, James Vickery, Jeff Wurgler, and seminar participants at the Federal Reserve Bank of St. Louis, the Florida Atlantic University, the International Monetary Fund, the second New York Fed – Princeton liquidity conference, Lehman Brothers, the Baruch-Columbia-Stern real estate conference, NYU Stern Research Day, Capula Investment Management, AQR Capital Management, and the Conference on the Subprime Crisis and Economic Outlook in 2008 at Lehman Brothers. The views expressed are those of the authors and do not

months later. The crisis spurred massive media attention; many different explanations of the crisis have been suggested. The goal of this paper is to answer the question: "What do the data tell us about the possible causes of the crisis?" To this end we use a loan-level database containing information on about half of all U.S. subprime mortgages originated between 2001 and 2006.

The relatively poor performance of vintage 2006 loans is illustrated in Figure 1. At every mortgage loan age, loans originated in 2006 show a higher delinquency rate (left panel) and a higher foreclosure rate (right panel) than loans originated in earlier years at the same ages. Note that 2001 was a fairly bad vintage year as well, ranking second, both in terms of the delinquency and the foreclosure rates.

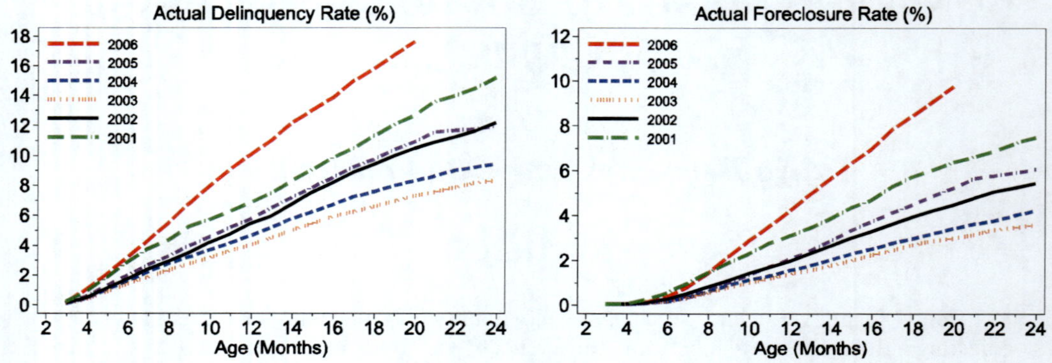

Figure 1. Actual Delinquency and Foreclosure Rate

The figure shows the age pattern in actual delinquency and foreclosure rates for the different vintage years. Delinquency is defined as being 60 days or more late with the monthly mortgage payment, in foreclosure, or real-estate owned. Foreclosure is defined as being in foreclosure or real-estate owned. Once a foreclosure procedure for a loan is finalized and/or the loan balance becomes zero, this loan is dropped from the analysis.

We document that the poor performance of the vintage 2006 loans was not confined to a particular segment of the subprime mortgage market. For example, fixed-rate, adjustable-rate, purchase-money, cash-out refinancing, low-documentation, and full-documentation loans originated in 2006 all showed substantially higher delinquency and foreclosure rates than loans made the prior five years. This contradicts a widely-held belief that the subprime mortgage crisis was mostly confined to adjustable-rate or low- documentation mortgages.

We explore to what extent the subprime mortgage crisis can be attributed to different loan characteristics, borrower characteristics, and subsequent house price appreciation. The subsequent house price appreciation is measured as the MSA-level house price change between the period of origination and the period of loan performance evaluation. For the empirical analysis, we run logit regressions with the probability of either delinquency or foreclosure being a function of these factors.

We find that loan and borrower characteristics are very important in terms of explaining the cross- section of loan performance. However, because these characteristics were not

necessarily reflect the official positions of the Federal Reserve Bank of St. Louis or the Federal Reserve System.

sufficiently different in 2006 compared with the prior five years, they cannot explain the unusually weak performance of vintage 2006 loans. For example, a one-standard-deviation increase in the debt-to-income ratio raises the probability of delinquency 12 months after origination by as much as 0.73 percentage points. However, because the average debt-to-income ratio was only 0.15 standard deviations higher in 2006 than its level in previous years, it contributes very little to explain the inferior performance of vintage 2006 loans. The only variable in the considered logit regression model that contributed substantially to the crisis is the low subsequent house price appreciation for vintage 2006 loans, which can explain about a 1.1 percentage points higherthan-average delinquency rate 12 months after origination.[1] Due to geographical heterogeneity in house price changes, some areas have experienced larger-than-average house price declines and therefore have a larger explained increase in delinquency and foreclosure rates.[2]

We analyze the quality of loans based on their performance, adjusted for differences in observed loan characteristics, borrower characteristics, and subsequent house price appreciation. For the analysis, we compute the prediction error as the difference between the actual delinquency or foreclosure rate and the estimated probability of delinquency or foreclosure based on the logit regression model. In Figure 2 we plot the adjusted delinquency (left panel) and adjusted foreclosure (right panel) rates, which are obtained by adding up the prediction errors and the weighted average actual rates. This ensures having the same weighted average for the actual (Figure 1) and adjusted (Figure 2) delinquency and foreclosure rates.

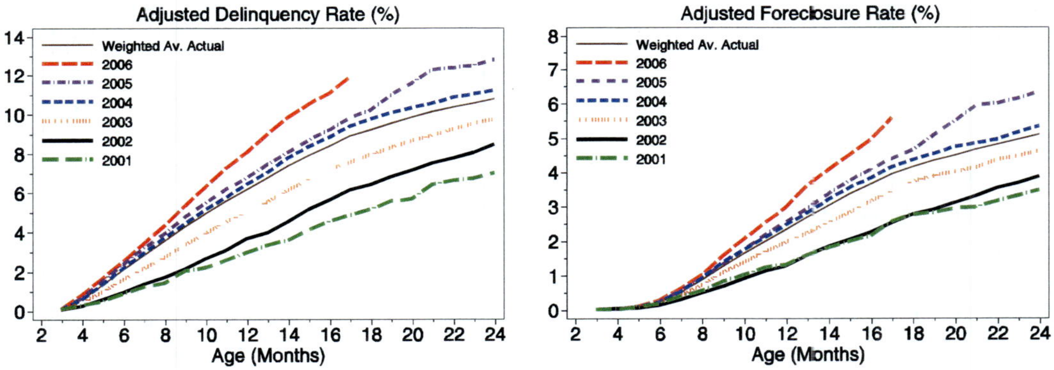

Figure 2. Adjusted Delinquency and Foreclosure Rate

As shown in Figure 2, adjusted delinquency and foreclosure rates have been steadily rising for the past six years, with no particularly large jump from 2005 to 2006. In other words, loan quality—adjusted for observed characteristics and subsequent house price appreciation—deteriorated monotonically between 2001 and 2006. Interestingly, 2001 was among the worst vintage years in terms of actual delinquency and foreclosure rates, but is in fact the best vintage year in terms of the adjusted rates. High interest rates, low average FICO

1 Other papers that research the relationship between house prices and mortgage financing include Genesove and Mayer (1997), Genesove and Mayer (2001), and Brunnermeier and Julliard (2007).

credit scores, and low house price appreciation created the "perfect storm" in 2001, resulting in a high actual delinquency rate; after adjusting for these unfavorable circumstances, however, the adjusted delinquency rates are low.

The figure shows the age pattern in the delinquency rate (left panel) and foreclosure rate (right panel) for the different vintages, after adjusting for variation in FICO scores, loan-to-value ratios, debt-to-income ratios, missing debt-to-income ratio dummies, cash-out refinancing dummies, owner-occupation dummies, documentation levels, percentage of loans with prepayment penalties, mortgage rates, margins, house price appreciation since origination, composition of mortgage contract types, and origination amounts.

In addition to the monotonic deterioration of loan quality, we show that over time the average combined loan-to-value ratio increased, the fraction of low documentation loans increased, and the subprime-prime rate spread decreased. The rapid rise and subsequent fall of the subprime mortgage market is therefore reminiscent of a classic lending boom-bust scenario.[3] The origin of the subprime lending boom has often been attributed to the increased demand for so-called private-label mortgage-backed securities (MBSs) by both domestic and foreign investors. Our database does not allow us to directly test this hypothesis,

but an increase in demand for subprime MBSs is consistent with our finding of lower spreads and higher volume. Mian and Sufi (2008) find evidence consistent with this view that increased demand for MBSs spurred the lending boom.

The logit regression specification used to compute the adjusted delinquency and foreclosure rates assumes that the regression coefficients on the different explanatory variables remain constant over time. We test the validity of this assumption for all variables and find that it is the most strongly rejected for the loan-to-value (LTV) ratio. High-LTV borrowers in 2006 were riskier than those in 2001 in terms of the probability of delinquency or foreclosure, for given values of the other explanatory variables. In fact, the increases in the adjusted delinquency and foreclosure rates are almost exclusively caused by the worsening performance of loans with a combined LTV of 80 percent or more.

Were securitizers aware of the increasing riskiness of high-LTV borrowers?[4] To answer this question, we analyze the relationship between the mortgage rate and LTV ratio (along with the other loan and borrower characteristics). We perform a cross-sectional ordinary least squares (OLS) regression, with the mortgage rate as the dependent variable, for each quarter from 2001Q1 to 2007Q2 for both fixed-rate mortgages and 2/28 hybrid mortgages. Figure 3 shows that the coefficient on the first-lien LTV variable, scaled by the standard deviation of the first-lien LTV ratio, has been increasing over time. We thus find evidence that securitizers were aware of the increasing riskiness of high-LTV borrowers, and adjusted mortgage rates accordingly.

---

2 Also, house price appreciation may differ in cities versus rural areas. See for example Glaeser and Gyourko (2005) and Gyourko and Sinai (2006).

3 Berger and Udell (2004) discuss the empirical stylized fact that during a monetary expansion lending volume typically increases and underwriting standards loosen. Loan performance is the worst for those loans underwritten toward the end of the cycle. Demirgüç-Kunt and Detragiache (2002) and Gourinchas, Valdes, and Landerretche (2001) find that lending booms raise the probability of a banking crisis. Dell'Ariccia and Marquez (2006) show in a theoretical model that a change in information asymmetry across banks might cause a lending boom that features lower standards and lower profits. Ruckes (2004) shows that low screening activity may lead to intense price competition and lower standards.

4 For loans that are securitized (as are all loans in our database), the securitizer effectively dictates the mortgage rate charged by the originator.

We show that our main results are robust when allowing for interaction effects between different loan and borrower characteristics. This includes taking into account risk-layering—the origination of loans that are risky in several dimensions, such as the combination of a high LTV ratio and a low FICO score. As an extension, we estimate our regression model using data just through year-end 2005 and again obtain the continual deterioration of loan quality since 2001. This means that the seeds for the crisis were sown long before 2007, but detecting them was complicated by high house price appreciation between 2003 and 2005—appreciation that masked the true riskiness of subprime mortgages. We also show that our results are robust to applying a different method for dealing with loan terminations (prepayments and defaults).

There is a large literature on the determinants of mortgage delinquencies and foreclosures, dating back to at least Von Furstenberg and Green (1974). Recent contributions include Cutts and Van Order (2005) and Pennington-Cross and Chomsisengphet (2007).[5] Our paper makes several novel contributions to this literature. First, we quantify how much different determinants have contributed to the observed high delinquency and foreclosure rates for vintage 2006 loans, which led up to the 2007 subprime mortgage crisis. Our data enables us to show that the effect of different loan-level characteristics as well as low house price appreciation was quantitatively too small to explain the bad performance of 2006 loans. Second, we uncover a downward trend in loan quality, determined as loan performance adjusted for differences in loan and borrower characteristics as well as subsequent house price appreciation. We further show that there was a deterioration of lending standards and a decrease in the subprime-prime mortgage rate spread during the 2001–2006 period. Together these results provide evidence that the rise and fall of the subprime mortgage market follows a classic lending boom-bust scenario, in which unsustainable growth leads to the collapse of the market. Third, we show that continual deterioration of loan quality could have been detected long before the crisis by means of a simple statistical exercise. Fourth, securitizers were, to some extent, aware of this deterioration over time, as evidenced by changing determinants of mortgage rates.

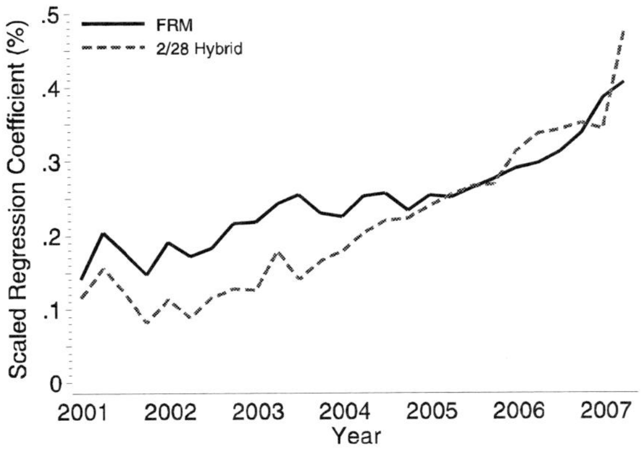

Figure 3. Sensitivity of Mortgage Rate to First-Lien Loan-to-Value Ratio

[5] Deng, Quigley, and Van Order (2000) discuss the simultaneity of the mortgage prepayment and default option. Campbell and Cocco (2003) and Van Hemert (2007) discuss mortgage choice over the life cycle.

The figure shows the effect of the first-lien loan-to-value ratio on the mortgage rate for first-lien fixed-rate and 2/28 hybrid mortgages. The effect is measured as the regression coefficient on the first-lien loan-to-value ratio (scaled by the standard deviation) in an ordinary least squares regression with the mortgage rate as the dependent variable and the FICO score, first-lien loan-to-value ratio, second-lien loan-to-value ratio, debt-to-income ratio, missing debt-to-income ratio dummy, cash-out refinancing dummy, owner-occupation dummy, prepayment penalty dummy, origination amount, term of the mortgage, prepayment term, and margin (only applicable to 2/28 hybrid) as independent variables. Each point corresponds to a separate regression, with a minimum of 13,281 observations.

The structure of this paper is as follows. In Section 2 we show the descriptive statistics for the subprime mortgages in our database. In Section 3 we present the econometric results and discuss explanatory factors for delinquency and foreclosure. In Section 4 we discuss the increasing riskiness of high-LTV borrowers, and the extent to which securitizers were aware of this risk. In Section 5 we analyze the subprime-prime rate spread and in Section 6 we provide robustness checks. In Section 7 we conclude.

2 Descriptive Analysis

In this paper we use and analyze a loan-level database that covers more than half of the U.S. subprime mortgage market.[6] There is no consensus on the exact definition of a subprime mortgage loan. The term subprime can be used to describe certain characteristics of the borrower (e.g., a FICO credit score less than 620),[7] lender (e.g., specialization in high-cost loans),[8] security of which the loan can become a part (e.g., high projected default rate for the pool of underlying loans), or mortgage contract type (e.g., no money down and no documentation provided). The common element across definitions of a subprime loan is a high default risk. In this paper, subprime loans are those underlying subprime securities. We do not include less-risky Alt-A mortgage loans in our analysis. We focus on first-lien loans and consider the 2001 through 2007 sample period.

We first discuss the main characteristics of the loans in our database at origination. Second, we discuss the delinquency and foreclosure rates of these loans for various segments of the subprime mortgage market.

2.1 Loan Characteristics at Origination

Table 1 provides the descriptive statistics for the subprime mortgage loans in our database that were originated between 2001 and 2006. The subprime mortgage market grew

[6] We use the First American LoanPerformance database, which contains about 85 percent of all securitized subprime mortgages. Mortgage Market Statistical Annual (2007) reports securitization shares of subprime mortgages each year from 2001 to 2006 equal to 54, 63, 61, 76, 76, and 75 percent respectively.

[7] The Board of Governors of the Federal Reserve System, The Office of the Controller of the Currency, the Federal Deposit Insurance Corporation, and the Office of Thrift Supervision use this definition.

[8] The U.S. Department of Housing and Urban Development uses HMDA data and interviews lenders to identify subprime lenders among them. There are, however, some subprime lenders making prime loans and some prime lenders originating subprime loans.

dramatically over this period. In the first block of Table 1 we see that over the sample period, the annual number of originated loans more than quadrupled and the average loan size almost doubled. The total dollar amount originated in 2001 was $94 billion. By 2006, originations had increased more than seven-fold, to $685 billion.

Table 2-1. Loan Characteristics at Origination for Different Vintages

Descriptive statistics for the first-lien subprime loans in the LoanPerformance database. We do not report other mortgage types, which amount to less than 0 1%.

	2001	2002	2003	2004	2005	2006
			Size			
Number of Loans (*1000)	624	974	1676	2743	3440	2646
Average Loan Size (*$1000)	151	168	180	201	234	259
			Mortgage Type			
FRM (%)	41.4	39.9	43.3	28.2	25.1	26.1
ARM (%)	0.9	1.9	1.3	4.3	10.3	12.8
Hybrid (%)	52.2	55.9	54.7	67.3	62.0	46.2
Balloon (%)	5.5	2.2	0.8	0.2	2.6	14.9
			Loan Purpose			
Purchase (%)	35.1	33.9	32.9	42.0	45.7	45.4
Refinancing (cash out) (%)	52.1	51.2	51.6	47.9	45.7	44.8
Refinancing (no cash out) (%)	12.3	14.6	15.1	10.0	8.6	9.8
			Variable Means			
FICO Score	620.1	630.5	641.4	645.9	653.7	654.7
Combined Loan-to-Value Ratio (%)	80.0	79.9	80.6	82.8	83.5	84.4
Debt-to-Income Ratio (%)	37.8	38.1	38.2	38.5	39.1	39.8
Missing Debt-to-Income Ratio Dummy (%)	41.6	44.1	38.3	35.1	39.2	31.7
Investor Dummy (%)	10.0	12.0	14.0	14.0	15.0	15.0
Documentation Dummy (%)	68.5	63.4	59.8	57.2	51.8	44.7
Prepayment Penalty Dummy (%)	66.3	63.8	61.4	60.1	60.6	61.6
Mortgage Rate (%)	9.4	8.3	7.3	6.7	6.6	7.2
Margin for ARM and Hybrid Mortgage Loans (%)	6.2	6.3	5.9	5.3	5.0	4.9

In the second block of Table 1, we split the pool of mortgages into four main mortgage contract types. Most numerous are the hybrid mortgages, accounting for about half of all our subprime loans. A hybrid mortgage carries a fixed rate for an initial period (typically 2 or 3 years) and then the rate resets to a reference rate (often the 6-month LIBOR) plus a margin. The fixed-rate mortgage contract has become less popular in the subprime market over time and accounted for just 26 percent of the total number of loans in 2006. In contrast, in the prime mortgage market, most mortgage loans are of the fixed-rate type.[9]

The proportion of balloon mortgage contracts jumped substantially in 2006, and accounted for 15 percent of the total number of mortgages originated that year. A balloon mortgage does not fully amortize over the term of the loan and therefore requires a large final (balloon) payment. About 13 percent of the mortgages originated in 2006 were adjustable-rate (non-hybrid) mortgages.

In the third block of Table 1, we report the purpose of the mortgage loans. In about 30 to 45 percent of cases, the purpose is to finance the purchase of a house. Approximately 50 percent of our subprime mortgage loans were originated to extract cash, by refinancing an existing mortgage loan into a larger new mortgage loan. Cash-out refinancing loans were particularly prevalent between 2001 and 2003. The share of loans originated in order to refinance with no cash extraction is relatively small.

In the final block of Table 1, we report the mean values for the variables that we will use in the regression analysis (see Table 2 for a definition of these variables). The average FICO credit score actually rose over the sample period. The combined loan-to-value (CLTV) ratio, which measures the value of all- lien loans divided by the value of the house, slightly increased over time, primarily because of the increased popularity of second-lien and third-lien loans. The (back-end) debt-to-income ratio (if provided) and the fraction of loans with a prepayment penalty were fairly constant. For about a third of the loans in our database, no debt-to-income ratio was provided; this is captured by the missing debt-to-income ratio dummy variable. The share of loans with full documentation fell sharply over the sample period, from 69 percent in 2001 to 45 percent in 2006.

The mean mortgage rate fell substantially from 2001 to 2004, consistent with sharp declines in both the 1-year and 10-year Treasury yields over the same period. Between 2004 and 2006, both the 1-year and 10- year Treasury yield increased again, but the mortgage rate on subprime mortgages, remarkably, remained fairly constant. Finally, the margin (over a reference rate) for adjustable-rate and hybrid mortgages declined from 2001 to 2004 and remained fairly constant afterward.

We do not report summary statistics on the loan source, such as whether a mortgage broker intermediated, as the broad classification used in the database rendered this variable less informative.

---

[9] For example Koijen, Van Hemert, and Van Nieuwerburgh (2007) show that the fraction of conventional, single-family, fully amortizing, purchase-money loans reported by the Federal Housing Financing Board in its Monthly Interest Rate Survey that are of the fixed-rate type fluctuated between 60 and 90 percent from 2001 to 2006. Vickery (2007) shows that empirical mortgage choice is affected by the eligibility of the mortgage loan to be purchased by Fannie Mae and Freddie Mac.

2.2 Performance of Loans by Market Segments

In Figure 1 we showed that for the subprime mortgage market as a whole, vintage 2006 loans stand out in terms of high delinquency and foreclosure rates (for variable definitions, see Table 2). In Figure

4, we again plot the age pattern in the delinquency rate for vintages 2001 through 2006 and split the subprime mortgage market into various segments. As the figure shows, the poor performance of the 2006 vintage is not confined to a particular segment of the subprime market, but rather reflects a market-wide phenomenon.

In the lower four panels of Figure 4 we see that for purchase-money, cash-out refinancing, low- documentation, and full-documentation mortgage loans, the 2006 vintage shows the highest delinquency rate pattern. In general, vintage 2001 loans show the second-highest delinquency rates, and vintage 2003 loans have the lowest delinquency rates.

In the upper right panel, we see that for adjustable-rate mortgages (ARMs), the 2006 vintage clearly stands out with higher delinquency rates, while 2001 again ranks as the second worst vintage year. In the upper left panel of Figure 4 we see that, in general, the delinquency rate for fixed-rate mortgages (FRMs) is lower than that for ARMs. As with the ARMs in our sample, the delinquency rate for FRMs originated in 2006 is substantially higher than the delinquency rates of the loans originated between 2001 and 2005.

In Figure 5 we plot the delinquency and foreclosure rates of all *outstanding* mortgages. Notice that the fraction of FRMs that are delinquent or in foreclosure remained fairly constant at about five percent from 2005 on. These rates are consistent with those used in an August 2007 speech by the Chairman of the Federal Reserve System (Bernanke (2007)), who said "For subprime mortgages with fixed rather than variable rates, for example, serious delinquencies have been fairly stable at about 5-1/2 percent." It is important, though, to realize that this result is driven by an aging effect of the FRM pool, caused by a recent decrease in the popularity of FRMs (see Table 1). In other words, FRMs originated in 2006 in fact performed unusually poorly (Figure 4, upper-left Panel), but if one plots the delinquency rate of outstanding FRMs over time (Figure 5, left Panel), the weaker performance of vintage 2006 loans is masked by the aging of the overall FRM pool.

3 Empirical Analysis of Delinquency and Foreclosure Determinants

In this section we investigate to what extent a logit regression model can explain the high levels of delinquencies and foreclosures for the vintage 2006 mortgage loans in our database. The regression coefficients are assumed to be constant over time, which allows us to interpret the time variation in the regression error term. All results in this section will be based on a random sample of one million first-lien subprime mortgage loans, originated between 2001 and 2006.

The Figure shows the actual delinquency and foreclosure rates of all outstanding FRMs and hybrids from January 2000 through September 2007.

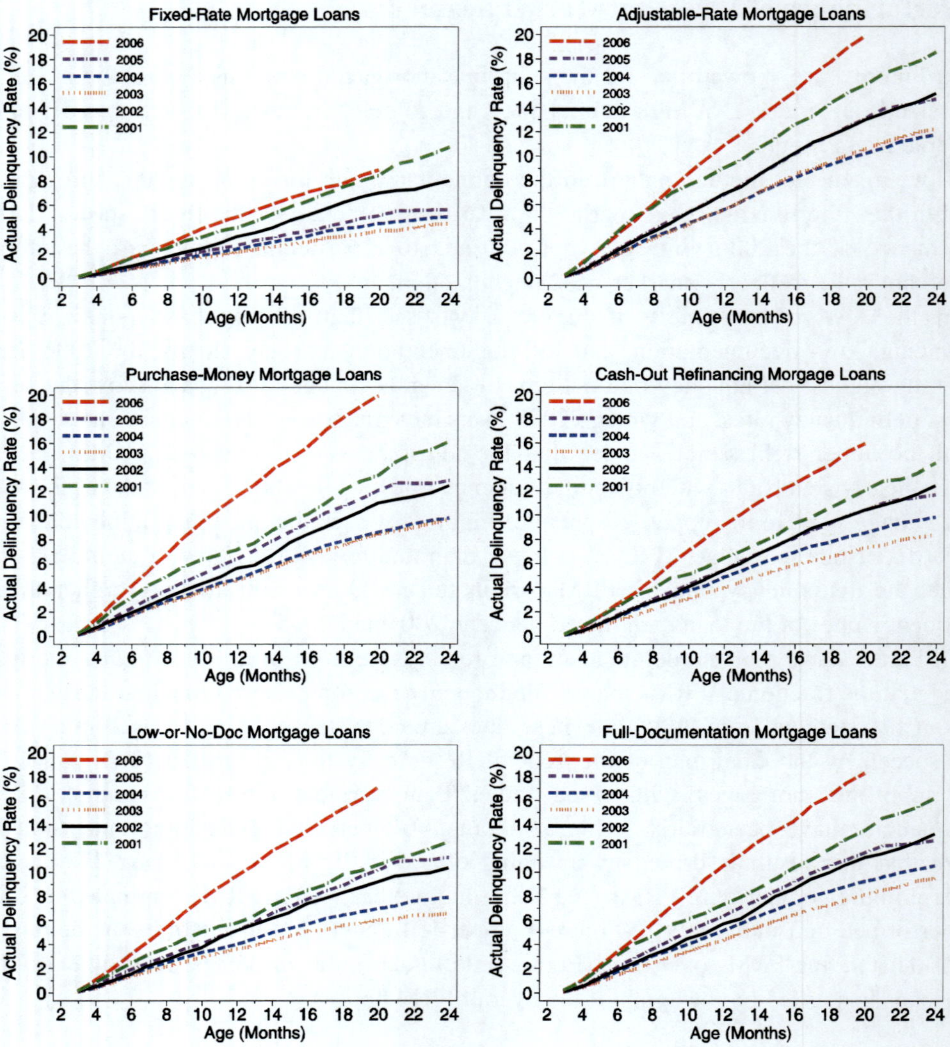

Figure 4. Actual Delinquency Rate for Segments of the Subprime Mortgage Market

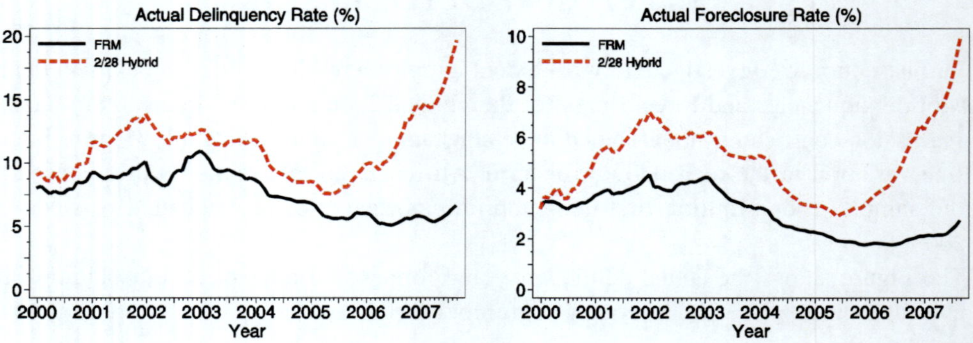

Figure 5. Actual Delinquency and Foreclosure Rates of Outstanding Mortgages

3.1 Empirical Model Specification

We run the following logit regression

$$\Pr(event) = \Phi(\beta' X), \tag{1}$$

where the *event* is either delinquency or foreclosure of a subprime mortgage loan after a given number of months; $\Phi(x) = 1/(1 + \exp(-x))$ is the logit function; X is the vector of explanatory variables, including a constant; and β is the vector of regression coefficients. We will report the following statistics for each explanatory variable i:

$$marginal_i = \Phi(\beta' + X_i\sigma_i) - \Phi(\beta' X) \tag{2}$$

$$deviation06_i = \left(\overline{X06_i} - \overline{X}_i\right)\sigma_i \tag{3}$$

$$contribution06_i = \Phi\left(\beta' X + \overline{X06_i}\right)/\sigma_i \tag{4}$$

$$\approx \text{marginal}_i \times \text{deviation06}_I \tag{5}$$

where $\overline{X}$ is the vector with mean values, σ is the standard deviation of the i-th variable, and $\overline{X06}$ is the mean value of the i-th variable for vintage 2006 loans. We define *deviation*01 and *contribution*01 for vintage 2001 loans in a similar fashion. Equation (5) emerges from a first-order Taylor approximation with the derivative of the logit function with respect to the i-th variable approximated by $marginal_i$.[10] The *marginal* statistic measures the effect of a one-standard-deviation increase in a variable (from its mean) on the probability of an event. The *deviation* statistic measures the number of standard deviations that the mean value of a variable in 2006/2001 was different from the mean value measured over the entire sample. The *contribution* statistic measures the deviation of the (average) event probability in 2006/2001 from the (average) event probability over the entire sample that can be explained by a particular variable.

For any subgroup of loans, such as a particular vintage, we can determine the predicted probability of an event by computing:

$$predicted = \sum_{j=1}^{L} \Phi(\beta' X^j)/L \tag{6}$$

where the superscript j refers to the loan number and L is the total number of loans in the subgroup.

[10] Technically, we first change units by multiplying by σ in Equation (2) and diving by σ in Equation (3).

3.2 Variable Definitions

Table 2 provides the definitions of the dependent and independent (explanatory) variables used in the empirical analysis. We use either the delinquency or the foreclosure dummy variable as the dependent variable. We define a loan to be delinquent if payments on the loan are 60 or more days late, the loan is in foreclosure, or the associated house is real estate owned by a lender. We define a loan to be in foreclosure if the reported status is in foreclosure or real estate owned by a lender. Once a foreclosure procedure for a loan is finalized and/or the loan balance becomes zero, we drop this loan from our analysis. In Subsection 6.3 we show that our main results are robust to incorporating loan terminations.

The borrower and loan characteristics we use in the analysis are: the FICO credit score, the combined loan-to-value ratio, the value of the debt-to-income ratio (when provided), a dummy variable indicating whether the debt-to-income ratio was missing, a dummy variable indicating whether the loan was a cash-out refinancing, a dummy variable indicating whether the borrower was an investor (as opposed to an owner-occupier), a dummy variable indicating whether full documentation was provided, a dummy variable indicating whether there is a prepayment penalty on a loan, the (initial) mortgage rate, and the margin for adjustable-rate and hybrid loans.[11]

In addition, we construct a variable that measures house price appreciation from the time of origination until the time we evaluate whether the loan is delinquent or in foreclosure. To this end we use metropolitan statistical area (MSA) level house price indexes from the Office of Federal Housing Enterprise Oversight (OFHEO) and match loans with MSAs by using the zip code provided by LoanPerformance.

We also considered the change in the unemployment rate from the period of origination until the period of loan performance evaluation, which we could only measure accurately at the state-level for the entire sample. It turned out that the unemployment variable mainly picked up the time trend in the delinquency or foreclosure rate. The relationship between the (trending) unemployment rate and the (trending) loan performance, however, is spurious. When vintage dummy variables are included in the regression, the unemployment rate becomes insignificant, both statistically and economically. We therefore decided to omit the change in the unemployment rate as an explanatory variable.

In Table 2 we report the expected sign for the regression coefficient on each of the explanatory variables in parentheses.

This table presents definitions of the variables used in the regression analysis. The first two variables are used as dependent variables. The other variables are used as independent variables. We report the expected sign for the independent variables in parentheses and sometimes provide a brief motivation.

---

[11] We also studied specifications that included loan purpose, reported in Table 1, and housing outlook, defined as the house price accumulation in the year prior to the loan origination. These variables were not significant and did not materially change the regression coefficients on the other variables.

Table 2-2. Variable Definitions

Variable (Expected Sign)	Explanation
Delinquency Dummy	Payments on the loan are 60 or more days late, the loan is in foreclosure, or the loan is real estate owned.
Foreclosure Dummy	The loan is in foreclosure or is real estate owned.
FICO Score (-)	Fair, Isaac and Company (FICO) credit score at origination.
Combined Loan-to-Value Ratio (+)	Combined values of all liens divided by the value of the house at origination. A higher combined loan-to-value ratio makes default more attractive.
Debt-to-Income Ratio (+)	Back-end debt-to-income ratio, defined by the total monthly debt payments divided by the gross monthly income, at origination. A higher debt-to-income ratio makes it harder to make the monthly mortgage payment.
Missing Debt-to-Income Dummy (+)	Equals one if the back-end debt-to-income ratio is missing and zero if provided. We expect the lack of debt-to-income information to be a negative signal on borrower quality.
Cash-Out Dummy (-)	Equals one if the mortgage loan is a cash-out refinancing loan. Pennington-Cross and Chomsisengphet (2007) show that the most common reasons to initiate a cash-out refinancing are to consolidate debt and to improve property.
Investor Dummy (+)	Equals one if the borrower is an investor and does not owner-occupy the property.
Documentation Dummy (-)	Equals one if full documentation on the loan is provided and zero otherwise. We expect full documentation to be a positive signal on borrower quality.
Prepayment Penalty Dummy (+)	Equals one if there is a prepayment penalty and zero otherwise. We expect that a prepayment penalty makes refinancing less attractive.
Mortgage Rate (+)	Initial interest rate as of the first payment date. A higher interest rate makes it harder to make the monthly mortgage payment.
Margin (+)	Margin for an adjustable-rate or hybrid mortgage over an index interest rate, applicable after the first interest rate reset. A higher margin makes it harder to make the monthly mortgage payment.
House Price Appreciation (-)	MSA-level house price appreciation from the time of loan origination, reported by the O±ce of Federal Housing Enterprise Oversight (OFHEO). Higher housing equity leads to better opportunities to refinance the mortgage loan.
Product Type Dummies (+)	We consider four product types: FRMs, Hybrids, ARMs, and Balloons. We include a dummy variable for the latter three types, which therefore have the interpretation of the probability of delinquency or foreclosure relative to FRM. Because we expect the FRM to be chosen by more risk-averse and prudent borrowers, we expect positive signs for all three product type dummies.
Origination Amount (?)	Size of the mortgage loan. We have no clear prior on the effect of the origination amount on the probability of foreclosure and delinquency, holding constant the loan-to-value and debt-to-income ratio.

3.3 Results

Table 3 shows the results of the logit regression described in Section 3.1 with the delinquency (panel A) or foreclosure (panel B) dummy variables 12 months after origination as the dependent variables. The explanatory variables are listed in the first column. Focusing on the marginal effect of the regression coefficients, defined in Equation 2, we see that the mortgage rate is the most important factor explaining cross-sectional differences in loan performance. The positive sign means that a higher mortgage rate increases the probability of delinquency (panel A) and foreclosure (panel B). Based on the point estimate in panel A, a one standard deviation increase in the mortgage rate increases the probability of delinquency by 1.9 percentage points 12 months after origination.

Table 2-3. Logit Rgression

	Panel A: Delinquency Rate			Panel B: Foreclosure Rate			Panel C: Deviations	
Explanatory Variable	Marginal Effect (%)	Contribution 2001 (%)	Contribution 2006 (%)	Marginal Effect (%)	Contribution 2001 (%)	Contribution 2006 (%)	Deviation 2001	Deviation 2006
Fico Score	– 1:75	1:03	– 0:26	– 0:45	0:24	– 0:06	– 0:37	0:11
Combined Loan-to-Value Ratio	1:60	– 0:26	0:16	0:58	– 0:09	0:06	– 0:20	0:12
Debt-to-Income Ratio	0:73	– 0:07	0:10	0:19	– 0:02	0:03	– 0:11	0:15
Missing Debt-to-Income Ratio	0:57	0:04	– 0:06	0:11	0:01	– 0:01	0:08	– 0:12
Cash-Out Dummy	– 0:32	– 0:04	0:02	– 0:12	– 0:01	0:01	0:11	– 0:07
Investor Dummy	0:37	– 0:04	0:01	0:18	– 0:02	0:00	– 0:12	0:03
Documenta-tion Dummy	– 0:68	– 0:22	0:15	– 0:25	– 0:08	0:06	0:30	– 0:20
Prepayment Penalty Dummy	0:10	0:01	0:00	0:05	0:01	– 0:00	0:12	– 0:01
Mortgage Rate	1:90	2:22	0:10	0:94	1:11	0:05	1:14	0:07
Margin	0:68	– 0:07	– 0:01	0:23	– 0:02	– 0:00	– 0:11	– 0:02
House Price Apprecia-tion	– 1:01	0:62	1:10	– 0:44	0:31	0:56	– 0:48	– 0:80
Hybrid Dummy	0:07	– 0:01	– 0:02	0:08	– 0:01	– 0:02	– 0:12	– 0:23
ARM Dummy	0:04	– 0:01	0:01	0:00	0:00	– 0:00	– 0:23	0:20
Balloon Dummy	0:21	0:01	0:11	0:09	0:01	0:05	0:06	0:52
Origination Amount	0:77	– 0:26	0:20	0:32	– 0:10	0:08	– 0:39	0:27

The second most important marginal effect is associated with the FICO score. A higher FICO score decreases the probability of delinquency (panel A) and foreclosure (panel B), as one would expect. In general all the variables have the expected signs (as discussed in Table 2) and all variables are statistically significant at the 1% level. We also experimented with several interaction and quadratic terms, which yielded very similar results, both qualitatively and quantitatively (see also Section 6.1).

The table shows the output of the the logit regression defined in Equation 1, where the event is that a loan is delinquent (panel A) or in foreclosure (panel B), 12 months after origination. The first column reports the explanatory variables (constant not reported). In panels A and B we report the marginal effect of a variable, defined in Equation 2, and the contribution of a variable to explain a different probability of delinquency or foreclosure in 2001/2006, defined in Equation 4. Panel C reports the deviation of the 2001/2006 value of a variable from the average over 2001{2006, defined in Equation 3. We have the first-order approximation contribution ≈ marginal × deviation. All coefficients are statistically significant at the 1% level.

In panel C of Table 3 we report the "Deviation," defined as the difference between the average value of a variable in 2001/2006 and the average value over the whole sample, expressed in standard deviations (see Equation 3). In particular, the average mortgage rate was high in 2001 and the average house price appreciation was low in 2006, both compared with the average values over the whole sample period.

In panels A and B, "Contribution" measures to what extent a variable can explain why the delinquency and foreclosure rates in 2001 or in 2006 differed from the average over the entire period. We see that the high mortgage rate for vintage 2001 loans was quantitatively the most important factor explaining high observed delinquency and foreclosure rates for that year. Additionally, the low average FICO score for 2001 loans and the low house price appreciation in the months following origination help explain the poor performance of 2001. One could say that in 2001 we had "the perfect storm."

For vintage 2006 loans, low subsequent house price appreciation, in particular, contributed to their weak performance, and accounted for a 1.1 percentage point increase in delinquency rate and a 0.6 percentage point increase in foreclosure rate, 12 months after origination. The mean values in 2006 for the other variables were not sufficiently different from the sample mean to contribute much to a different delinquency or foreclosure rate in 2006. It is worth noting that the increase in the average CLTV ratio and the decrease in the fraction of loans with full documentation over time does not contribute a lot to the high delinquency and foreclosure rates in 2006.

We also computed the contributions of all explanatory factors for the other vintage years (the results are not reported). For loans originated in 2003 and 2004, the high subsequent house price appreciation between 2003 and 2005 contributed to a lower actual delinquency rate. For example, the explained change in the delinquency rate 12 months after origination was –0.3 percentage points and –0.6 percentage points for 2003 and 2004, respectively. The house price appreciation variable had the largest (absolute) contribution among all variables considered for those years. Therefore, we can say that high house price appreciation between 2003 and 2005 masked the true riskiness of subprime mortgages.[12]

The product type has a relatively small effect on the performance of a loan, beyond what is explained by other characteristics (see Table 3). In Figure 4 we showed that FRMs experience a much lower delinquency rate than ARMs, which must be driven by borrowers with better characteristics selecting into FRMs.[13]

To examine to what extent the logit regression model is capable of explaining the large observed delinquency and foreclosure rates in 2006, we compare the adjusted delinquency and foreclosure rates for different ages and different vintages in Figure 2. The adjusted rate at a given age equals the prediction error (the actual rate minus the predicted rate) plus the weighted average rate over the 2001–2006 period, with weights equal to the number of loans originated in each year. The predicted delinquency and foreclosure rates are determined using Equation 6. We add up the weighted-average actual rates to facilitate the comparison with the actual rates plotted in Figure 1. Interestingly, both the adjusted delinquency and foreclosure rates have been increasing over the past six years. In other words, loan quality deteriorated monotonically between 2001 and 2006. This picture is in sharp contrast with that obtained from actual rates, depicted in Figure 1, where 2003 was the year with the lowest delinquency and foreclosure rates, and 2001 was the year with the second-highest rates.

4 Non-Stationarity of the Loan-to-Value Effect

The logit regression specification used in Section 3 assumes that the regression coefficients are constant over time. That is, the effect of a unit change in an explanatory variable on the delinquency or the foreclosure rate is the same in, for example, 2006 as it is in 2001, holding constant the values of the other explanatory variables. We test the validity of this assumption for all variables in our analysis by running cross-sectional OLS regressions for each calendar month from 2001 to 2006 and checking the stability of the regression coefficients. It turns out that the strongest rejection of a constant regression coefficient is for the CLTV ratio. In this section we first discuss this finding and then turn to the question of whether lenders were aware of the non-stationarity of the loan-to-value effect, by investigating the relationship between the loan-to-value ratio and mortgage rates over time.

4.1 Loan-to-Value Ratio and the Delinquency Rate

Figure 6 shows the distribution of the CLTV ratio for all first-lien loans. About 30 percent have a CLTV smaller than 80 percent, about 20 percent have a CLTV of exactly 80 percent, and about 50 percent have a CLTV greater than 80 percent. The average CLTV increased slightly from 80 percent in 2001 to 84 percent in 2006 (see Table 1). In addition,

---

[12] Shiller (2007) argues that house prices were too high compared to fundamentals in this period and refers to the house price boom as a classic speculative bubble largely driven by an extravagant expectation for future house price appreciation.

[13] Consistent with this finding, LaCour-Little (2007) shows that individual credit characteristics are important for mortgage product choice.

the distribution shifted slightly to the right over time: In 2001 the percentages of loans in these three CLTV categories was 35, 20, and 45 percent, respectively; in 2006 they were 28, 14, and 58 percent, respectively.

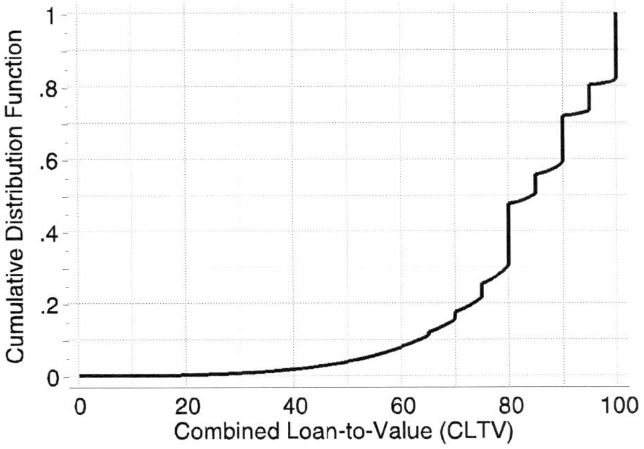

Figure 6. Cumulative Distribution of the Combined Loan-to-Value Ratio (CLTV)

The figure shows the cumulative distribution of the combined loan-to-value ratio for all first-lien subprime mortgage loans originated between 2001 and 2006. Loans with a combined loan-to-value ratio greater than 100 account for less than 05% of all loans and are omitted from the Figure.

Table 4 reports the actual minus the predicted delinquency rate for different CLTV value categories and different vintage years, estimated using Equation 6. In other words, the table reports the average prediction error for the three CLTV subgroups discussed above and for each origination year of loans. A positive prediction error means that the actual delinquency rate was higher than the rate predicted by the logit regression model. Consistent with Figure 2, the error increased over time. However, for the low CLTV group, the increase in the error was much smaller and, in fact, had been slightly decreasing from 2004 onward. For a CLTV ratio of 80 percent, the increase in the error was 43 percent, and for the CLTV ratio above 80 percent, the increase was 71 percent. Therefore, high CLTV ratios were increasingly associated with higher delinquency rates, beyond what is captured by the logit regression model.

4.2 Loan-to-Value Ratio and the Mortgage Rate

The combined LTV ratio rather than the first-lien LTV ratio is believed to be the main determinant of delinquency and foreclosure, because it is the burden of all the debt together that may trigger financial problems for the borrower. In contrast, the first-lien LTV is the more important determinant of the mortgage rate on a first-lien mortgage, because it captures the dollar amount at stake for the first-lien lender.[14]

[14] This is confirmed by our empirical results. To conserve space the results are not reported.

Table 2-4: Actual Minus Predicted Delinquency Rate

	2001	2002	2003	2004	2005	2006	2006–2001
$CLTV < 80\%$	–1.7%	–1.4%	–0.4%	0.6%	0.4%	0.5%	2.2%
$CLTV = 80\%$	–2.7%	–2.1%	–0.7%	0.4%	1.0%	1.6%	4.3%
$CLTV > 80\%$	–4.4%	–3.3%	–1.6%	0.2%	0.7%	2.7%	7.1%

This table presents the actual minus the predicted delinquency rate 12 months after origination for different vintages and combined loan-to-value (CLTV) ratios.

In this subsection we try to determine whether lenders were aware that high LTV ratios were increasingly associated with riskier borrowers. Specifically, we test whether the sensitivity of the lender's interest rate to the first-lien LTV ratio changed over time. We perform a cross-sectional OLS regression with the mortgage rate as the dependent variable and loan characteristics, including the first-lien LTV and second-lien LTV (CLTV minus first-lien LTV), as independent variables.[15] We perform one such regression for each calendar quarter in our sample period. We can only expect to get accurate results when using relatively homogeneous groups of loans, and therefore consider fully amortizing FRM and 2/28 hybrid loans separately. Together these two contract types account for about half of all mortgage loans in our database. Each cross-sectional regression is based on a minimum of 13,281 observations.

Figure 3 shows the regression coefficient on the first-lien LTV ratio for each quarter from 2001Q1 through 2007Q2.[16] We scaled the coefficients by the standard deviation of the first-lien LTV ratio, and they can therefore be interpreted as the changes in the mortgage rates when the first-lien LTV ratios are increased by one standard deviation. In the fourth quarter of 2006, a one-standard-deviation increase in the first-lien LTV ratio corresponded to about a 35-basis-point increase in the mortgage rate for both FRMs and 2/28 hybrid mortgages, keeping constant other loan characteristics. In contrast, in the first quarter of 2001, the corresponding rate increase was around 13 basis points. This provides evidence that lenders were to some extent aware of high LTV ratios being increasingly associated with risky borrowers.[17] Finally, notice that the effect of a one-standard-deviation increase in the first-lien LTV ratio on the 2/28 mortgage rate increased substantially in the wake of the subprime mortgage crisis: from 34 basis points in 2007Q1 to 47 basis points in 2007Q2.

5 Subprime-Prime Rate Spread

In general, interest rates on subprime mortgages are higher than on prime mortgages to compensate the lender for the (additional) default risk associated with subprime loans. In this section we analyze the time series of the subprime-prime rate spread, both with and without

[15] Specifically, we use the FICO score, first-lien loan-to-value ratio, second-lien loan-to-value ratio, debt-to-income ratio, a dummy for a missing debt-to-income ratio, a cash-out refinancing dummy, a dummy for owner occupation, documentation dummy, prepayment penalty dummy, margin, origination amount, term of the mortgage, and prepayment term as the righthand-side variables.

[16] Our data extends to 2007Q3, but due to a near shutdown of the securitized subprime mortgage market we lack statistical power in this quarter.

[17] The effects of other loan characteristics on mortgage rates have been much more stable over time, as unreported results suggest.

adjustment for changes in loan and borrower characteristics. We focus on fixed-rate mortgages for this exercise. For hybrid mortgages the subprime-prime comparison is more complicated because (i) both the initial (teaser) rate and the margin should be factored in, and (ii) we don't have good data on the prime initial rates and margins.

In Figure 7 we show the actual subprime-prime rate spread. The subprime rate is from the LoanPerformance database, the prime rate is the contract rate on fixed-rate mortgages reported by the Federal Housing Finance Board (FHFB) in its Monthly Interest Rate Survey.[18] The subprime-prime spread decreased substantially over time, with the largest decline between 2001 and 2004, which coincides with the most rapid growth in the number of loans originated (see Table 1). In Figure 7 we also plot the yield spread between 10-year BBB and AAA corporate bonds, which we obtained from Standard and Poor's Global Fixed Income Research. Compared to the corporate BBB-AAA yield spread, the actual subprime-prime rate spread declined much more and more steadily, hence the decline cannot just be attributed to a change in the overall level of risk aversion.

We perform an OLS regression with the spread as dependent variable and the prime rate and various subprime loan and borrower characteristics as explanatory variables, using data from 2001 through 2006.[19]

$$spread = \beta_0 + \beta_1 prime + \beta_2' characteristics + error \tag{7}$$

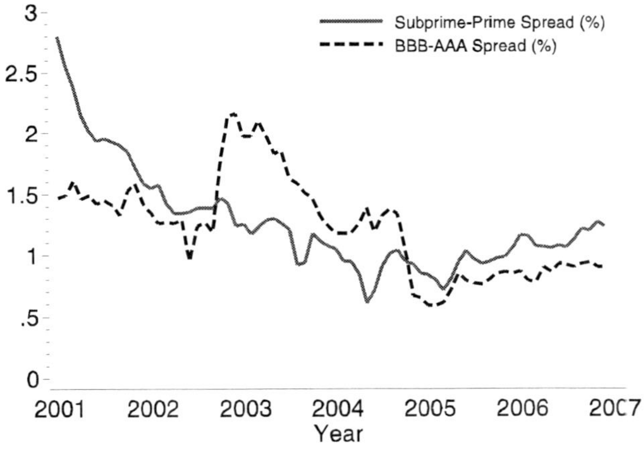

Figure 7. FRM Rate Spread and Corporate Bond Yield Spread

The figure shows the FRM subprime-prime rate spread and the yield spread between 10-year BBB and AAA corporate bonds.

---

[18] Available at http://www.fhfb.gov/GetFile.aspx?FileID=6416.

[19] The explanatory factors in the regression are the FICO credit score, a dummy variable that equals one if full documentation was provided, a dummy variable that equals one if prepayment penalty is present, origination amount, value of debt-to-income ratio, a dummy variable that equals one if debt-to-income was not provided, a dummy variable that equals one if loan is a refinancing, a dummy variable that equals one if a borrower is an investor, loan-to-value ratio based on a first-lien, and loan-to-value ratios based on a second, third, etc. liens if applicable.

Notice that the $\beta_1 prime$ term corrects for the fact that the spread is affected by the prime rate itself, and thus changes over the business cycle, because a higher prime rate increases the default probability on subprime loans for a given spread. In Figure 8 we plot the prediction error, averaged per origination month, along with a fitted linear trend.

The downward trend in Figure 8 indicates that the subprime-prime spread, after adjusting for differences in observed loan and borrower characteristics, declined. In Figure 2 we showed that loan quality, obtained by adjusting loan performance for differences in loan and borrower characteristics and subsequent house price appreciation, deteriorated over the period, and thus the (adjusted) riskiness of loans rose. Therefore, on a per-unit-of-risk basis, the subprime-prime mortgage spread decreased even more than the level of the spread.

6 Robustness and Extensions

In this section we discuss the robustness of reported results and extensions of the empirical model used in Sections 3 and 4.

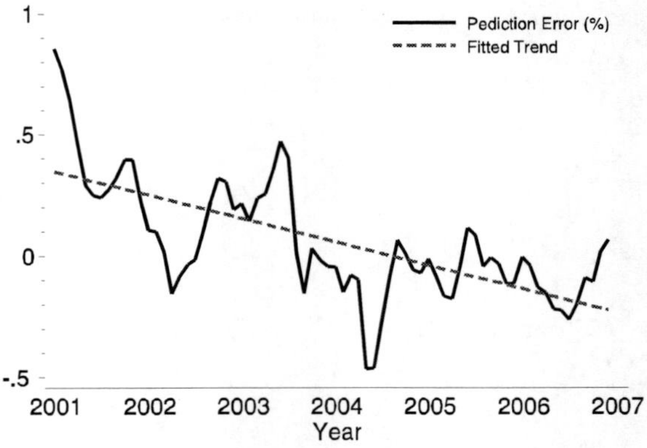

Figure 8. Prediction Error in the Subprime-Prime Rate Spread

The figure shows the prediction error in the subprime-prime rate spread, determined in a regression of the spread on the prime rate and the following loan and borrower characteristics: FICO credit score, a dummy variable that equals one if full documentation was provided, a dummy variable that equals one if a prepayment penalty is present, origination amount, value of debt-to-income ratio, a dummy variable that equals one if debt-to-income was not provided, a dummy variable that equals one if the loan is a refinancing, a dummy variable that equals one if a borrower is an investor, loan-to-value ratio based on a first lien, and loan-to-value ratio based on a second, third, etc. liens if applicable.

6.1 Allowing for Interaction Terms

In this subsection we consider a logit regression with the delinquency rate as the dependent variable. As independent variables we use those from the baseline case presented in Table 3, plus the 10 interaction and quadratic terms that can be constructed from the four most important independent variables: the FICO score, the CLTV ratio, the mortgage rate, and subsequent house price appreciation.

Allowing for the above interaction terms, we take into account the effect of risk-layering—such as, for example, the effect of a combination of a borrower's low FICO score and a high CLTV ratio—on the probability of delinquency. In the above example, it is a priori not clear what the sign on the FICO-CLTV interaction variable is. A negative sign means that a low FICO and a high CLTV reinforce each other and give rise to a predicted delinquency probability that is higher than when the interaction is ignored. A positive sign could be explained by lenders who originate a low FICO and high CLTV loan only if they have positive private information on the loan or borrower quality. It turns out that the coefficient on the FICO-CLTV interaction term is positive and significant at the 1% level for delinquency 12 months after origination.

More certain is the sign we expect on the HPA-CLTV variable. Low house price appreciation is expected to especially give rise to a higher delinquency probability for a high CLTV ratio, because the borrower is closer to a situation with negative equity in the house (combined value of the mortgage loan larger than the market value of the house). Consistent with this intuition, we find a negative and significant (at the 1 percent level) coefficient on this interaction term for delinquency 12 months after origination.

Using this alternative regression specification, we plot in Figure 9 (left panel) the adjusted delinquency rates, as we did in Figure 2 (left panel) for the baseline case specification. Comparing Figure 2 (left panel) and Figure 9 (left panel) we see that adding the interaction and quadratic terms hardly changes the adjusted delinquency rates. Therefore, our result of a continual increase in the adjusted delinquency rate is robust to explicitly taking into account the effect of risk-layering and other interaction effects.

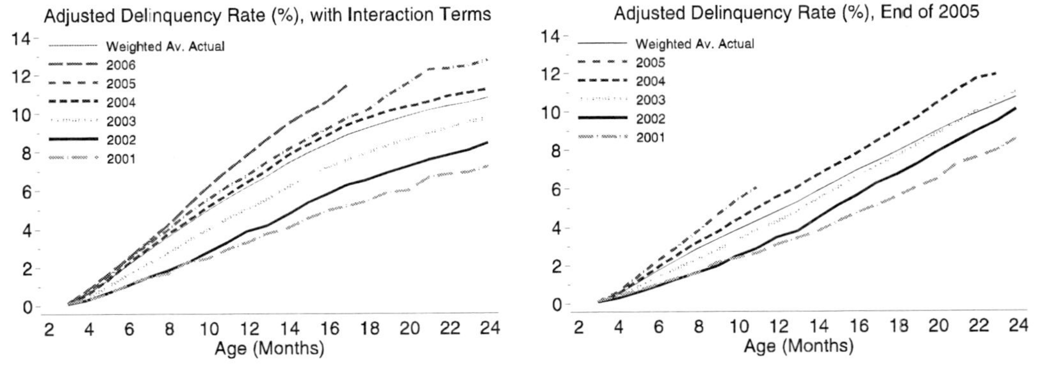

Figure 9. Adjusted Delinquency Rate, Alternative Specifications.

The figure shows the adjusted delinquency rate under two alternative specifications; it should be compared to the adjusted delinquency rates presented in Figure 2, the baseline case. In the left panel, the adjusted delinquency rates are obtained using the variables of the baseline case plus 10 additional quadratic and interaction terms that can be constructed from the four most important independent variables—the FICO score, the CLTV, the mortgage rate, and house price appreciation. In the right panel, we estimated the baseline case regression using the data from 2001 to 2005 only.

6.2 Adjusted Delinquency Rate as Observed Year-End 2005

In this subsection we study the following question: Based on information available at the end of 2005, was the dramatic deterioration of loan quality since 2001 already apparent? Notice that we cannot answer this question by simply inspecting vintages 2001 through 2005 in Figure 2 (left panel), because the computation of the adjusted delinquency rate for, say, vintage 2001 loans, makes use of a regression model estimated using data from 2001 through 2006.

Hence, we re-estimate the logit regression model underlying Figure 2 (left panel) making use of only 200 1–2005 data. The resulting age pattern in delinquency rates is plotted in Figure 9 (right panel). We again obtain the result that the adjusted delinquency rate rose monotonically from 2001. We therefore conclude that the dramatic deterioration of loan quality should have been apparent by the end of 2005.[20]

6.3 Including Terminated Loans

For the regressions in Section 3 we used as dependent variable the probability that a loan of a particular age is delinquent or in foreclosure, conditional on the loan not being terminated (prepaid or defaulted) before that age. Since the focus in this paper is on young loans (age below 24 months), we do not expect terminations to play an important role for the questions we address. We confirm in this subsection that our main results are robust to explicitly taking into account terminations.

The fraction of loans that terminate in the first 12 months is 10%, 13%, 14%, 17%, 14%, 13% for 200 1-2006 vintage loans respectively. This fraction peaks in 2004, during the heyday of the house price boom, which created favorable refinancing opportunities. Remarkably, it is lowest for vintage 2001 loans, which were originated prior to interest rate declines. This result might be particular for loans of age below 24 months. For hybrid mortgage loans many refinances may occur at or after the moment of the rate reset, which is typically at a loan age of 24 or 36 months.[21]

We re-estimate the results presented in Table 3—analyzing the effects of loan characteristics, borrower characteristics, and economic circumstances on the probability of

[20] One reason why investors did not massively start to avoid or short subprime-related securities is that the timing of the subprime market downturn may have been hard to predict. Moreover, a short position is associated with a high cost of carry (Feldstein (2007)).

[21] Gabaix, Krishnamurthy, and Vigneron (2007) argue that the risk associated with mortgage prepayments is priced in the mortgage-backed securities market.

delinquency and foreclosure—but this time include loans that are terminated prior to the moment of loan performance evaluation.

Specifically, we define a delinquent loan as a loan that 12 months after origination is either delinquent (or in foreclosure, or real estate owned), or terminated due to default. We define a loan terminated due to default when the month prior to termination the loan was in foreclosure or real-estate owned. Similarly, the new definition for foreclosure is that a loan is in foreclosure (or real estate owned), or terminated due to default. Using this alternative definitions for delinquency and foreclosure, all explanatory variables we use in the regression (see Table 3) have the same sign and remain statistically significant, except for the ARM dummy. The mortgage rate, FICO score, the CLTV ratio, and the subsequent house price appreciation remain the most important explanatory variables, measured by the absolute size of the marginal effect.

In Figure 10 we plot the actual delinquency rate (left panel) and adjusted delinquency rate (right panel) based on the definition above that includes terminated loans. In general the delinquency rate is somewhat lower than based on the baseline case definition of delinquency, in particular at older loan ages, see left panels of Figures 1 and 2 (left panel). Terminations due to a prepayment will lower the delinquency rate compared to the baseline case. Terminations due to a default have the opposite effect. Hence we find that the prepayment effect dominates the default effect. Importantly, both for the actual and the adjusted delinquency rate the order of the lines for the different vintage years remain unchanged. We again have the result that the adjusted delinquency rate has been steadily rising over the past six years.

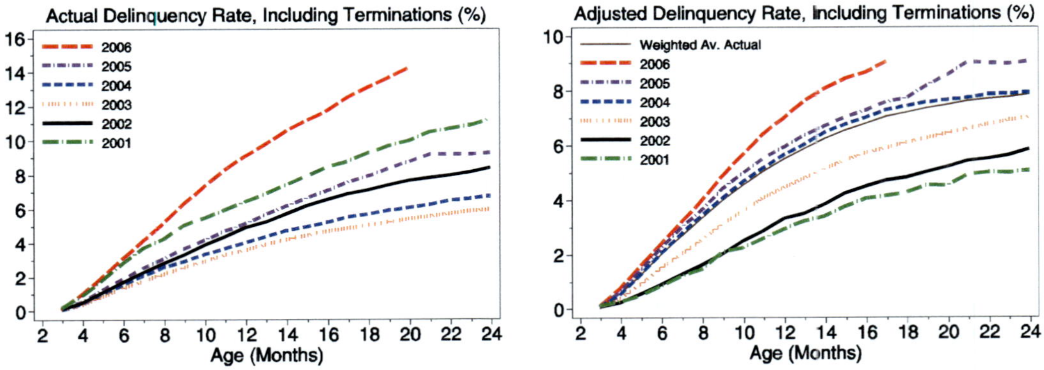

Figure 10. Actual and Adjusted Delinquency Rates, Including Terminated Loans

The figure shows the actual delinquency rates (left panel) and adjusted delinquency rates (right panel) including terminated (prepaid and defaulted) loans for the different vintage years. Delinquency is defined as being 60 days or more late with the monthly mortgage payment, in foreclosure, real-estate owned or defaulted. Foreclosure is defined as being in foreclosure or real-estate owned or defaulted. The corresponding figures that exclude terminated loans are Figure 1 (left panel) for the actual delinquency rates and Figure 2 (left panel) for the adjusted delinquency rates.

6.4 Non-Linearity in the Sensitivity of the Mortgage Rate to the LTV

In Figure 3 we plotted the sensitivity of the fixed-rate and 2/28 hybrid mortgage rates to the first- lien LTV ratio. The sensitivity is defined as the regression coefficient on the first-lien LTV (scaled by the standard deviation) in a regression with the mortgage rate as dependent variable and the first-lien LTV, the second-lien LTV, and the other loan and borrower characteristics listed in Subsection 4.2, as independent variables.

In this subsection we study the robustness of this result to adding the square of the first-lien LTV and the square of the second-lien LTV as independent variables, therefore allowing for a non-linear functional form. In Figure 11 we report the resulting scaled marginal effect of the first-lien LTV for fixed-rate and 2/28 hybrid mortgages evaluated at a first-lien LTV of 80 percent (left panel) and 90 percent (right panel). Without non-linear terms the marginal effect is simply given by the regression coefficient. This is what we plotted in Figure 3. With the quadratic terms, the marginal effect is given by $\beta_{LTV} + 2\beta_{LTV2}X,$ where the βs are the regression coefficients and X is the first-lien LTV ratio at which the marginal effect is evaluated.

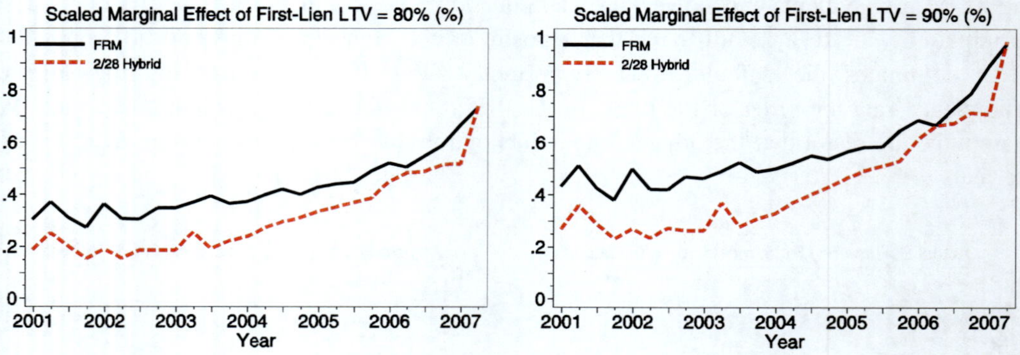

Figure 11: Sensitivity of Mortgage Rate to First-Lien LTV Ratio Allowing for Non-Linearity

The figure shows the scaled marginal effect of the first-lien loan-to-value (LTV) ratio on the mortgage rate for first-lien fixed-rate and 2/28 hybrid mortgages, evaluated at a first-lien LTV of 80% (left panel) and 90% (right panel). The effect is determined using an OLS regression with the interest rate as dependent variable and the FICO score, first-lien LTV (and the square), second-lien LTV (and the square), debt-to-income ratio, missing debt-to-income ratio dummy, cash-out refinancing dummy, owner-occupation dummy, prepayment penalty dummy, origination amount, term of the mortgage, prepayment term, and margin as independent variables.

As shown in Figure 11, the marginal effect is rising over time, consistent with the baseline case results presented in Figure 3. Moreover, we find that there is a statistically and economically significant nonlinear effect of the first-lien LTV on the mortgage rate. Comparing the left and right panels in Figure 11, the higher the first-lien LTV ratio, the more sensitive is the mortgage rate to changes in the first-lien LTV. The largest difference between the results based on specifications with and without non-linearity is observed for 2/28 hybrid mortgages in 2007 at a first-lien LTV of 90 percent (right panel). The scaled marginal effect increases by 27 basis points over the course of 3 months in 2007 when a model allows for non-linearity. In contrast, ignoring the non-linearity, as in Figure 3, the increase in the scaled marginal effect is only 13 basis points.

7 Concluding Remarks

The subprime mortgage market experienced explosive growth between 2001 and 2006. Angell and Rowley (2006) and Kiff and Mills (2007), among others, argue that this was facilitated by the development of private-label mortgage backed securities, which do not carry any kind of credit risk protection by the Government Sponsored Enterprises. Investors in search of higher yields kept increasing their demand for private-label mortgage-backed securities, which also led to sharp increases in the subprime share of the mortgage market (from around 8 percent in 2001 to 20 percent in 2006) and in the securitized share of the subprime mortgage market (from 54 percent in 2001 to 75 percent in 2006).

In this paper we show that during the dramatic growth of the subprime (securitized) mortgage market, the quality of the market deteriorated dramatically. We analyze loan quality as the performance of loans, adjusted for differences in borrower characteristics (such as credit score, level of indebtedness, ability to provide documentation), loan characteristics (such as product type, amortization term, loan amount, interest rate), and subsequent house price appreciation.

The decline in loan quality has been monotonic, but not equally spread among different types of borrowers. Over time, high-LTV borrowers became increasingly risky (their adjusted performance worsened more) compared to low-LTV borrowers. Securitizers seem to have been aware of this particular pattern in the relative riskiness of borrowers: We show that over time mortgage rates became more sensitive to the LTV ratio of borrowers. In 2001, for example, the premium paid by a high LTV borrower was close to zero. In contrast, in 2006 a borrower with a one standard deviation above-average LTV ratio paid a 30 basis point premium compared to an average LTV borrower.

In principal, the subprime-prime mortgage rate spread (subprime mark-up) should account for the default risk of subprime loans. For the rapid growth of the subprime mortgage market to have been sustainable, the increase in the overall riskiness of subprime loans should have been accompanied by an increase in the subprime mark-up. In this paper we show that this was not the case: Subprime markup—adjusted and not adjusted for changes in differences in borrower and loan characteristics—declined over time. With the benefit of hindsight we now know that indeed this situation was not sustainable, and the subprime mortgage market experienced a severe crisis in 2007. In many respects, the subprime market experienced a classic lending boom-bust scenario with rapid market growth, loosening underwriting standards, deteriorating loan performance, and decreasing risk premiums.[22] Argentina in 1980, Chile in 1982, Sweden, Norway, and Finland in 1992, Mexico in 1994, Thailand, Indonesia, and Korea in 1997 all experienced the culmination of a boom-bust scenario, albeit in different economic settings.

---

[22] A more detailed discussion, theory, and empirical evidence on such episodes is available in Dell'Ariccia and Marquez (2006), Demirgüç-Kunt and Detragiache (2002), Gourinchas, Valdes, and Landerretche (2001), and Kamisky and Reinhart (1999), among many others.

Were problems in the subprime mortgage market apparent before the actual crisis showed signs in 2007? Our answer is yes, at least by the end of 2005. Using the data available only at the end of 2005, we show that the monotonic degradation of the subprime market was already apparent. Loan quality had been worsening for five consecutive years at that point. Rapid appreciation in housing prices masked the deterioration in the subprime mortgage market and thus the true riskiness of subprime mortgage loans. When housing prices stopped climbing, the risk in the market became apparent.

REFERENCES

Angell, Cynthia & Clare D. Rowley (2006). Breaking new ground in U.S. mortgage lending, FDIC: Outlook Summer 2006 Federal Deposit Insurance Corporation.

Berger, Allen & Gregory Udell (2004). The institutional memory hypothesis and the procyclicality of bank lending behavior, *Journal of Financial Intermediation, 12,* 458–495.

Bernanke, Ben (2007). Housing, housing finance, and monetary policy, Speech Federal Reserve Bank of Kansas City's Economic Symposium.

Brunnermeier, Markus & Christian Julliard (2007). Money illusion and housing frenzies, *Review of Financial Studies* forthcoming.

Campbell, John Y. & João F. Cocco (2003) Household risk management and optimal mortgage choice, *Quarterly Journal of Economics, 118,* 1449–1494.

Cutts, Amy Crews & Robert A. Van Order (2005). On the economics of subprime lending, *The Journal of Real Estate Finance and Economics, 30,* 167–196.

Dell'Ariccia, Giovanni & Robert Marquez (2006). Lending booms and lending standards, *Journal of Finance, 61,* 2511–2546.

Demirg¨uç-Kunt, Asli & Enrica Detragiache (2002). Does deposit insurance increase banking system stability? An empirical investigation, *Journal of Monetary Economics, 49,* 1373–1406.

Deng, Yongheng, John M. Quigley & Robert A. Van Order, (2000). Mortgage terminations, heterogeneity and the exercise of mortgage options, *Econometrica, 68,* 275–308.

Feldstein, Martin S. (2007). Housing, credit markets and the business cycle, NBER working paper 13471.

Gabaix, Xavier, Arvind Krishnamurthy & Olivier Vigneron (2007). Limits of arbitrage: Theory and evidence from the mortgage-backed securities market, *Journal of Finance, 62,* 557–596.

Genesove, David & Christopher Mayer (1997). Equity and time to sale in the real estate market, *American Economic Review, 87,* 255–269.

———. (2001). Loss aversion and seller behavior: Evidence from the housing market, *Quarterly Journal of Economics, 116,* 1233–1260.

Glaeser, Edward & Joseph Gyourko (2005). Urban decline and durable housing, *Journal of Political Economy, 113,* 345–375.

Gourinchas, Pierre-Oliver, Rodrigo Valdes & Oscar Landerretche (2001). Lending booms: Latin America and the world, *Economia, 1,* 47–99.

Gyourko, Joseph, Mayer Christopher & Todd Sinai (2006). Superstar cities, NBER working paper 12355.

Kamisky, Graciela L & Carmen M. Reinhart (1999). The twin crises: The causes of banking and balance-ofpayment problems, *American Economic Review, 89,* 473–500.

Kiff, John & Paul Mills (2007). Money for nothing and checks for free: Recent developments in U.S. subprime mortgage markets, IMF working paper.

Koijen, Ralph, Otto Van Hemert, & Stijn Van Nieuwerburgh (2007). Mortgage timing, NBER working paper 13361.

LaCour-Little, Michael (2007). The home purchase mortgage preferences of low-and-moderate income households, *Real Estate Economics* forthcoming.

Mian, Atif & Amir Sufi (2008). The consequences of mortgage credit expansion: Evidence from the 2007 mortgage default crisis, Working paper.

Pennington-Cross, Anthony & Souphala Chomsisengphet (2007). Subprime refinancing: Equity extraction and mortgage termination, *Real Estate Economics, 35,* 233–263.

Ruckes, Martin (2004). Bank competition and credit standards, review of financial studies, *Review of Financial Studies, 17,* 1073–1102.

Shiller, Robert J. (2007). Understanding recent trends in house prices and home ownership, NBER working paper 13553.

Van Hemert, Otto (2007). Household interest rate risk management, Working paper.

Vickery, James (2007). Interest rates and consumer choice in the residential mortgage market, Working paper.

Von Furstenberg, George M. & Jeffery Green, R. (1974). Home mortgage delinquencies: A cohort analysis, *Journal of Finance, 29,* 1545–1548.

In: Securitization of Subprime Mortages
Editor: Milton R. Spotgeste
ISBN: 978-1-60692-200-2

Chapter 3

INFORMATION ON RECENT DEFAULT AND FORECLOSURE TRENDS FOR HOME MORTGAGES AND ASSOCIATED ECONOMIC AND MARKET DEVELOPMENTS*

United States Government Accountability Office

October 16, 2007

The Honorable Barney Frank Chairman Committee on Financial Services House of Representatives
The Honorable Spencer Bachus Ranking Member Committee on Financial Services House of Representatives

Subject: Information on Recent Default and Foreclosure Trends for Home Mortgages and Associated Economic and Market Developments

Substantial growth in the mortgage market in recent years has helped many Americans become homeowners. However, as of the latest quarterly data available, June 2007, more than 1 million mortgages were in default or foreclosure, an increase of 50 percent compared with June 2005.[1] Defaults and foreclosures on home mortgages can impose significant costs on borrowers, lenders, mortgage investors, and neighborhoods. Additionally, recent increases in defaults and foreclosures have contributed to concern and increased volatility in certain U.S.

* This is an edited, reformatted and augmented version of a United States Government Accountability Office publication GAO-08-78R, dated October 16, 2007

1 Although definitions vary, a mortgage loan is commonly considered in default when the borrower has missed three or more consecutive monthly payments (i.e., is 90 or more days delinquent). At this point, foreclosure proceedings against the borrower become a strong possibility. Foreclosure is a legal, and often lengthy, process with several possible outcomes, including that the borrower sells the property or the lender repossesses the home. Unless noted otherwise, we treat loans in default and loans in foreclosure as mutually exclusive categories.

and global financial markets. These developments have raised questions about the extent and causes of problems in the mortgage market.

To provide some insights on these issues, you asked us to analyze (1) the scope and magnitude of recent default and foreclosure trends, and how these trends compare with historical values, and (2) developments in economic conditions and the primary and secondary mortgage markets associated with these trends. On October 10, 2007, we briefed your offices on the results of this work. This letter provides a brief summary of those results, and the enclosures contain the more detailed briefing materials and a bibliography of related research.

BACKGROUND

The primary mortgage market has several segments and offers a range of loan products:

- The prime market serves borrowers with strong credit histories and provides the most competitive interest rates and mortgage terms. In 2006, the prime market segment accounted for about 58 percent of mortgage originations (in dollar terms).[2]
- The Alt-A market (accounting for about 16 percent of mortgage originations) generally serves borrowers whose credit histories are close to prime, but the loans often have one or more higher-risk features such as limited documentation of income or assets.
- The subprime market (about 24 percent of mortgage originations) generally serves borrowers with blemished credit and features higher interest rates and fees than the prime market.
- Finally, the government-insured or -guaranteed market (about 3 percent of mortgage originations) primarily serves borrowers who may have difficulty qualifying for prime mortgages but features interest rates competitive with prime loans in return for payment of insurance premiums or guarantee fees. The Federal Housing Administration and Department of Veterans Affairs operate the two main federal programs that insure or guarantee mortgages.

Across all of these market segments, two types of loans are common: fixed-rate mortgages (FRM), which have interest rates that do not change over the life of the loans; and adjustable-rate mortgages (ARM), which have interest rates that change periodically based on changes in a specified index.

One of the main sources of information on the status of mortgage loans is the Mortgage Bankers Association's (MBA) quarterly National Delinquency Survey (NDS), which represents about 80 percent of the mortgage market.

The NDS provides national and state-level information on mortgage delinquencies, defaults, and foreclosures back to 1979 (a 28-year span) for first-lien purchase and refinance

[2] We excluded home equity loans from our calculation of market shares. Percentages do not add to 100 due to rounding. A graph showing market shares for the various market segments from 2001 through 2006 appears in slide 11 of enclosure I.

mortgages on one-to-four family residential units.[3] The data are disaggregated by market segment and loan type (FRM or ARM) but do not contain information on other loan or borrower characteristics. NDS data provide two measures of foreclosure: (1) foreclosure starts, which are loans that entered the foreclosure process during the quarter and (2) foreclosure inventory, which represents the aggregate number of loans that were in the foreclosure process during the quarter (regardless of when they entered the process).

The secondary mortgage market plays an important role in providing liquidity—that is, supplying capital—for mortgage lending by bundling mortgages into securities (called residential mortgage-backed securities or RMBS) that are bought and sold by investors. The secondary market consists of (1) Ginnie Mae securities, which are backed by government-guaranteed mortgages; (2) government-sponsored enterprise (GSE) securities backed by mortgages that meet the requirements for purchase by Fannie Mae and Freddie Mac;[4] and (3) private label securities, which are backed by mortgages that do not conform to GSE purchase requirements because they are too large or do not meet GSE underwriting criteria. Investment banks bundle most subprime and Alt-A loans into private label RMBS.

SUMMARY

Overall, the number and percentage of mortgages in default or foreclosure rose sharply from the second quarter of 2005 through the second quarter of 2007 to levels at or near historical highs, but there was significant variation among market segments, loan types, and states.[5] More specifically:

- The overall default rate grew by 29 percent, reaching a point at which just over 1 in every 100 mortgages was in default, almost a 28-year high. The foreclosure start rate did reach a 28-year high, rising by 55 percent. (See graph on slide 14 in enclosure I for additional details.)
- The subprime market experienced substantially steeper increases in default and foreclosure start rates than the prime or government-insured markets, accounting for two-thirds or more of the overall increase in the number of loans in default or foreclosure during this time frame.
- Among types of loans, ARMs experienced relatively steeper growth in default and foreclosure rates, compared with FRMs which experienced no or modest increases.
- Several "Sun Belt" states such as Arizona, California, Florida, and Nevada experienced some of the largest increases in the number and percentage of defaults and foreclosures. Industrial midwest states such as Michigan and Ohio saw more

[3] NDS data do not separately identify Alt-A loans but include them among loans in the prime and subprime categories. State-level breakouts are based on the address of the property associated with each loan. The NDS presents default and foreclosure *rates* (i.e., the number of loans in default or foreclosure divided by the number of loans being serviced).

[4] Fannie Mae and Freddie Mac are congressionally chartered, private corporations that are publicly owned that purchase mortgages from lenders. To be eligible for purchase by the GSEs, loans (and borrowers receiving the loans) must meet specified criteria.

[5] In the second quarter of 2005, foreclosure start rates began to rise after remaining relatively stable for about 2 years.

modest growth in default and foreclosure rates but accounted for a significant part of the increase in the number of troubled loans in part because their default and foreclosure rates started at higher levels. Other states, such as New Mexico, Oregon, and Utah experienced little or no growth in default and foreclosure rates.

According to mortgage industry researchers and participants, the number and percentage of loans in default and foreclosure are likely to worsen through the end of 2007 and into 2008, due partly to scheduled payment increases for many ARMs.

A number of studies and industry data indicate that a combination of economic and market developments contributed to recent increases in default and foreclosure rates:

- First, the rapid decline in the rate of home price appreciation throughout much of the nation beginning in 2005 may have reduced incentives for borrowers to keep current on their mortgages and made it more difficult for borrowers to refinance or sell their homes to avoid default or foreclosure. Our analysis found that states that experienced a sharp decline in house price appreciation following a period of strong growth (e.g., California, Florida, and Nevada) generally experienced larger percentage increases in foreclosure start rates from the second quarter of 2005 through the second quarter of 2007.
- Second, in some states with foreclosure rates that were already relatively high in 2005, weak labor market conditions likely contributed to mortgage problems. For example, the two states with the lowest rates of employment growth in recent years—Michigan and Ohio—experienced the third- and sixth- largest increases in the number of foreclosure starts.
- Third, more aggressive lending practices—an easing of underwriting standards and wider use of certain loan features associated with poorer loan performance—reduced the likelihood that some borrowers would be able to meet their mortgage obligations, particularly in times of economic hardship or limited house price appreciation. For example, data on private label securitized loans show significant increases from 2000 through 2006 in the percentage of mortgages with higher loan-to-value ratios (the amount of the loan divided by the value of the home), adjustable interest rates, limited or no documentation of borrower income or assets, and deferred payment of principal or interest.
- Fourth, growth in the market for private label RMBS beginning in 2003 provided liquidity to some brokers and lenders to support these more aggressive lending practices. Investors were attracted to these securities because of their seemingly high risk-adjusted returns.

A number of other factors—including incentives that potentially emphasized loan volume over loan quality and growth in the incidence of mortgage fraud—may have contributed to recent default and foreclosure trends, but additional information would be needed to fully assess their impact.

SCOPE AND METHODOLOGY

To assess the scope and magnitude of recent trends in defaults and foreclosures and compare these trends to historical values, we analyzed NDS data from 1979 through the second quarter of 2007 (the most recent quarter for which data were available). The NDS data provide information on first-lien purchase and refinance mortgages on one- to four-family residential properties. For the entire period, we examined national and state-level trends in the number and percentage of loans that were in default, starting the foreclosure process, and in the foreclosure inventory each quarter. We also identified historical maximums and calculated long-run medians for these measures. For the second quarter of 2005 through the second quarter of 2007, we disaggregated the data by market segment and loan type, calculated absolute and percentage increases in default and foreclosure measures, compared and contrasted trends for each state, and compared default and foreclosure start rates at the end of this period to historical maximums and medians. We assessed the reliability of the NDS data by reviewing existing information about the quality of the data, performing electronic testing to detect errors in completeness and reasonableness, and interviewing MBA officials knowledgeable about the data. We determined that the data were sufficiently reliable for purposes of this report.

To analyze developments in economic conditions and the primary and secondary mortgage markets that may be associated with recent default and foreclosure trends, we analyzed NDS data, the Office of Federal Housing Enterprise Oversight's (OFHEO) quarterly house price index (HPI) for purchase transactions, and data on employment growth from the Bureau of Labor Statistics.[6] For each state, we calculated the average rate of growth in the HPI from the third quarter of 2003 through the first quarter of 2006 (a period of relatively steady growth in the HPI at the national level) and projected what the HPI would have been had this rate of growth continued through the second quarter of 2007. We then divided the projected HPI by the actual HPI as of the second quarter of 2007, with higher ratios indicating states that experienced relatively sharp drop-offs in house price appreciation after a period of strong growth. We ranked the states based on this ratio and determined the extent to which states with higher rankings had also experienced relatively greater percentage increases in foreclosure start rates from the second quarter of 2005 through the second quarter of 2007.

With regard to labor market conditions, we ranked states based on their percentage change in employment from the fourth quarter of 2001 (the end of the last recession) through the second quarter of 2007 and examined the relationship between this measure and changes in the number and percentage of loans entering foreclosure from the second quarter of 2005 through the second quarter of 2007. Additionally, we reviewed relevant industry, government, and academic data and research on factors that may have contributed to recent default and foreclosure trends. We did not independently confirm the accuracy of the information and analysis that we obtained from third parties. However, we took steps to ensure that the data we used from these sources were sufficiently reliable for our purposes, such as reviewing existing information about data quality, interviewing officials familiar with the data, and corroborating key information. Finally, we interviewed officials from bank regulatory institutions, the Department of Housing and Urban Development, Federal Trade Commission,

---

[6] In the second quarter of 2005, foreclosure start rates began to rise after remaining relatively stable for about 2 years.

Securities and Exchange Commission, mortgage lenders, investment banks, credit rating agencies, academia, and industry and consumer groups.

We performed our work from June 2007 through October 2007 in accordance with generally accepted government auditing standards. We provided a draft of the briefing materials to the Board of Governors of the Federal Reserve System, the Federal Deposit Insurance Corporation, the Office of the Comptroller of the Currency, and the Office of Thrift Supervision for their technical comments, which we incorporated where appropriate.

Enclosure I: Briefing to the Committee on Financial Services, House of Representatives

Home Mortgage Defaults and Foreclosures Recent Trends and Associated Economic and Market Developments

Briefing to the Committee on Financial Services House of Representatives October 10, 2007

Overview

- Objectives
- Scope and methodology
- Summary
- Background
- Recent default and foreclosure trends
- Developments associated with recent trends

Objectives

- Analyze the scope and magnitude of recent trends in home mortgage defaults and foreclosures, and how these trends compare with historical values.
- Evaluate developments in economic conditions and the primary and secondary mortgage markets associated with recent default and foreclosure trends.

Scope and Methodology

- Scope
  - First-lien purchase and refinance mortgages on one-to-four family residential properties, second quarter of 2005 through the second quarter of 2007.
- Methodology
- Analysis of data collected by the Mortgage Bankers Association's (MBA) quarterly National Delinquency Survey (NDS), which
  - contains national and state-level information on mortgage delinquencies, defaults, and foreclosures back to 1979, disaggregated by market segment and loan type, and
  - represents about 80 percent of the mortgage market.
- Analysis of state-level data on house price appreciation and employment growth.
- Review of relevant industry, government, and academic research.
- Interviews with officials from bank regulatory institutions, theDepartment of Housing and Urban Development, FederalTrade Commission, Securitiesand Exchange Commission, mortgage lenders, investment banks, credit rating agencies, academia, and industry and consumer groups.

Summary

- Overall, defaults and foreclosures have risen sharply over the last 2 years but they have varied significantly among market segments, loan types, and states.
  - Default and foreclosure rates grew to levels at or near historical highs.
  - Subprimeand adjustable-rate mortgages accounted for most of the overall increase.
  - While foreclosure rates more than doubled in eight states, they remained flat or declined in nine states.
- A combination of economic and market developments contributed to these trends:
  - House price changes reduced incentives for borrowers to keep current on their mortgages or made it more difficult to avoid foreclosure.
  - Aggressive lending practices reduced the likelihood that some borrowers would be able to meettheir mortgage obligations.
  - Growth in the private mortgage-backed securities market provided liquidity to support these lending practices.

BACKGROUND

- The mortgage market grew rapidly in the early part of the decadeas long-term mortgage interest rates fell.
- The nation's homeownership rate increased from about 67.4 percent in 2000 to 68.8 percent in 2006.
- The percentage of home purchase mortgage originations for borrowers who were not owner-occupants (e.g., investors) increased from about 8 to 16.5 percent over the same period.

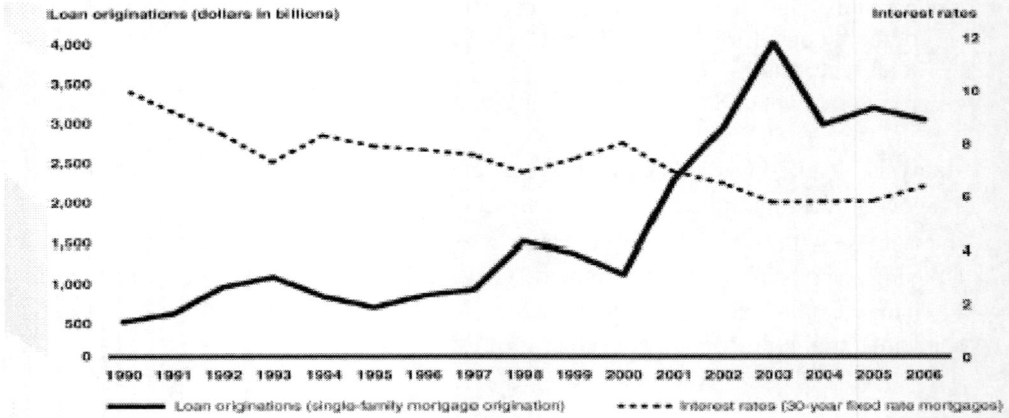

Source: GAO analysis of data from Inside Mortgage Finance

- The primary mortgage market has several segments.
  - *Prime*—Serves borrowers with strong credit histories and provides the most competitive interest rates and mortgage terms.
  - *Alternative—A (Alt-A)*-Generally serves borrowers whose credit histories are close to prime, but loans often have one or more higher-risk features such as limited documentation of income or assets.
  - *Subprime*—Generally serves borrowers with blemished credit and features higher interest rates and fees than the prime market.
  - *Government-insured or –guaranteed*—Primarily serves borrowers who may have difficulty qualifying for prime mortgages but features interest rates competitive with prime loans in return forpayment of insurance premiums or guarantee fees. The Federal Housing Administration (FHA) and Department of Veterans Affairs (VA) operate the two main federal programs that insure or guarantee mortgages.

Note: There is no uniform definition across the lending industryfor what characterizes a loan as subprimeor Alt-A.

- The mortgage market offers a range of loan products, which may be available in more than one market segment.

- *Fixed-rate mortgage (FRM)*–interest rate does not change over the life of the loan.
- *Adjustable-ratemortgage (ARM)*–interest rate changes periodically over the life of the loan based on changes in a specified index
- *Hybrid ARM*–interest rate is fixed and relatively low during an initial period then "resets" to an adjustable rate for the remaining term of the loan. In the subprime market, 2/28 loans (fixed rate for 2 years, adjustable rate for 28 years) are a common type of hybrid ARM.
- *Option ARM*–borrower has multiple payment options each month, which may include payments lower than needed to cover interest (deferred interest is added to the loan balance).
- *Interest-only mortgage*–borrower pays just the interest on the loan for a specified period, thereby deferring payment of principal.
- *Piggyback loan*–simultaneous second mortgage that allows the borrower to make little or no down payment on the first mortgage.
- *Jumbo mortgage*–loan amount is larger than the maximum eligible for purchase byFannie Mae and Freddie Mac (currently $417,000).
- *Nonconforming mortgage*–does not meet the purchase requirements of Fannie Mae or Freddie Mac because it is too large or does not meet their underwriting criteria.

Note: Unless stated otherwise, we use "mortgage market" to meanthe primary mortgage market, including loans for purchase and loans for refinancing.

- Mortgages are originated through three major channels:
    - *Mortgage brokers*–Independent contractors that originate loans for multiple lenders who underwrite and close the loans.
    - *Loan correspondents*–Generally smaller lenders that originate, underwrite, and close loans and immediately sell them to other (generally larger) lenders.
    - *Retail lenders*–Lenders that originate, underwrite, and close loans without reliance on brokers or correspondents.
- Large mortgage lenders may originate loans through a combination of these channels.
- In dollar terms, subprime lending grew from about 9 to 24 percent of mortgage originations (excluding home equity loans) from 2003 through 2006.
- Over the same period, Alt-A lending grew from about 2 to almost 16 percent of mortgage originations, and the share for loans with government insurance or guarantees fell from about 6 to 3 percent.
- As we reported in June 2007, in terms of number of loans, the subprime share of the market for home purchase mortgages grew most rapidly in census tracts with lower median incomes and higher concentrations of minorities, the same areas where FHA's share dropped most sharply.

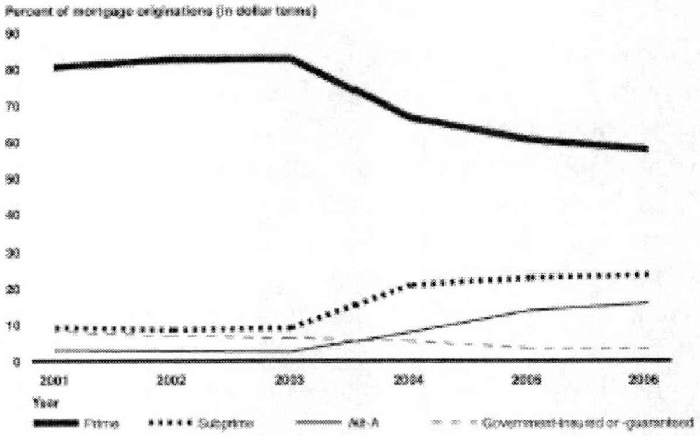

Source: GAO analysis of data from Inside Mortgage Finance.

Note: Data exclude home equity loans.

- The secondary mortgage market plays an important role in providing liquidity for mortgage lending by bundling mortgages into securities (residential mortgage-backed securities or RMBS) that are bought and sold by investors.

    - GinnieMae, government-sponsored enterprises (GSE), and private label RMBS are the major segments of this market.
    - Private label RMBS, also called "nonagencyRMBS," are backed by jumbo and other nonconforming mortgages securitized primarily by investment banks.
    - Purchasers of RMBS include hedge funds, pension funds, insurance companies, banks, and managers of other complex structured finance products known as collateralized debt obligations.

- Delinquency, default, and foreclosure rates are common measures of loan performance.

    - Delinquency is the failure of a borrower to meet one or more scheduled monthly payments.
    - Default generally occurs when a borrower is 90 or more days delinquent. At this point, foreclosure proceedings against the borrower become a strong possibility.
    - Foreclosure is a legal (and often lengthy) process with several possible outcomes, including that the borrower sells the property or the lender repossesses the home.

        - Two measures of foreclosure are (1) foreclosure starts(loans that entered the foreclosure process during a particular time period) and (2)foreclosure inventory(loans that were in, but had not exited, the foreclosure process during a particular time period)

Note: There is no uniform definition of default across the lending industry. The NDS data measure the percentage of loans serviced each quarter that were 30, 60, or 90 days delinquent; entered foreclosure; or were in the process of foreclosure.

DEFAULT AND FORECLOSURE TRENDS

National Level (1979-2007)

- Default and foreclosure rates for home mortgages have varied over time and have increased during both recessionary and nonrecessionary periods.

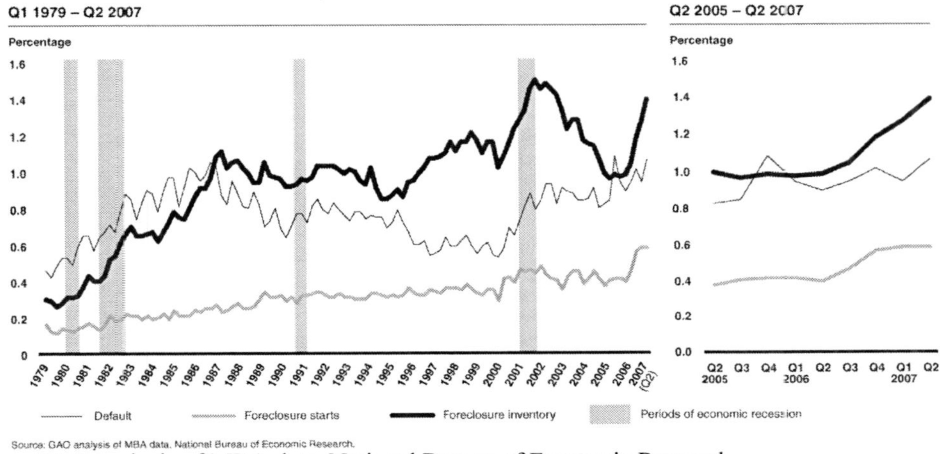

Source: GAO analysis of MBA data, National Bureau of Economic Research

National Level (2005-2007)

- The number and percentage of mortgages in default or foreclosurerose sharply from the second quarter of 2005 (the most recent "low" level) through thesecond quarter of 2007 (the most recent quarter for which NDS data are available).

	Q2 2005	Q2 2007	Percentage increase
Number of defaults	331,000	473,000	43%
Default rate	0.83%	1.07%	29%
Number of foreclosure starts	151,000	261,000	73%
Foreclosure start rate	0.38%	0.59%	55%
Foreclosure inventory	399,000	619,000	55%
Foreclosure inventory rate	1.0%	1.4%	40%

Source: GAO analysis of MBA data.

Note: Defaults do not include loans in foreclosure. We calculated the number of defaults and foreclosures by multiplying default and foreclosure rates by the number of loansthat the NDS showed as being serviced and rounding to the nearest thousand.

National Level (Market Segments)

- Changes in foreclosure start rates have varied by market segment.

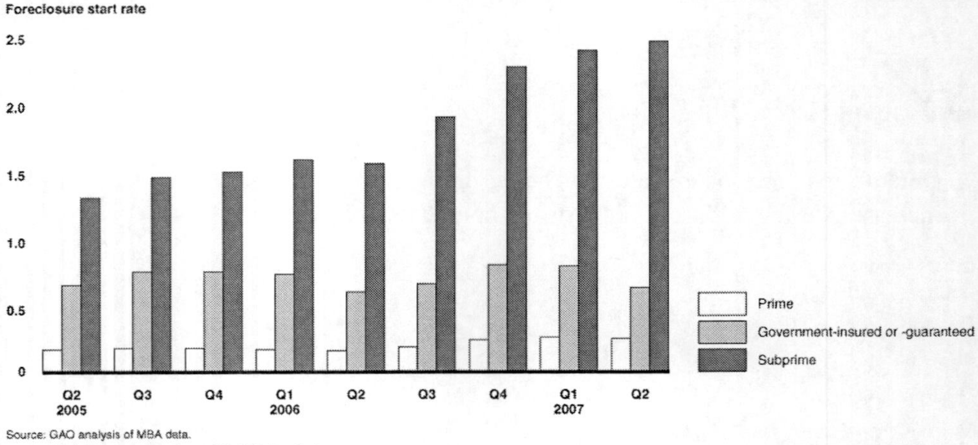

Source: GAO analysis of MBA data.

Note: NDS data do not separately identify Alt-A loans but include them in the prime and subprimecategories.

- According to NDS data, subprimeloans accounted for less than 15 percent of the loans serviced but about two-thirds of the overall increase in the number of mortgages in default and foreclosure from the second quarter of 2005 through the second quarter of 2007.

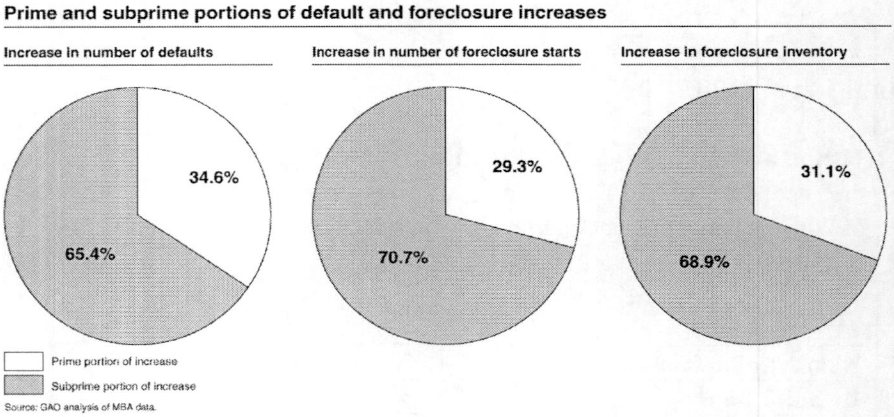

Source: GAO analysis of MBA data.

Note: We excluded government-insured or -guaranteed loans because they did not contribute to the increasein foreclosure starts over the period we examined.

National Level (Market Segments)

- Subprimeloans originated in late 2005 and 2006 are playing a major role in recent defaults and foreclosures.

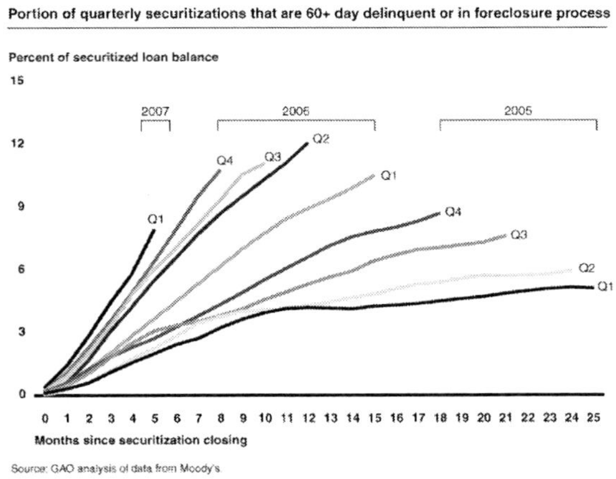

- According to researchers at the financial services firm UBS, 2005 and 2006 originations accounted (in dollar terms) for roughly three-quarters of the subprimeloans in foreclosure as of September 2007.

  - An analysis by Moody's Investors Service of subprime mortgages securitized each quarter from 2005 through the first quarter of 2007 shows that the rate of serious delinquency among similarly aged loans worsened for each successive quarterly group.

National Level (FRMsand ARMs)

- Across market segments, ARMsexperienced relatively steeper increases in default and foreclosure rates (compared with flat or modest growth for FRMs) and accounted for a disproportionate share of the increase in the number of loans in default and foreclosure.

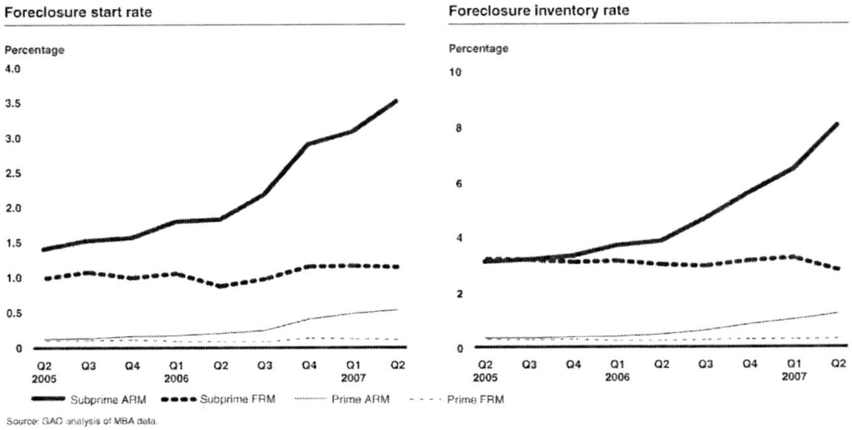

Source: GAO analysis of MBA data.

State Level

- While foreclosure start rates varied among the states, in most states (41 states and the District of Columbia), they were higher in the second quarter of 2007 than in the second quarter of 2005.

- However, the magnitude of the increases variedsubstantially by state.

  - Several "Sun Belt" states such as Arizona, California, Florida, and Nevada have experienced some of the largest increases in the number and percentage of defaults and foreclosures.
  - States in the industrial midwest(e.g., Michigan, Ohio, and Indiana) have seen more modest growth in default and foreclosure rates but account for a significant part of the increase in the number of troubled loans, in part because their default and foreclosure rates started at higher levels.
  - Some states, such as Utah, New Mexico, and Oregon, have seen much smaller increases or even declines in default and foreclosure rates.

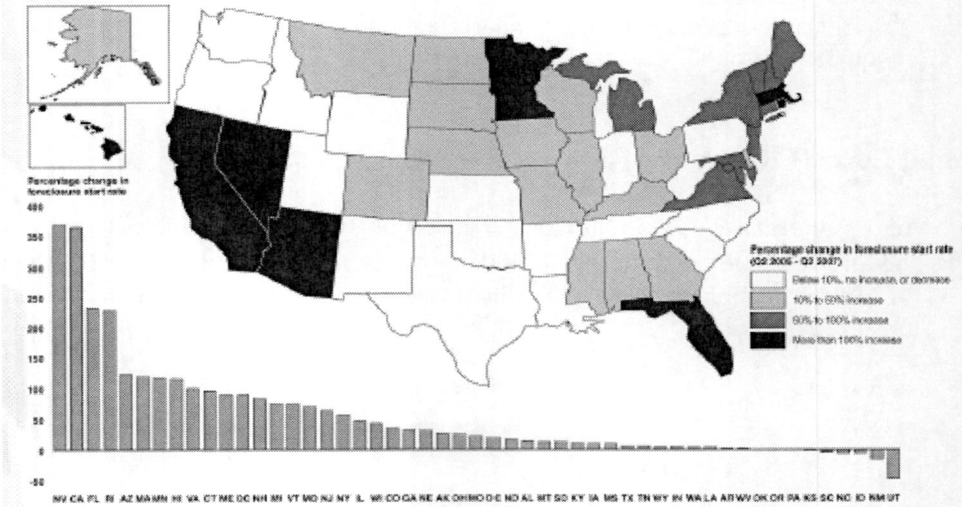

Source: GAO analysis of MBA data; Art Explosion (map).

National and State Historical Comparisons

- As of the second quarter of 2007, the number and percentage of mortgages nationwide that were in default and foreclosure were near or above their highest levels since 1979 (the first year covered bythe NDS data set).

  - Default rate of 1.07 percent (second highest level);
  - Foreclosure start rate of 0.59 percent (highest level); and
  - Foreclosure inventory rate of 1.40 percent (below the historicalmaximum of 1.51 percent, which occurred in 2002).

- Also as of the second quarter of 2007,
  - the foreclosure start and foreclosure inventory rates were abovetheir long-run historical medians in 47 and 40 states (including the District of Columbia), respectively.
  - foreclosure start rates were at their historical maximums in four states (Florida, Maine, Minnesota, and Nevada), as were foreclosure inventory rates in five states (Maine, Michigan, Minnesota, Ohio, and Rhode Island).

Outlook

- Mortgage industry researchers told us that the number and percentage of loans in default and foreclosure were likely to worsen through the end of this year and into 2008, due partly to forthcoming interest rate resets on hybrid ARMs.
- In a 2007 study, Caganestimated that about 13 percent of ARMs(1.1 million loans) originated from 2004 through 2006 would foreclose over a 6-to 7-year period as a result of interest rate resets.
- The extent to which current default and foreclosure trends continue depends on a number of factors, including lenders' willingness to modify loan terms, the amount of liquidity available for refinancing, changes in home prices and interest rates, and general economic conditions.

Developments Associated with Recent Trends

Overview

- A number of studies and industry data indicate that a combination of economic and market developments contributed to recent default and foreclosure increases, including:
  - the rapid decrease in home price appreciation (HPA) throughout much of the nation beginning in 2005 and weak labor market conditionsin certain states;
  - an easing of underwriting standards and wider use of certain loan features that, while potentially helping to expand homeownership, also reduced the likelihood that some borrowers would be able to meettheir mortgage obligations, particularly in times of economic hardship or limited HPA; and
  - growth in the private label RMBS market, which provided liquidity to some brokers and lenders to support more aggressivelending practices.
- Other developments may have played a role, but additional information would be needed to fully assess their impact.

Decline in HPA

- Rapid HPA from 2003 into 2005 (which has been associated with several factors, including low interest rates, expectation of continued price increases, and a plentiful supply of credit) likely helped to mitigate defaults and foreclosures.

  - Growth in homeowner equity created incentives for borrowers to keep their mortgages current.
  - Borrowers could refinance or sell their homes to avoid default or foreclosure.

- According to industry researchers, the stagnation or decline in home prices in much of the country beginning in 2005 changed this scenario.

  - Borrowers lost this "equity cushion" and had more difficulty refinancing or selling their homes.
  - Borrowers who hadpurchased homes (particularly homes for investment purposes) but now owed more than the properties were worth, had incentives to stop making mortgage payments in order to minimize their financial losses.

- Several factors may have contributed to the slowdown in HPA, including a rising supply of homes and a decline in speculative activity.
- States with a sharp drop-off in HPA following a period of strong growth generally experienced larger percentage increases in foreclosure start rates.

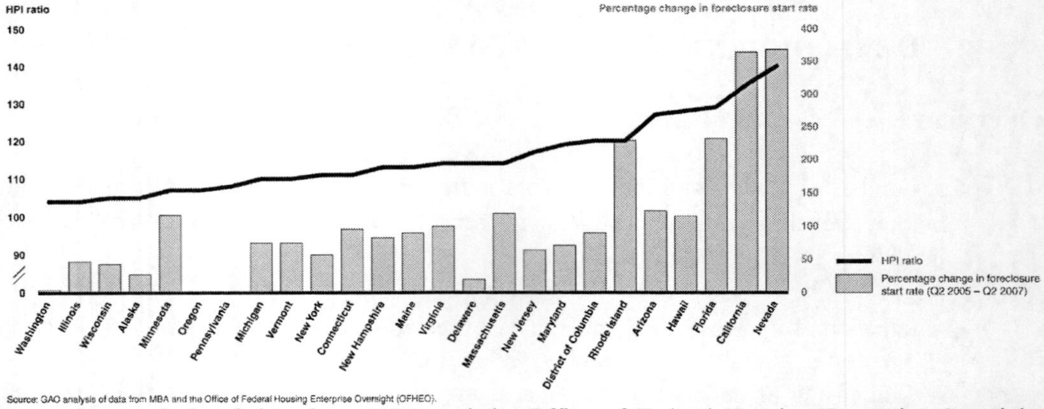

Source: Gao analysis of data from MBA and the Office of Federal Housing Enterprise Oversight (OFHEO)

Note: The HPI ratio is the ratio of (1) the projected OFHEO house price index for purchase transactions, assuming average Q3 2003 – Q1 2006 appreciation continued through Q2 2007 to (2) the actual OFHEO house price index as of Q2 2007. The figure covers the 25 states with the highest HPI ratio.

- Recent analysis has examined the relationship between HPA and loan performance.

  - Zandiet al (2007) estimated that changes in HPA explained about three-quarters of the nationwide increase in mortgage delinquency rates from the fourth quarter of 2005 through the first quarter of 2007.

- The Federal Reserve Bank of San Francisco (2007) found a strong and statistically significant relationship between increases in delinquency rates on subprime loans from 2005 through 2006 and house price deceleration. The analysis covered 309 metropolitan areas and controlled for changes in economic conditions.

Weak Regional Labor Market Conditions

- Job loss is a common "trigger event" that can lead to default and foreclosure because of its direct impact on a borrower's ability to make mortgage payments.

- Although the national unemployment rate is relatively low and has declined in recent years, parts of the industrial midwesthave experienced job losses, particularly in the manufacturing sector.

    - Michigan's rate of employment growth from the fourth quarter of 2001 (the end of the last recession) through the second quarter of 2007 was -4.6 percent, the worst in the nation.
    - The corresponding figure for Ohio was -0.9 percent, the second worst.

- From the second quarter of 2005 through the second quarter of 2007,

    - Michigan had the third highest rate of foreclosure starts for most of the period and the third largest increase in the total number of foreclosure starts (behind California and Florida).
    - Ohio had the second highest rate of foreclosure starts (behind Indiana) throughout the period and the sixth largest increase in the total numberof foreclosure starts.

- Zandiet al (2007) estimated that employment growth trends in certain metropolitan areas explained a substantial portion of the change in mortgage delinquency rates in those areas from the fourth quarter of 2005 through the first quarter of 2007, but had little impact nationally.

    - Negative employment growth explained about 32percent of the change in delinquency rates in Detroit-Livonia-Dearborn, Michigan, and 20 percent of the change in Cleveland-Elyria-Mentor, Ohio.
- In a separate analysis of securitized subprime loans, Zandiet al (2007) found that erosion in labor market conditions increased foreclosure rates.

Easing of Underwriting Standards and Wider Use of Certain Loan Features

- Strong house price appreciation in much of the country beginning in 2003 made home purchases less affordable for many buyers.

- According to several industry observers and participants, an increasingly competitive environment led lenders to lower underwriting standards and offer products that lowered monthly payments, which in turn helped feed housing price appreciation.
- According to the Office ofthe Comptroller of the Currency's *Survey of Credit Underwriting Practices*(October 2006), the 73 large banks surveyed reported "a third consecutive year of easing underwriting standards, as banks continued to stretch for volume and yield."

The easing of underwriting standards and wider use of certain loan features, as evidenced by data on private label securitized mortgages (representing about 56 percent of RMBS issuances in 2006), resulted in more loans with features that may increase the risk of default and foreclosure.

- Higher loan-to-value (LTV) ratios (i.e., the amount of the loan divided by the value of the home)
    - As we reported in February 2005, a substantial amount of research indicates that LTV ratio is one of the most important factors in assessingmortgage risk.
    - The higher the LTV ratio, the less cash borrowers will have invested in their homes and the more likely it is that they may default on mortgage obligations, especially during times of financial hardship.
- Piggyback loans
    - Borrowers use these to finance all or part of their down payment, which can result in higher combined LTV (CLTV) ratios—that is, the LTV ratio taking both the first mortgage and piggyback loan into account.

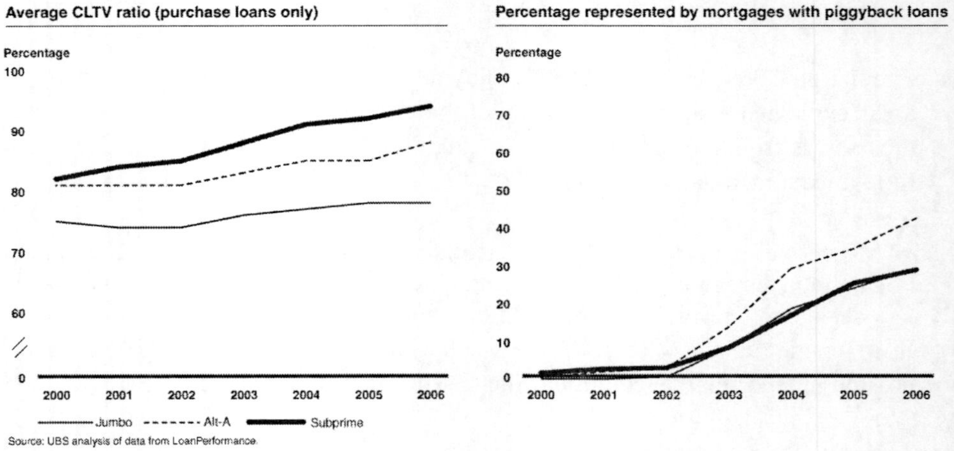

Note: Loan characteristics are for mortgages originated in the year indicated and pooled into private label securities. The CLTV figure reflects purchase loans only, while the piggyback loan figure reflects both purchase and refinance loans. The percentages in the figure on piggyback loans represent the dollar amount of first-lien mortgages with anassociated piggyback loan. In dollar terms, jumbo, Alt-A, and subprimemortgages represented about 19, 16, and 24 percent of mortgage originations in 2006 (excluding home equity loans), respectively.

- Adjustable interest rates

  - ARMsare generally considered to carry a higher default risk than otherwise comparable FRMs, in part because borrowers are subject to higher payments if interest rates rise.
  - Hybrid ARMscan lead to "payment shock" for some borrowers because of interest rate adjustments following the initial fixed-rate period.

- Prepayment penalties

  - Can be an obstacle to refinancing because borrowers must pay a penalty if they pay off the original loan before the prepayment period expires.

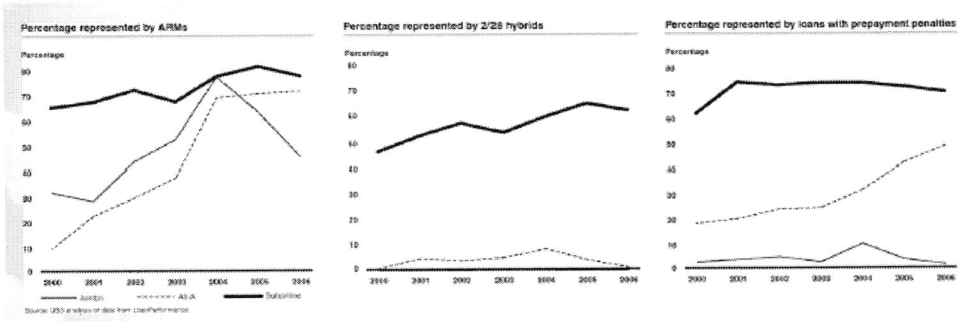

Note: Percentages represent the dollar amount of purchase and refinance mortgages originated in the year indicated and pooled into private label securities that have certain characteristics. In dollar terms, jumbo, Alt-A, and subprimemortgages represented about 19, 16, and 24 percent of mortgage originations in 2006 (excluding home equity loans), respectively.

- Limited or no documentation of income or assets

  - Allows borrowers to provide less detailed financial information than traditionally required.
  - Originally intended for borrowers who may have difficulty documenting income, such as the self-employed.
  - Problematic if borrowers or loan originators overstate income orassets to qualify borrowers for mortgages they cannot afford.

- High debt service-to-income ratio (the percentage of a borrower's income that goes toward paying all recurring debt payments)

  - The higher the ratio, the greater the risk the borrower will have cash-flow problems and miss mortgage payments.

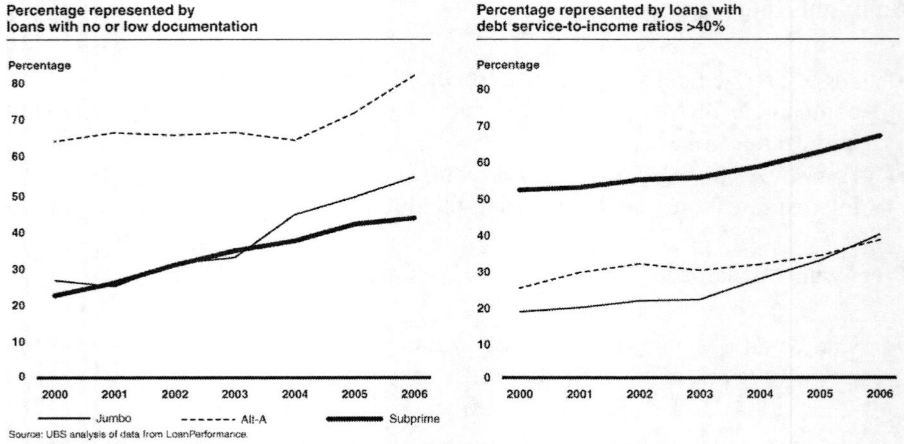

Source: UBS analysis of data from Loan Performance.

Note: Percentages represent the dollar amount of purchase and refinance mortgages originated in the year indicated and pooled into private label securities that have certain characteristics. In dollar terms, jumbo, Alt-A, and subprimemortgages represented about 19, 16, and 24 percent of mortgage originations in 2006 (excluding home equity loans), respectively.

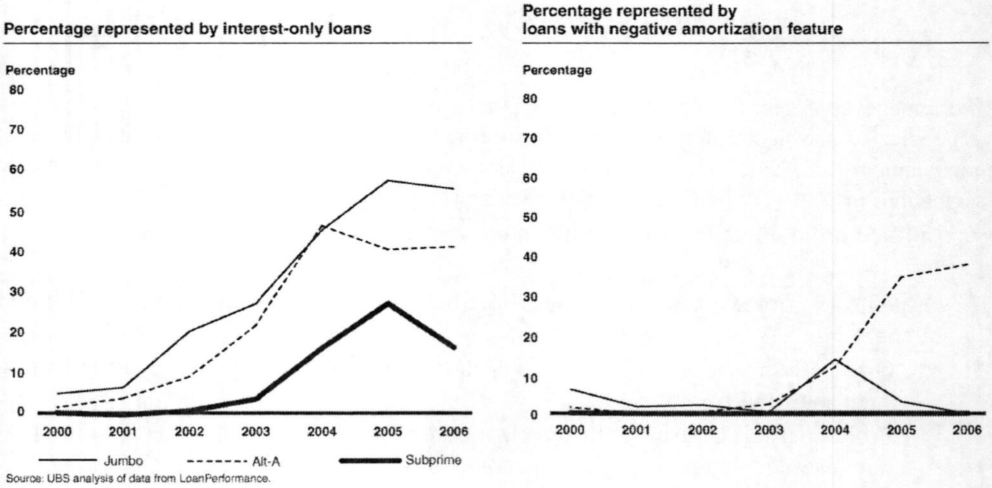

Note: Percentages represent the dollar amount of purchase and refinance mortgages originated in the year indicated and pooled into private label securities that have certain characteristics. In dollar terms, jumbo, Alt-A, and subprimemortgages represented about 19, 16, and 24 percent of mortgage originations in 2006 (excluding home equity loans), respectively.

Deferred payment of principal or interest

- As we reported in September 2006, interest-only loans and loans with payment options that allow for negative amortization (by adding deferred interest payments to the loan balance) can lead to payment shock when the interest-only or payment-option period expires.
- Borrowers may build less home equity than they would with a traditional loan.

- Borrowers may not be well-informed about the risks of these products, due to their complexity and because promotional material by somelenders and brokers do not provide balanced information on the risks and benefits.Several econometric studies have examined the relationship between some of the previously noted loan features and loan performance, particularly among subprime mortgages. For example:

- Danisand Pennington-Cross (forthcoming) found for fixed-rate securitized subprime loans that (1) higher LTVsand the presence of prepayment penalties were positively correlated with default and (2) loans with limited or no documentation had substantially higher default and foreclosure rates than full documentation loans.
- Querciaet al (2005) found that securitized subprime refinance loans with prepayment penalties were more likely to experience a foreclosure than loans without such penalties.
- The Center for Responsible Lending (2006) found that securitizedsubprime loans withfeatures such as adjustable rates, prepayment penalties, and no or low documentation had a higher likelihood of default than loans without those features, controlling for differences in borrower credit scores.
- Zandiet al (2007) estimated that rising debt-service burdens explained about 9 percent of the change in mortgage delinquency rates nationally and 18 percent in California from the fourth quarter of 2005 through the first quarter of 2007.
- Many recent Alt-A and subprime loans were originated with multiple features thatare associated with a greater risk of delinquency, a practice known as risk layering.
- FitchRatingsanalysis of securitized subprime loans from 2005 shows the impact of risk layering on mortgage delinquency rates after 1 year of seasoning.

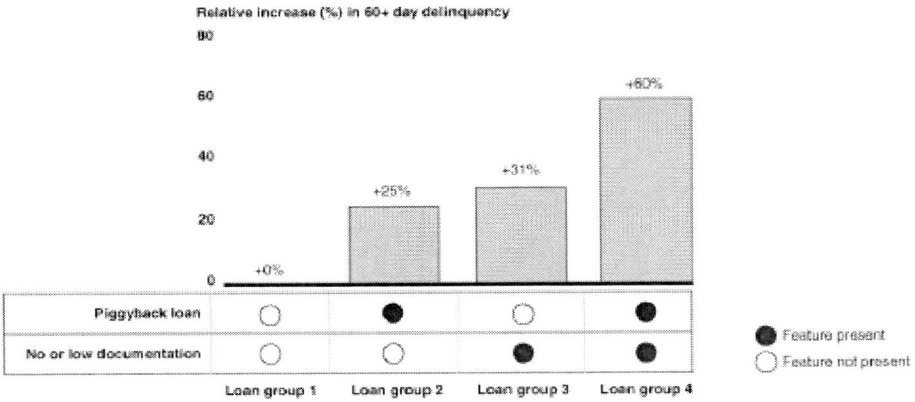

Source: FitchRatings.

DEVELOPMENTS ASSOCIATED WITH RECENT TRENDS

Growth in Private Label RMBS Market

- As previously noted, the increase in defaults and foreclosures has been concentrated among subprime loans, and to a lesser extent Alt-A loans, which are primarily pooled into private label RMBS (as opposed to GinnieMae or GSE securities).
- From 2002 to 2006, the share of private label RMBS comprised of subprimeand Alt-A loans increased from 43 percent to 71 percent by dollar volume.
- Investors were attracted to these securities because of their seemingly high risk-adjusted returns.
- The dollar volume of private label RMBS grew rapidly beginning in 2003, while GinnieMae and GSE volume fell sharply. The market share for private label RMBS surpassed the combined market shares of GinnieMae and the GSEsin 2005

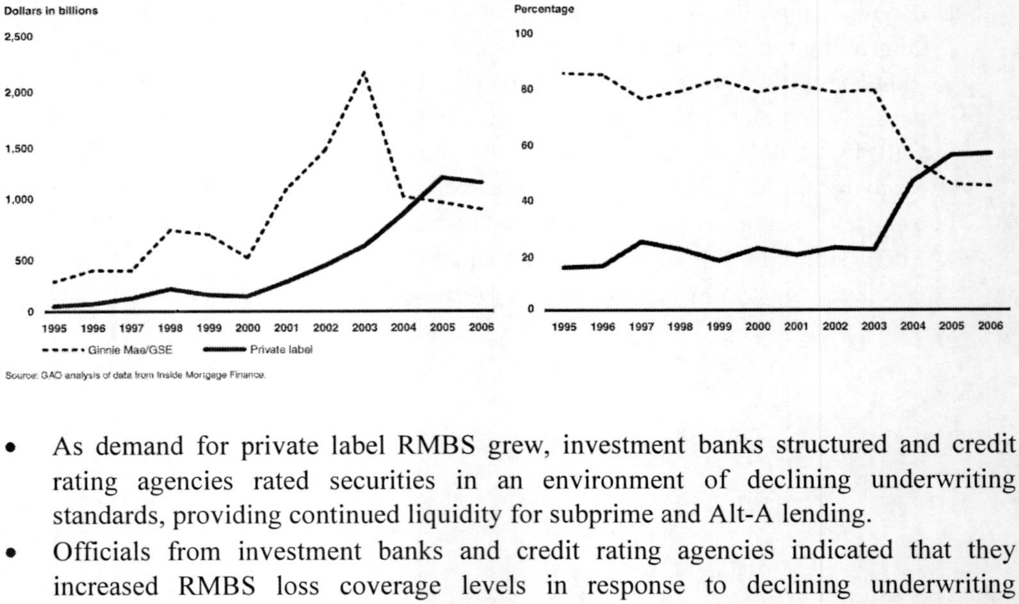

Source: GAO analysis of data from Inside Mortgage Finance.

- As demand for private label RMBS grew, investment banks structured and credit rating agencies rated securities in an environment of declining underwriting standards, providing continued liquidity for subprime and Alt-A lending.
- Officials from investment banks and credit rating agencies indicated that they increased RMBS loss coverage levels in response to declining underwriting standards. However, they also acknowledged that they were surprised by the speed andseverity of HPA declines and underestimated the risk of certain loan features such as low and no documentation and high LTV ratios.

- In mid-2007, credit rating agencies made changes to their ratings methodologies to reflect the worse-than-expected performance of subprime and Alt-A loans in particular.

  - Moody's Investors Service increased default and loss assumptionsby up to 25 percent for mortgages with low or no documentation, high LTVs, or piggyback loans.

- FitchRatingsrevised its ratings methodology to, among other things, place greater emphasis on regional economic risk and increase default assumptions for hybrid ARMs.

- Recent credit rating downgrades for RMBS have affected a relatively small portion of total private label RMBS issuances and have largely been limitedto lower-rated securities.

  - Standard & Poor's and Moody's downgraded securities representingabout 1 percent of the value of recently issued first-lien subprime RMBS rated by the agencies.
  - None of these downgrades affected triple-A securities.
  - However, downgrades of second-lien subprimeRMBS have been more extensive—for example, Moody's has downgraded about 60 percent of the dollar volume of these types of securities that it rated in 2006.

- Rating downgrades introduced uncertainty about the credit quality of subprime RMBS, contributing to financial market disruptions that reduced liquidity for borrowers seeking to refinance out of loans at risk of default or foreclosure.

Developments Associated with Recent Trends

Other Possible Factors

Other developments may have played a role in recent default and foreclosure increases, but additional information would be needed to fully assess their impact.

Misaligned Incentives and Lack of Accountability in the Origination and Distribution of Mortgages

- Some industry participants and observers have linked the declining credit quality of loans in recent years to market changes that have reduced incentives and accountability for prudent underwriting.
- Until the 1990s, lenders held most loans on their balance sheets, so the same entity that originated the loan and created the risk bore the risk.
- In recent years, lenders and mortgage brokers originated loans that were quickly sold down a chain of aggregators and investors.

  - Originators had financial incentives to increase loan volume, potentially at the expense of loan quality. As lenders sold loans on the secondarymarket, the risks were passed on to investors.
  - The private label RMBS market had more lenient underwriting standards than the GinnieMae and GSE portions of the secondary market.

    - Some originators, particularly independent mortgage companies, lacked sufficient capital to make good on representations and warranties designed to protect investors from imprudent and fraudulent lending practices.

- The role of mortgage brokers has grown in recent years.

    - By one estimate, the number of brokerages rose from about 30,000firms in 2000 to 53,000 firms in 2004.
    - In 2005, brokers accounted for about 60 percent of originations in the subprimemarket (compared with about 25 percent in the prime market).

Federal Regulation of Lenders

- Concerns exist that certain lenders (e.g., independent mortgage companies and nonbanksubsidiaries of banks, thrifts, or holding companies) that are not subject to routine monitoring and examination by federal bank regulators may tend to originate lower-quality loans.

    - Of the top 25 originators of subprimeand Alt-A loans in 2006 (which accounted for over 90 percent of the dollar volume of all such originations):

        - 21 were nonbanklenders, including 14 independent lenders and 7 nonbanksubsidiaries of banks, thrifts, or holding companies.
        - the 21 nonbanklenders accounted for 81 percent of the dollar volume (44 percent was originated by independent lenders and 37 percent by nonbanksubsidiaries of banks, thrifts, or holding companies).
    - In prior work, we have raised concerns about nonbanklenders, noting that some have been targets of some of the most notable federal and state enforcement actions involving abusive lending.

- However, there has been limited analysis of differences in the performance of subprimeloans made by bank and nonbanklenders.

Mortgage Fraud

- Some industry participants and researchers have said that mortgage fraud has been a contributing factor in recent default and foreclosure trends.

    - Subprimeand Alt-A mortgages, which comprise a substantial portion of recent default and foreclosure increases, may be more likely to involve fraud because substantial percentages of these loans required no or little documentation or verification of income and assets, providing opportunities to misrepresent this information.
    - According to the Mortgage Asset Research Institute, the number of reported cases of mortgage fraud increased from about 3,500 in 2000 to about 28,000 in 2006.

- Florida and California, the states with the highest incidence ofreported mortgage fraud in 2006 (adjusted for loan volume), also experienced among the largest percentage increases in foreclosure start rates from the second quarter of 2005 through the second quarter of 2007.

- According to some industry researchers, growth in early payment defaults in recent years (i.e., defaults occurring within a few months of loan origination) are an indicator of increasing mortgage fraud.

Interest Rates

- Rising interest rates can increase the probability of default and foreclosure for borrowers with adjustable-rate mortgages because their monthly payments grow as rates climb.

  - The Federal Open Market Committee raised the federal funds rate from 1 percent to 5.25 percent from 2004 through 2006 (although it has since reduced it to 4.75 percent).
  - Major rate indexes used to set adjustable-rate mortgages followed this upward trend, while long-term mortgagerates did not increase until late 2005.
  - Zandiet al (2007) estimated that changes in interest rates explaineda modest portion (about 6 percent) of the change in delinquency rates for all mortgage loans from the fourth quarter of 2005 through the first quarter of 2007.

Enclosure II: Staff Acknowledgments

In addition to the individual named above, Steve Westley (Assistant Director), Kevin Averyt, Steve Brown, Marta Chaffee, Steve DelGrosso, Randy Fasnacht, Marc Molino, and Jim Vitarello made key contributions to this report.

Enclosure III – Selected Bibliography

Cagan, C. "Mortgage Payment Reset: The Issue and the Impact." First American CoreLogic, Inc. (Santa Ana, California: March 19, 2007).

Danis, M., & A. Pennington-Cross. "The Delinquency of Subprime Mortgages." Journal of Economics and Business (forthcoming).

Doms, M., Furlong, F. & J. Krainer. "House Prices and Subprime Mortgage Delinquencies." Federal Reserve Bank of San Francisco Economic Letter No. 2007-14 (June 2007).

GAO, *Alternative Mortgage Products: Impact on Defaults Remains Unclear, but Disclosure of Risks to Borrowers Could Be Improved*, GAO-06-1021 (Washington, D.C.: Sept. 19, 2006).

GAO, *Consumer Protection: Federal and State Agencies Face Challenges in Combating Predatory Lending*, GAO-04-280 (Washington, D.C.: Jan. 30, 2004).

GAO, *Federal Housing Administration: Decline in the Agency's Market Share Was Associated with Product and Process Developments of Other Mortgage Market Participants*, GAO-07-645 (Washington, D.C.: June 29, 2007).

GAO, *Mortgage Financing: Actions Needed to Help FHA Manage Risks from New Mortgage Loan Products*, GAO-05-194 (Washington, D.C.: Feb. 11, 2005).

Pavlov, A., & S. Wachter. "Aggressive Lending and Real Estate Markets." Samuel Zell and Robert Lurie Real Estate Center Working Paper, Wharton School, University of Pennsylvania. (Apr. 10, 2007).

Quercia, R., Stegman, M. & W. Davis. "The Impact of Predatory Loan Terms on Subprime Foreclosures: The Special Case of Prepayment Penalties and Balloon Payments." Center for Community Capitalism, Kenan Institute for Private Enterprise, University of North Carolina at Chapel Hill (Jan. 25, 2005).

Schloemer, E., Li, W., Ernst, K. & Keest, K. "Losing Ground: Foreclosures in the Subprime Market and Their Cost to Homeowners." Center for Responsible Lending. (Durham, North Carolina: December 2006).

Zandi, M., Hughes, T., Licari, J. & Faucher, A. "Into the Woods: Mortgage Credit Quality, Its Prospects, and Implications." Moody's Economy.com. (West Chester, Pennsylvania: July 2007).

GAO's Mission

The Government Accountability Office, the audit, evaluation, and investigative arm of Congress, exists to support Congress in meeting its constitutional responsibilities and to help improve the performance and accountability of the federal government for the American people. GAO examines the use of public funds; evaluates federal programs and policies; and provides analyses, recommendations, and other assistance to help Congress make informed oversight, policy, and funding decisions. GAO's commitment to good government is reflected in its core values of accountability, integrity, and reliability.

In: Securitization of Subprime Mortages
Editor: Milton R. Spotgeste
ISBN: 978-1-60692-200-2

Chapter 4

SUBPRIME MORTGAGES: PRIMER ON CURRENT LENDING AND FORECLOSURE ISSUES*

Edward Vincent Murphy

SUMMARY

Subprime mortgages are loans extended to borrowers with weak credit profiles. Subprime mortgages entail higher risk of delinquency and default. Recent increases in subprime borrower foreclosures and lender bankruptcies have prompted concerns that some lenders' underwriting guidelines are too loose and that some borrowers may not have fully understood the risks of the mortgage products they chose. Regulatory agencies are revisiting the guidance they provide lenders and are reevaluating required disclosures to consumers. In addition, Congress is holding hearings on the subject and may consider consumer protection legislation. Subprime foreclosures have reached the highs of the 2000-2001 recession but delinquency rates are not the same across mortgage features. The adjustable interest rate (ARM) feature is currently associated with higher delinquency rates than comparable fixed rate loans. However, the delinquency rate of loans with the negative amortization (NegAm) feature has remained below 1%, the range normally associated with less risky loans. NegAm is a loan that allows a monthly payment less than the current interest on the loan with the remaining interest added to the principal, thus increasing the loan balance.

Financial regulators issued a guidance for alternative mortgage products in October 2006 and issued a proposed statement for subprime lending in March 2007. The guidances require that consumers be given plain-language explanations of the risks of their mortgages. Borrowers must be qualified for mortgage loans based on the ability to repay the loan, not based on speculation about future increases in the value of the real estate collateral. The proposed guidance also seeks to limit payment shock and prepayment penalties. Policymakers are faced with the challenge of balancing the benefits of access to credit against the costs of potential foreclosures.

---

* This is an edited, reformatted and augmented edition of a Congressional Research Service publication, Report RL33930, dated Marach 19, 2007.

Background

Subprime mortgage lending can benefit consumers by allowing greater access to credit, and thus homeownership, but can also impose costs on consumers through defaults and foreclosures. Subprime refers to people who have no credit history, have a blemished credit record, and/or have a weak debt-service-to-income ratio. A generation ago, subprime loan applicants were generally denied credit and neither enjoyed homeownership nor risked default. Policymakers evaluating subprime lending issues will be called on to consider the benefits of increased access to credit markets which can lead to homeownership as well as the costs of increased debt burdens and potential foreclosure. To that end, this report describes the subprime market, presents delinquency and foreclosure data, and summarizes banking agency guidance on subprime lending.

The rise of risk-based pricing encouraged growth of the subprime market during the mid-1990s.[1] For example, the number of subprime refinance loans increased nearly tenfold between 1993 and 1998.[2] Subprime loans increased from an estimated 5% of the mortgage market in 1994 to as much as 20% in 2005.[3] After retreating during the recession of 1999-2001, subprime lending expanded rapidly during 2002-2005. In 2006, the housing market slowed and there was a rise in late mortgage payments and foreclosures. The rise in delinquencies and foreclosures continues to be more severe in the subprime market than the prime market but both rates are growing. Several prominent subprime lenders are experiencing financial difficulties, including the recent bankruptcy of Ownit and investigations into New Century. Potential negative consequences for consumers, banks, and financial markets have drawn renewed attention to government policies related to subprime lending.

Government policies play a role at each stage of the mortgage lending process. When a borrower takes out a mortgage loan, the Truth in Lending Act (TILA) and the Home Ownership Equity Protection Act (HOEPA) provide rules for disclosure and limitations on the terms of certain high cost loans. When lenders originate loans, the regulatory agencies of the Federal Financial Institutions Examinations Council (FFIEC) supervise their portfolios to

---

[1] Risk-based pricing refers to assessing a borrower's risk and then charging higher-risk borrowers a higher interest rate rather than simply refusing to qualify them for a loan. In contrast, pool-based pricing accepts a range of borrowers into a pool which is charged the same rate based on the average credit quality of the pool. Borrowers outside the pool are simply denied credit.

[2] "Unequal Burden in New York: Income and Racial Disparities in Subprime Lending," Department of Housing and Urban Development (HUD), May 2000, p.1. The study cites the Home Mortgage Disclosure Act (HMDA) database as reporting 80,000 subprime loans in 1993 and 790,000 in 1998.

[3] Robert Avery et al., "Higher-Priced Home Lending and the 2005 HMDA Data," Federal Reserve Bulletin, September, 2006 (rev.), p. A125. There is no single accepted source for subprime market share. The Federal Reserve collects loan information through the Home Mortgage Disclosure Act (HMDA), which does not currently require lenders to report a borrower's credit score and only requires interest rate information if the rate is more than 3% above a comparable Treasury rate. The proportion of loans that exceed HMDA's 3% threshold, and are thus considered high cost, is sensitive to changes in the proportion of loans that are adjustable rate and to the difference between short-term and long-term interest rates. Alternatively, the Department of Housing and Urban Development maintains a list of lenders who specialize in loans to consumers with weaker credit. The market share of these lenders can vary significantly over time. Private financial consultants with access to more detailed lender loan information provide a third set of estimates.

ensure safe and sound banking practices.[4] When lenders sell some of their loans to secondary markets through the government sponsored enterprises (GSEs), Fannie Mae and Freddie Mac, the Office of Federal Housing Enterprise Oversight (OFHEO) supervises the GSEs for safety and soundness and the Department of Housing and Urban Development (HUD) regulates the GSE's charter compliance. When investors purchase mortgage-backed securities (MBS) issued by the GSEs or their competitors, the Securities and Exchange Commission (SEC) enforces the anti-fraud provisions of the securities laws.

Government policies designed to aid lower-income consumers achieve homeownership may have contributed to the expansion of subprime lending. For example, the Community Reinvestment Act (CRA) encourages lenders to provide loans in the poorer areas of their market where subprime borrowers are more likely to reside. Similarly, increases in HUD's Affordable Housing Goals encourage the GSEs to expand their purchases of loans originated from lower-income and minority borrowers who are more likely to be subprime. Federal Housing Administration (FHA) slowness to adopt some of the nontraditional mortgage products that became popular when house prices were rising rapidly may have resulted in some FHA-eligible borrowers turning to subprime lenders.

THE SUBPRIME MARKET AND ALTERNATIVE MORTGAGES

Generally, subprime mortgages are defined in terms of the credit bureau risk score (FICO) of the borrower.[5] Other credit imperfections, however, can also cause borrowers to be categorized as subprime for a particular loan. For example, the addition of the mortgage loan might increase the borrower's debt-to-income level above traditionally prudent thresholds. Generally, bank supervisors look for one or more of the following credit-risk characteristics when deciding to label a loan subprime:[6]

- Recent payment delinquencies (30-day or 60-day depending on recency)
- Judgment, foreclosure, repossession, or charge-off within prior two years
- Bankruptcy in the last five years
- Relatively high default probability (FICO below 660 or similar measure)
- Limited ability to cover living expenses after debts (debt-service-toincome ratio of 50% or more)

Subprime loans are disproportionately used by the elderly and members of minority groups. The elderly are more likely to own a home and to have accumulated significant equity and therefore are more likely to qualify for a refinance loan despite, perhaps, having imperfect credit. Minorities, on average, have lower incomes and therefore are often more

[4] The FFIEC includes the Federal Reserve Board (FRB), the Federal Deposit Insurance Corporation (FDIC), The Office of Thrift Supervision (OTS), the Office of the Comptroller of the Currency (OCC), and the National Credit Union Administration (NCUA).

[5] A FICO score is an estimate of a borrowers creditworthiness provided by credit rating agencies that monitor consumer payment histories. The term comes from the company, Fair Isaacs, that originated the score and continues to provide it to lenders.

[6] "Subprime Lending (Risk Management and Internal Controls)," *Bank Holding Company (BHC) Supervision Manual*, Section 2128.08, Dec. 2002, pp1-2.

likely to have credit blemishes. In addition, there is some evidence that minorities who could qualify for cheaper prime loans are sometimes borrowing in the more expensive subprime market.[7]

In recent years, subprime borrowers increasingly used alternative mortgage products that had previously been used primarily by sophisticated investors. Interest only (I-O) mortgages provide an introductory period during which monthly payments cover only the loan interest. After the introductory period, loan payments reset to a higher amount to also cover the loan's principal. Negative amortizing mortgages (NegAms) allow borrowers to pay less than current interest due and result in a higher loan balance and higher future payments. In contrast to fixed rate mortgages (FRM), which have fixed interest rates and constant monthly payments, adjustable rate mortgages (ARMs) reset the interest rate with changes in market interest rates and therefore can result in higher or lower monthly payments depending on market conditions. Because alternative mortgage products allow monthly payments to rise, some policymakers are concerned that subprime borrowers in particular may not have fully understood the risks associated with non-traditional features.

GROWTH, FORECLOSURES, AND RISK IN SUBPRIME MORTGAGES

Expansion of the subprime market may have benefited some consumers by improving access to credit and facilitating homeownership. he timing of the growth of the subprime market corresponds to growth in homeownership. The U.S. homeownership rate increased from 64.1% in 1993 to 68.9% in 2005.[8] Homeownership among minority groups increased at a faster rate, from 42.4% in 1993 to 51.3% in 2005. Recall that subprime lending is more prevalent in minority communities. The homeownership gap between white-non-hispanics and allminorities dropped from 27.8 percentage points in 1993 to 24.5 percentage points in 2005.

Expansion of the subprime market may have increased the costs associated with greater debt burdens. Subprime foreclosures increased faster than prime foreclosures during the 2000-2001 recession and are again rising faster than prime foreclosures in the current housing slowdown. **Figure 1** presents data from the Mortgage Bankers Association mortgage delinquency survey. Subprime loans in this sample are several times more likely to go into foreclosure and are far more sensitive to the credit cycle than prime loans. **Figure 1** shows that less than 1% of prime loans were in foreclosure during 1998-2006. In contrast, at least 3% of subprime loans were generally in foreclosure. During the 2000-2001 recession, subprime foreclosures reached almost 10%. In the current housing downturn, subprime foreclosures are again rising rapidly.

Although higher subprime foreclosures confirm that subprime loans are riskier than prime loans, the evidence for alternative mortgage products depends on the particular feature. **Figure 2** shows that the adjustable rate feature appears to be under significant stress for both

[7] Unequal Burden: Income and Racial Disparities in Subprime Lending in America, HUD, 2000.

[8] U.S. Department of Commerce, Bureau of the Census. The year 1993 is chosen as the beginning point both because Census data reflect a changed weighting procedure in that year and because the subprime market grew rapidly during 1993-1998.

interest-only loans and fully amortizing loans.[9] Loan Performance, a financial consulting firm, has found that among subprime loans, adjustable rate products appear to have increased their delinquency rate faster than fixed rate products since 2005.[10] During the period Loan Performance studied, the 60-day delinquency rate for subprime fixed rate mortgages remained close to 9%, but the 60-day delinquency rate for subprime adjustable rate mortgages rose from under 2% during the summer of 2004 to over 14% in November 2006.

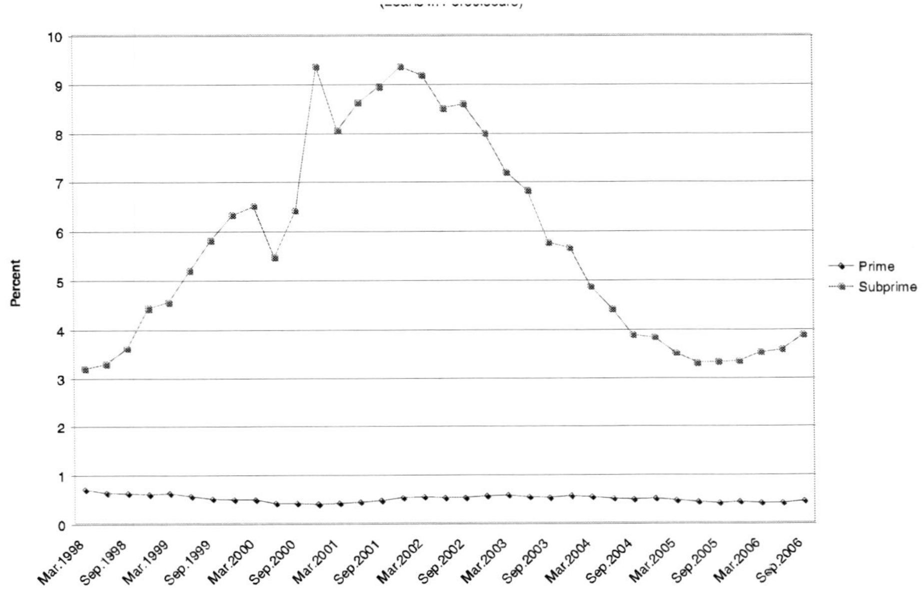

Figure 1. Prime and Subprime Loans in Foreclosure, 1998-2006

Source: Mortgage Bankers Association Delinquency Survey

The 60-day delinquency rate for negative amortizing (NegAm) loans is rising but remains relatively low. NegAm loans give the borrower the option of paying less than the interest owed in any month and therefore can increase the loan balance. In the sample analyzed by Loan Performance, most NegAm ARMs originated during 2004-2006 have increased their balance but the delinquency rate for these products has not risen as fast as subprime delinquency rates. The 60-day delinquency rate for all NegAm ARMs originated in 2006 remained below 1%, but the 60-day delinquency rate for subprime ARMs originated in 2006 exceeds 8%.[11]

[9] A fully amortizing loan pays off the loan balance using the traditional method of constant monthly payments. An interest-only loan has an introductory period of lower payments during which the monthly payments do not pay down the loan balance.

[10] Loan Performance calculations cited in Economic Commentary, Fannie Mae, February 20, 2007, p.2. A 60-day delinquent loan is not yet a loan in foreclosure. Loan Performance's definition of subprime does not necessarily match the Mortgage Bankers Association survey.

[11] Loan Performance calculations cited in *Economic Commentary*, Fannie Mae, February 20, 2007, p.2. Not all subprime loans are NegAm loans and not all NegAm loans are subprime loans.

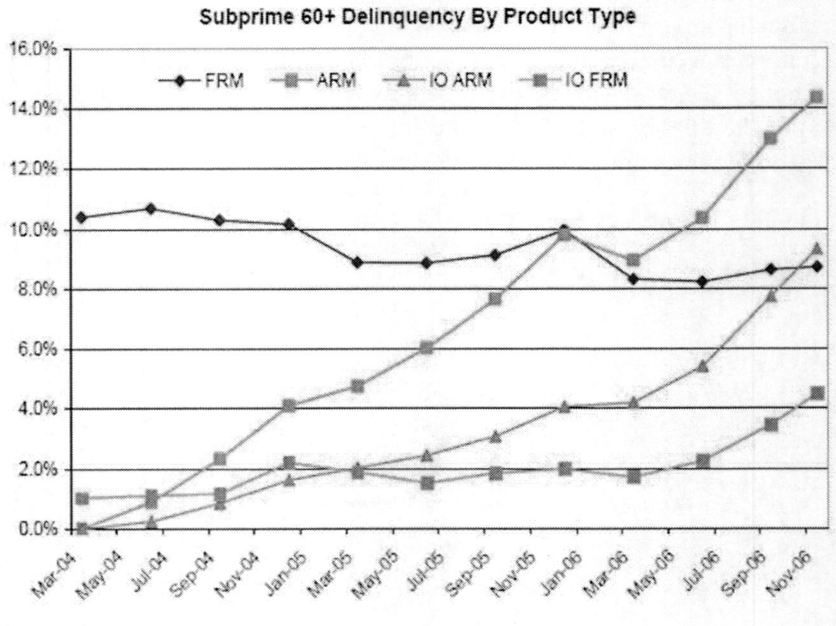

Figure 2. Delinquency Rate of Subprime Mortgages by Feature

Stress on Subprime Lenders

In addition to rising foreclosures among subprime borrowers, the slowdown in the housing market has also challenged subprime lenders. Many subprime lenders raise funds by selling their loans to investors in the secondary market and using the proceeds to make new loans. These lenders can suffer significant hardship if investors downgrade the value of subprime debt. For example, Ownit Mortgage declared bankruptcy in December 2006, reportedly after it lost financing from Merrill Lynch and other investors.[12] New Century is under investigation for accounting and other improprieties connected to its subprime business. Several other lenders have shut their doors or restricted their subprime lending.

Stress on subprime financing is not confined to just a few lenders. A key indicator of investor estimation of the risk associated with funding loans through secondary markets, the ABX index, declined suddenly and significantly for subprime loans in February 2007 (see **Figure 3**). The ABX index is based on the cost of hedging purchases of mortgage loans that are packaged into securities and sold to investors in the secondary market.[13] According to Markit, an independent provider of data for derivatives trades, the price that investors were willing to pay for the BBB- rated portion of the index (part of the subprime market) fell from

---

[12] Julie Creswell and Vikas Bajaj, "A Mortgage Crisis Begins to Spiral and Casualties Mount," *New York Times*, Mar. 5, 2007, p. C1.

[13] Investors can use insurance and other financial instruments to reduce their exposure to the risk that their investment will go sour. A traditional hedge occurs when someone simultaneously invests in two instruments

just over 97% on January 19, 2007, to under 70% by February 26, 2007.[14] The decline in the ABX index reflects the reduced willingness of investors to accept the risks associated with subprime loans. As a result, funds for additional subprime loans are decreasing.

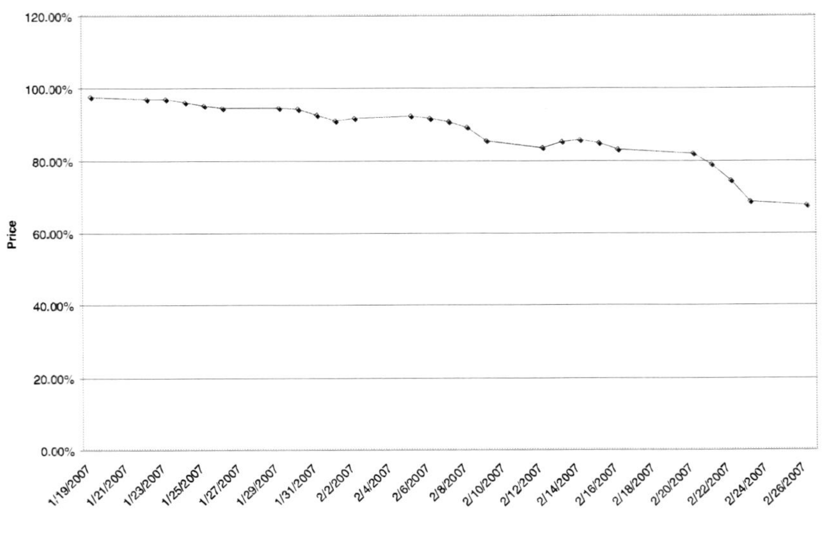

Source: Markit Group Limited

Figure 3. ABX Index of BBB- Rated Mortgage Derivatives

Source: Markit group limited

The safety and soundness of subprime lenders has been a concern for many policymakers because some believe that disruptions in financial markets could have wider effects on the economy. For example, some believe that banking disruptions can make the business cycle more volatile. Federal responses to the Savings and Loan Crisis in the 1980s may have been due in part to concerns for the larger economy. The Federal Reserve itself was created because of a congressional commission to study banking issues in the Panic of 1907. While disruptions in the current subprime market do not rise to the level of historic banking panics, financial regulatory agencies have made public their intention to closely watch the subprime sector. The FFIEC agencies have issued new inter-agency guidance "to address emerging issues and questions relating to certain subprime mortgage lending practices."[15]

that move in opposite directions so that if one goes bad, the other partially compensates. The ABX index is one measure of the price investors are willing to pay to hedge mortgage backed securities.

14 Data provided by Markit Group, Limited. The company receives daily data contributions from over 70 firms dealing in related securities. See [http://www.Markit.com]. A decline in the index percentage represents an increase in the cost to hedge the investment.

15 "Proposed Statement on Subprime Mortgage Lending," Federal Register, Vol 72, No. 45, Mar. 8, 2007, p. 10533.

BANKING AGENCY GUIDANCE

Financial regulators have recognized the increased risks of subprime lending. Rising subprime foreclosures during 2000 prompted the OCC to tighten oversight of subprime lending programs in January 2001. "Institutions with significant subprime lending activities will be subject to closer scrutiny to ensure that their programs have appropriate risk management controls and capital support."[16] The guidance covered capital maintenance, standards for individual loan review by examiners, documentation requirements for delinquent subprime accounts, and policies to curb potentially abusive lending practices.

Since 2001, as mortgage markets have continued to evolve, and housing markets have expanded, subprime lending has drawn renewed attention. In October 2006, the lending regulators of the FFIEC issued guidance for alternative mortgage products. The guidance reiterated that lenders must qualify loans based on the borrower's ability to repay the loan balance, not based on the value of the loan collateral in sale or foreclosure. The October 2006 guidance also reminded lenders of Truth in Lending Act requirements to explain payment terms in plain language in order to curb abusive lending practices.

With subprime delinquencies and foreclosures mounting again, the FFIEC has issued a new interagency guidance for comment. The proposed guidance "reiterates many of the principles addressed in existing guidance relative to prudent risk management practices and consumer protection laws."[17] Concerning risk management, the proposed guidance states that predatory lending typically involves at least one of (1) lending on collateral value rather than borrower ability to repay, (2) inducing repeated refinances to charge high points and fees, or (3) using deceptive marketing to conceal the true nature of the mortgage obligation. Concerning consumer protection, the proposed guidance states that mortgage product descriptions and advertisements should provide clear, detailed information on the costs, terms, features, and risks of the loan to the borrower, including any payment shock or prepayment penalty.

In the proposed guidance, the FFIEC asks for comments concerning restrictions on planned refinances because "the structural evolution of subprime mortgage lending in recent years has introduced some products that are intended at their outset to be temporary credit accommodations in anticipation of early sale or refinancing, rather than longer-term amortizing accounts."[18] Commentors are asked to address the following:

- Do planned subprime refinances always present inappropriate risks that should be discouraged? If not, under what circumstances are they appropriate?
- Will the proposed guidance restrict existing subprime borrowers' attempts to refinance and avoid payment shock?
- Should restrictions on planned refinances apply beyond subprime markets?
- Should prepayment penalties be restricted to the introductory period?

[16] "Subprime Lending: Expanded Guidance for Subprime Lending Programs," OCC 2001-6, Jan. 31, 2001. This bulletin supplements OCC Bulletin 1999-15, "Subprime Lending, Risks and Rewards."

[17] "Proposed Statement on Subprime Mortgage Lending," Federal Register, Vol 72, No. 45, Mar. 8, 2007, p. 10533.

[18] "Proposed Statement on Subprime Mortgage Lending," Federal Register, Vol 72, No. 45, Mar. 8, 2007, p. 10533.

POLICY CONSIDERATIONS

Subprime loans, which are extended to borrowers with weaker credit conditions, have higher delinquency and foreclosure rates. Policies that facilitate subprime lending have to balance the benefits of homeownership against the risks of increased debt. More complex mortgage products may facilitate homeownership under some conditions but may be more difficult for consumers to understand.[19] Restrictions on mortgage products may insulate credit-impaired borrowers from default risk but may make it more difficult for these potential borrowers to own a home. Federal and state authorities also protect consumers through anti-predatory lending initiatives.[20] The recent rise in subprime delinquencies illustrates the trade-off between encouraging greater access to credit markets and risking increased defaults and foreclosures. Policymakers decide the role of government agencies and government sponsored enterprises (GSEs) in the subprime sector.[21] Some argue that greater GSE presence in the subprime market could help reduce instability in that market by helping to standardize underwriting procedures. Raising the GSEs' housing goals may direct their programs to lower-income households but may increase the flow of funds to risky mortgages.[22] Reforming the loan programs of the Federal Housing Administration (FHA) could provide lower-income borrowers with an alternative to subprime lenders but may be less flexible in changing market conditions.[23] FHA makes it easier for borrowers to obtain loans by insuring the loan payments. On the other hand, some argue that granting FHA greater flexibility could increase the amount of risky mortgages.

---

[19] CRS Report RL33775, Alternative Mortgages: Risks to Consumers and Lenders in the Current Housing Cycle, by Edward Vincent Murphy.

[20] CRS Report RL32784, Predatory Lending: A Comparison of State Laws to the Federal Home Ownership and Equity Protection Act, by Kamilah M. Holder, Kate M. Manuel.

[21] CRS Report RS22336, GSE Reform: A New Affordable Housing Fund, by N. Eric Weiss.

[22] The GSE housing goals refer to the percentage of housing units financed by the GSEs' loan purchases that must be for low income groups and underserved areas. The housing goals are set by HUD.

[23] CRS Report RS20530, FHA Loan Insurance Program: An Overview, by Bruce E. Foote, Meredith Peterson.

In: Securitization of Subprime Mortages
Editor: Milton R. Spotgeste

ISBN: 978-1-60692-200-2

Chapter 5

POLICY OPTIONS FOR THE HOUSING AND FINANCIAL MARKETS*

Congressional Budget Office

INTRODUCTION

Problems in the housing and mortgage markets have now spread to a broader array of financial markets. At this point, the nation faces a serious disruption to the functioning of its financial markets that could substantially impair economic activity in the near term. Since the end of the unusual housing boom from 2003 to early 2006, delinquencies and foreclosures on mortgages have risen, particularly on subprime adjustable-rate mortgage loans (ARMs), reflecting a retreat of house prices from unsustainable levels, the use of lax credit standards to make the loans, weak local economies, and in some cases, higher interest rates on ARMs whose interest rates had reset as scheduled in their loan contracts.[1] (Subprime loans are made to borrowers with low credit scores or other impairments to their credit histories.) The problems are not limited to subprime ARMs, however. Delinquencies have also risen for prime ARMs and on so-called alt-A mortgage loans, which are often made on the basis of little or no documentation of the borrower's income and may include low-downpayment loans, loans that are not for the owner's principal residence, interest-only loans, and loans whose balances rise over time. Because most mortgages are resold as mortgage-backed securities (MBSs), the rise in delinquencies has caused the value of MBSs to decline, in some cases quite sharply.

The problems in mortgage markets have spread to the wider financial markets for several reasons. Although highly uncertain, the number of bad mortgages and, consequently, losses on MBSs are expected to be large. The use of complex instruments to fund subprime lending,

* This is an edited, reformatted and augmented version of a Congressional Budget Office publication, dated April 11, 2008.

[1] The percentage of homes with subprime ARMs entering foreclosure was a record 5.3 percent in the fourth quarter of 2007, up from 2.7 percent at the end of 2006 and 1.6 percent at the end of 2005. At the end of 2007, more than 13 percent of subprime ARMs were in the process of foreclosure.

such as collateralized debt obligations (CDOs), also has made it difficult for participants in financial markets to identify the magnitude of the exposure of other participants to losses.[2] Moreover, a number of financial institutions borrowed heavily to finance their mortgage holdings, further increasing their risk exposure.

Those losses on mortgage assets, and the resulting contraction of the availability of credit to businesses and households, pose a significant threat to the pace of economic activity. Given the elevated uncertainty about their exposure to risk, financial institutions have tightened their lending standards and pulled back from all types of risky lending, preferring to conserve capital to guard against potential losses. Following a period in which the risk premium (the higher return required to compensate investors for assuming the risk of default) had been unusually low, the price of risk has risen, in some cases significantly. That pullback has extended to short-term lending between banks. In response, the Federal Reserve and some foreign central banks have intervened to provide large infusions of liquidity (that is, short-term financing) to keep financial markets from freezing up. Moreover, large numbers of foreclosures could trigger a downward spiral of house prices that could take them below what would be justified on the basis of normal relationships to income and production costs. Such a downward spiral would exacerbate the problems in the financial markets and could reduce consumption spending by reducing household wealth, increasing the likelihood and severity of a recession.

Policymakers have already taken steps to help the housing and financial markets cope with the aftereffects of the housing boom. In the wake of continuing weakness in those markets, though, additional actions have been proposed. (See Box 1-1 for a discussion of current federal housing policy.) Some of those actions would involve lenders (seeking to promote the modification of troubled mortgages), while others would expand the role of the federal government (providing or guaranteeing credit to mortgage markets). Such actions could help reduce the number of foreclosures, attenuating one source of downward pressure on house prices—although they would not address more important influences on prices. Many policy options, moreover, would significantly shift the risk involved in mortgage losses from current lenders and investors to taxpayers. (Policymakers are also considering new supervisory guidelines and regulations for financial institutions to address weaknesses that contributed to the problems in financial markets; this paper does not address those potential changes.)

Box 1-1. Federal Support for Housing

The government currently supports homeownership through various channels. The effects of that support in normal times are to increase the number of people who own their homes rather than rent and also to increase land prices, the average size and price of houses, and the proportion of wealth that is in the form of housing (as opposed to other forms of investment). There are also distributional consequences that favor homeowners relative to renters.

[2] CDOs repackage assets such as mortgage bonds, buyout loans, and other debt (including other CDOs) into new securities.

The federal government, through the Department of Housing and Urban Development (HUD), undertakes activities that reduce mortgage rates. The Federal Housing Administration (FHA) provides mortgage insurance on loans made by FHA-approved lenders that meet certain requirements. The Government National Mortgage Association (Ginnie Mae) provides liquidity to the secondary mortgage market by guaranteeing investors the timely payment of principal and interest on mortgage-backed securities backed by federally insured or guaranteed loans— mainly loans insured by the FHA or guaranteed by the Department of Veterans Affairs. Other guarantors or issuers of loans eligible as collateral for securities guaranteed by Ginnie Mae include the Department of Agriculture's Rural Housing Service and HUD's Office of Public and Indian Housing.

In addition, two privately owned government-sponsored enterprises (GSEs), Fannie Mae and Freddie Mac, provide capital to the mortgage markets by purchasing conforming mortgages, securitizing them, and charging a guarantee fee to investors. Although there is no explicit government guarantee of those securities, it is commonly perceived that the government would prevent a default. That implicit guarantee makes the cost of funds to the GSEs lower than it otherwise would be.[1]

The tax system is a major source of support for homeownership. Owner-occupied housing receives more favorable tax treatment from the federal government than most other privately held assets.[2] Much of the income generated by assets owned by businesses is subject to corporate or personal income taxes. However, the value of the services generated by owner-occupied housing is excluded from taxable income. Even so, owners may deduct certain expenses, such as interest paid on mortgage and home-equity loans and property tax payments. Most capital gains from the sale of an owner-occupied house are also tax-exempt.

The tax advantages for investing in one's home have been estimated to increase homeownership by between 2.5 percent and 5.4 percent, depending on people's income.[3] Furthermore, those advantages have been estimated to increase the amount of housing purchased by homeowners by between 5 percent and 21 percent, again depending on owners' income. The study from which those estimates are derived assumes that additional land and other inputs for housing are available at no increase in cost, so none of the increase in purchases is absorbed in higher prices for houses and land. Those conditions seem more likely to exist on the outskirts of cities and in rural areas than in developed neighborhoods within large metropolitan areas, where limits on further development often exist. How much of the tax advantage is absorbed in higher prices inside metropolitan areas is disputed.[4]

1.Congressional Budget Office, *Federal Subsidies and the Housing GSEs* (May 2001).

2. See Congressional Budget Office, *Taxing Capital Income: Effective Rates and Approaches to Reform* (October 2005).

3. Harvey S. Rosen, "Housing Decisions and the U.S. Income Tax," *Journal of Public Economics*, vol. 11, no. 1 (February 1979), pp. 1–23. Rosen reports the amount by which taxing homeownership like other investments would reduce the rate of homeownership and the amount of housing purchased. The estimates in Table 4 under Regime 2 have been converted above to increases from the tax advantage.

4. Dennis R. Capozza, Richard K. Green, and Patric H. Hendershott, "Taxes, Mortgage Borrowing, and Residential Land Prices," in Henry J. Aaron and William G. Gale, eds., *Economics of*

Fundamental Tax Reform (Washington, D.C.: Brookings Institution Press, 1996), pp. 171–198. Also see Donald Bruce and Douglas Holtz-Eakin, "Fundamental Tax Reform and Residential Housing," *Journal of Housing and Economics*, vol. 8, no. 4 (December 1999), pp. 249–271; and Jane G. Gravelle, *The Flat Tax and Other Proposals: Effects on Housing*, CRS Report for Congress 96-379 (April 29, 1996).

Whether additional policy interventions in the housing and mortgage markets are advisable depends in part on their objective:

- If the objective is to assist homeowners in distress, some of the policies seem likely to succeed, at least to some degree. Many policies intended to help homeowners may produce significant benefits for lenders as well. Avoiding some unintended effects will be virtually impossible because it is difficult to distinguish among homeowners who were victims of their poor judgment or of predatory lenders, those who overstretched their finances for purchasing investment properties, and those who exploited poor underwriting standards.
- If the objective is to avoid foreclosures and abandonment of properties, intervention might break a downward spiral in which foreclosures put houses on the market, pushing down house prices and producing more foreclosures. Although many analysts believe that house prices remain too high relative to people's incomes, such a spiral, without intervention, could reduce prices even below their long-run ratio to incomes and production costs.
- If the objective is to arrest the decline in house prices, however, the policies are less likely to succeed. Perhaps the most important short-term influence on house prices is the elevated number of unoccupied houses for sale (the inventory overhang). That overhang is likely to remain until house prices fall enough to stimulate additional home sales. Put simply, none of the policies can (or presumably should) guarantee that house prices will stabilize in the near term. Furthermore, attempting to avoid (as opposed to attenuating) the market's necessary adjustments may not only be unrealistic, but even if it were to succeed, might ultimately serve only to delay the recovery of financial markets and impair the pace of economic activity.
- Finally, if the objective is to stabilize the overall economy, the policies under discussion will probably have only a limited effect because most of them are likely to exert only a modest influence directly on the housing market. (The Congressional Budget Office discussed policies more specifically related to general economic stimulus in a January 2008 paper, *Options for Responding to Short-Term Economic Weakness*.) They might affect the economy indirectly, through their effects on consumer and investor confidence, though that is harder to predict.

THE CURRENT ECONOMIC SITUATION

The current economic situation is quite fragile. The turmoil in financial markets, the drop in house prices, and the rise in energy prices have combined to slow economic activity. Credit flows have dropped significantly as financial institutions have reduced their activity; nonfinancial firms face new constraints on their borrowing as well. The outlook for economic activity in 2008 has worsened, with private-sector payroll employment falling for the past four months and a growing number of economists indicating that the economy is in a recession. Nevertheless, both the tax rebates that will begin arriving late this spring (as part of the recently enacted economic stimulus package) and the Federal Reserve's reduction of short-term interest rates and injections of liquidity will help boost the economy. It remains unclear at this point whether the National Bureau of Economic Research will ultimately determine officially that there was a recession.

Economic Activity

Economic activity has slowed sharply since last summer. Annualized growth of real (inflation-adjusted) gross domestic product (GDP) declined to just 0.6 percent in the fourth quarter of 2007 from a robust 4.9 percent in the third quarter, and growth appears to have slowed even further this year. Employment fell by 300,000 between November 2007 and March 2008; such a decline in employment over several months strongly suggests that the economy has entered a recession. Real consumer spending has been essentially flat between November and February. Some of that weakness is related to high energy prices and slower gains in real disposable income, but some may also be a result of the effect of lower house prices on households' wealth. The pace of residential construction has been decreasing rapidly, and declining numbers of building permits for new construction suggest that those declines will persist in the near term. Business fixed investment also appears to have contracted in the first quarter, partly because financing for new projects has become more difficult to obtain. Offsetting some of that weakness has been strong growth in exports.

Concerns about inflation may constrain policymakers' efforts to stimulate the economy further. The sharp drop in the value of the dollar over the past year and the increase in a broad array of commodity prices have raised fears of higher inflation this year. Although most forecasters do not anticipate an increase in inflation during 2008, further monetary stimulus may set the stage for higher inflation in 2009.

House Prices and Mortgage Markets

House prices are falling across the country, with some of the steepest declines occurring in areas that had experienced some of the largest gains. Delinquencies and foreclosures on mortgages are also rising across the nation. Some states experiencing large price declines have also experienced high rates of delinquencies and foreclosures. However, prices of mortgage-backed securities have stabilized close to their recent lows, suggesting that investors' expectations about future losses on MBSs are no longer worsening.

House Prices. Prices for houses have fallen sharply since their peak in the middle of 2006, and the decline appears to be accelerating. A number of indexes are available to track prices; each has its limitations, but together they give a sense of trends. One measure, the S&P/Case-Shiller national price index for single-family homes, was down by about 9 percent in the fourth quarter of 2007 as compared with the fourth quarter of 2006, after a 4.6 percent decline in the year ending in the third quarter of 2007. In real terms, the decline last year was almost 12 percent. Rapid declines in house prices continued in January: A narrower S&P/Case-Shiller index for 20 cities (reported monthly) fell by 10.7 percent in the year ending in January, while the monthly index for the S&P/Case-Shiller index for 10 cities was down by 11.4 percent over the same period. Those trends are generally confirmed by a third price index, published by Radar Logic, a real estate and data-analysis firm. Another widely used index, the purchase-only index published by the Office of Federal Housing Enterprise Oversight (OFHEO), did not begin to decline until May 2007. The difference between the movement of that index and the movement of the other indexes may reflect the fact that OFHEO's index excludes homes with nonconforming (for example, subprime) mortgages and thus omits the parts of the market that have seen the greatest difficulties in recent months.[3]

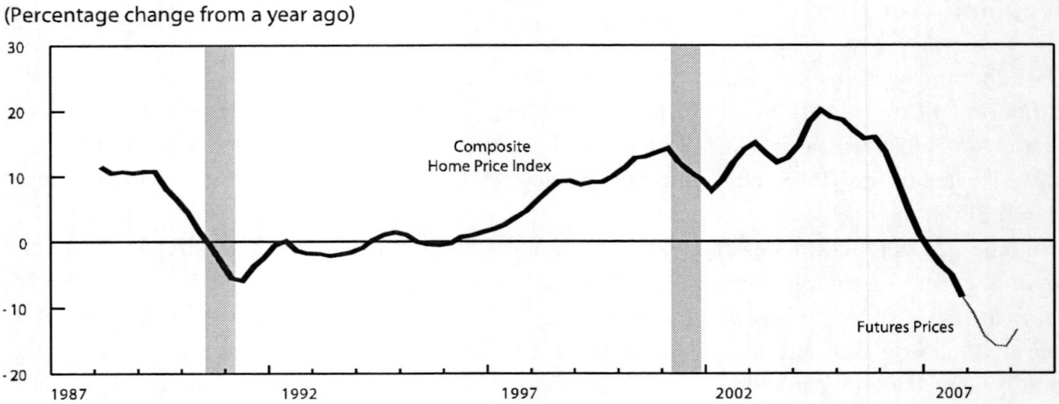

Figure 1. S&P/Case-Shiller 10-City Composite Home Price Index and Implied Values from Futures Prices

Sources: Congressional Budget Office; Bloomberg; Chicago Mercantile Exchange.

Note: The S&P/Case-Shiller 10-city composite home price index tracks price changes in 10 metropolitan areas on the basis of a house's previous sale. Data are quarterly and are plotted through the first quarter of 2009. The figure includes implied values from futures prices for the second quarter of 2008 through the first quarter of 2009.

The outlook for house prices is highly uncertain, but prices are likely to continue to fall, on average, at least through the end of 2008. Expectations of such a decline are widespread. Prices implied by futures contracts, for example, indicate that market participants expect large additional drops in house prices. Futures contracts on the S&P/Case-Shiller index for 10 cities project a decline of about 13 percent in nominal prices over the coming year and 16 percent by November 2009 (see Figure 2-1).[4]

3 Measures of house prices differ substantially in their coverage and how they handle changes in quality. OFHEO's index covers all areas of the country and has a relatively sophisticated adjustment for quality—which is a big issue in house prices—but it is restricted to houses with conforming mortgages (those eligible for purchase by Fannie Mae and Freddie Mac, two government-sponsored enterprises). The S&P/Case-Shiller indexes use the same adjustment for quality but cover fewer geographic areas. However, they include all homes in a covered area, whatever the type of mortgage. The Radar Logic composite index covers just 25 metropolitan housing markets and is not intended to represent the national market. It reflects all transactions, including sales of condominiums, and is updated daily. Its only quality adjustment, however, is for the size of the residence.

4 Futures contracts based on that index trade on the Chicago Mercantile Exchange. Trading in those contracts is akin to taking a position on what the value of the index will be in the future, say 12 months ahead. If, after that time, the value of the index is above the futures price the buyer paid, the seller pays the buyer the difference between the index and the futures price. However, if the value of the index is below the futures price, the

Another measure, based on Radar Logic's composite index of 25 cities, projects declines of 13 percent over the next year and 21 percent over the next three years. (However, those indexes may not indicate what is expected to happen to house prices nationwide.)

Private forecasters and investment firms also expect significant declines in nominal house prices. Macroeconomic Advisers, for its March 2008 forecast, assumed a 5.6 percent fall in prices from the end of 2007 to mid2009. Global Insight, another economic consulting firm, projects a 12 percent decline over the same period in its April forecast.

Delinquencies and Foreclosures of Mortgages. National delinquency and foreclosure rates are rising for both prime and subprime loans, particularly for adjustable-rate loans.[5] In the fourth quarter of 2007, 17.3 percent of all subprime loans were delinquent, up from 13.3 percent at the end of 2006. For subprime ARMs, 20 percent were delinquent in the fourth quarter of 2007, up from 14.4 percent in the fourth quarter of 2006. The delinquency rate on prime ARMs has also risen, from 3.4 percent at the end of 2006 to 5.5 percent at the end of last year (see Figure 2-2). In addition, the share of subprime ARMs entering foreclosure more than tripled, increasing from an average of 1.5 percent in 2004 and 2005 to 5.3 percent in the fourth quarter of 2007 (see Figure 2-3). Although the rate of delinquency on fixed-rate subprime loans has also grown, it is still much lower and has risen more slowly than that on subprime ARMs.

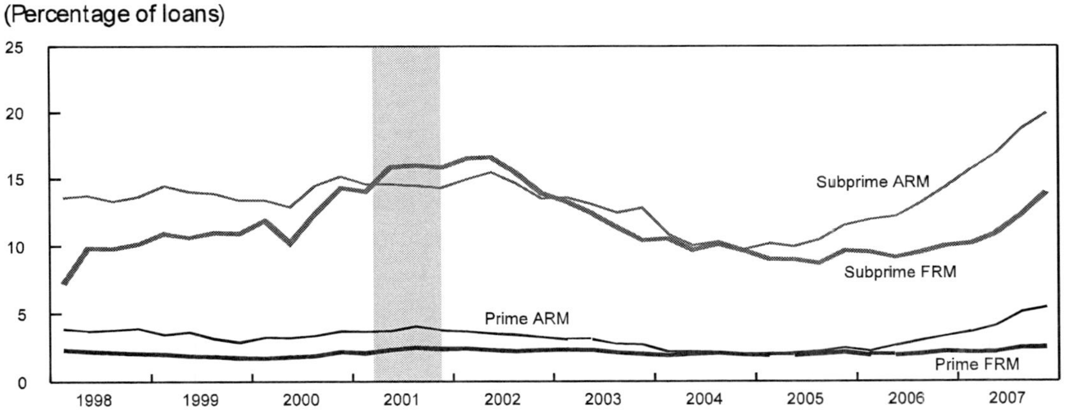

Figure 2. Mortgage Delinquencies
Sources: Congressional Budget Office; Mortgage Bankers Association.
Notes: Data are quarterly and are plotted through the fourth quarter of 2007.
ARM = adjustable-rate mortgage; FRM = fixed-rate mortgage.

---

buyer pays the seller the difference. Such contracts may be useful as a hedge against the real estate market. Futures prices may not be a reliable guide to expectations, though, particularly for longer periods. Futures contracts of this kind do not trade frequently or in large numbers and therefore may not represent a consensus of investors.

The S&P/Case-Shiller 10-City Composite Home Price Index tracks changes in the value of residential real estate in 10 metropolitan regions. No futures markets are associated with the S&P/ Case-Shiller 20-city or national price indexes.

5 A loan is delinquent when a borrower misses a contractual payment. The numbers cited in the text refer to loans that are at least 30 days overdue. Foreclosure is a legal proceeding to terminate a borrower's interest in a property, instituted by the lender either to gain title or to force a sale to satisfy the unpaid debt secured by the property.

Subprime loans are made to borrowers with low credit scores or other impairments to their credit histories.

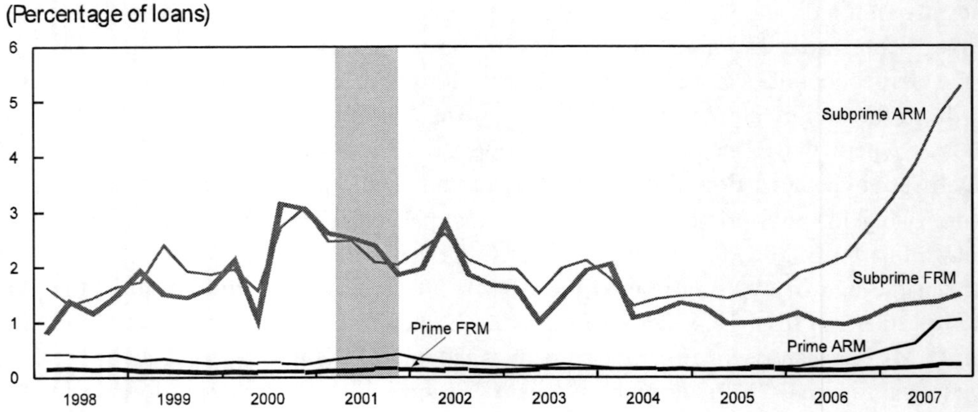

Figure 3. Mortgage Foreclosures Initiated

Sources: Congressional Budget Office; Mortgage Bankers Association.

Notes: Data are quarterly and are plotted through the fourth quarter of 2007.

ARM = adjustable-rate mortgage; FRM = fixed-rate mortgage.

Subprime loans are made to borrowers with low credit scores or other impairments to their credit histories

Rates of foreclosure are particularly high in areas experiencing economic weakness or large declines in house prices. Of the 10 states with the highest percentage of loans in foreclosure, 5 are among the 10 states with the largest declines in house prices.

Interest Rates on Mortgage Loans. Mortgage interest rates continue to reflect the heightened aversion to risk in financial markets. The interest rate on 30-year conforming mortgages, which can be securitized by the government-sponsored enterprises (GSEs) Fannie Mae and Freddie Mac, has fallen below 6 percent (see Figure 2-4). Although that rate is about one-half of a percentage point lower than it was in the past two years, the spread between that mortgage rate and the rate on seven-year Treasury notes—a measure of the market's current preference for the safest and most liquid collateral—continued to widen earlier this year.[6] Moreover, the rate on jumbo loans (those that exceed Fannie Mae's and Freddie Mac's loan limits) has moved up sharply since early February and currently is about 2 percentage points higher than the rate on conforming mortgages.

Initial rates for adjustable-rate mortgages, by contrast, dropped sharply earlier this year. In addition, the benchmark interest rate typically used for resetting the interest rate on subprime ARMs—the six-month Libor rate—has fallen significantly in the past few months and is now back down to levels last seen in the beginning of 2005 (see Figure 2-5).[7] That decline reflects the large amount of liquidity added by the Federal Reserve and other central banks in response to the turmoil in financial markets. As a result, the risk that resetting

---

6 On average, mortgages actually last only about seven years because people sell or refinance. Thus, the appropriate comparison is to a seven-year Treasury note rather than to an investment with a longer term to maturity.

7 Libor, the London Interbank Offered Rate, is the rate at which banks lend to each other for short terms.

interest rates on subprime ARMs will lead to a substantial number of additional mortgage defaults has fallen.

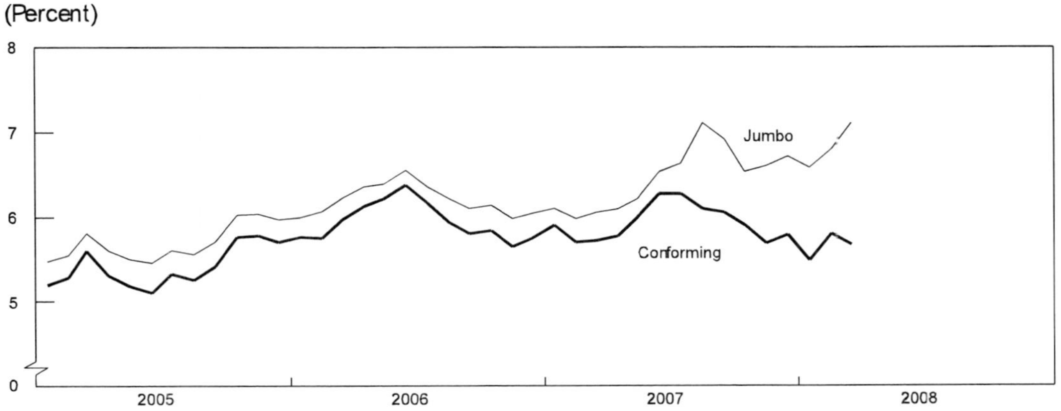

Figure 4. Rates on 30-Year Mortgages
Sources: Congressional Budget Office; Bankrate.com; Bloomberg.
Notes: Data are monthly and are plotted through March 2008. Jumbo loans exceed the loan limits of Fannie Mae and Freddie Mac

Prices of Mortgage-Backed Securities. The very high rates of delinquency on recent subprime mortgage loans surprised investors last year, who pulled back sharply from potential exposure to such lending in their investments during the summer. Lenders have virtually stopped making new subprime loans. Trading of existing subprime MBSs has diminished because of uncertainty about their value, particularly in view of investors' loss of confidence in the securities' credit ratings. Indeed, price declines on those MBSs have been striking, especially for subprime MBSs that were issued more recently and whose mortgages have experienced unusually high rates of defaults.

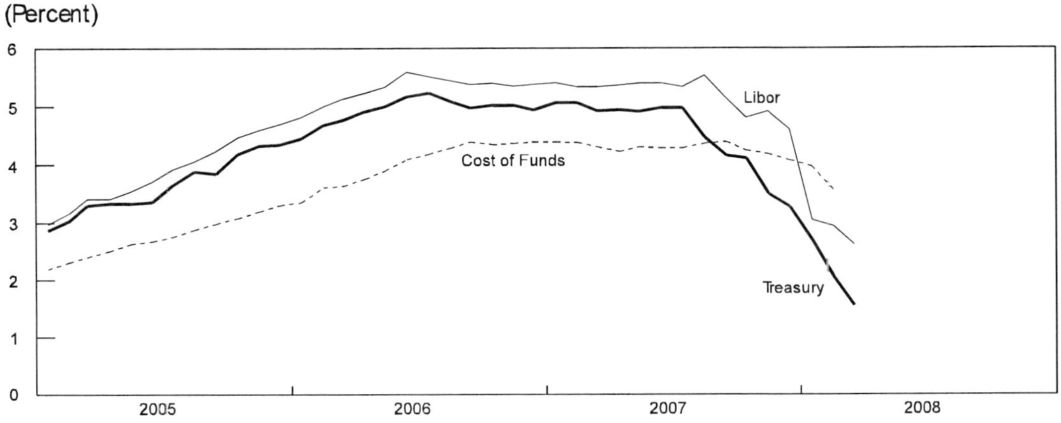

Figure 5. Popular Adjustable-Rate-Mortgage Indexes
Sources: Congressional Budget Office; Bloomberg.

Notes: The indexes shown are for the one-year constant maturity Treasury bill, the six-month Libor, and the 11th District Federal Home Loan Bank's cost of funds.

Data are monthly. The Libor and Treasury-bill rates are plotted through March 2008; the cost of funds rate is through February 2008.

The values of subprime mortgage securities (MBS tranches) can be inferred from ABX indexes related to those securities.[8] Those indexes are available for MBS tranches with different initial credit ratings.[9] As of late March 2008, the index for subprime MBSs issued in the second half of 2006 and initially rated BBB was 9 cents on the dollar, and the index for those initially rated AAA was 57 cents on the dollar (see Figure 2-6).[10] In both cases, index values a year ago were closer to 100 cents on the dollar. For subprime MBSs issued earlier, in the last half of 2005, prices have not fallen as much. Prices ranged from 17 cents on the dollar for the BBB-rated securities to 88 cents for the AAA-rated securities.

Financial Markets

The broader financial markets have also experienced significant turmoil recently. Lending in some markets remains depressed, as financial institutions continue to struggle to find ways of adequately dealing with losses on their leveraged financing of very risky mortgage loans and other risky assets.[11] Consequently, the risk of a systemic crisis in financial markets spurred by the collapse of one or more important financial institutions or markets remains elevated.

Subprime loans are made to borrowers with low credit scores or other impairments to their credit histories.

Credit Markets. Interest rates on investment-grade corporate bonds have remained relatively steady, but because the yield on the 10-year Treasury note has fallen sharply since last June, the interest rate spread has widened. Investors' tolerance for risk appears to have decreased as yields on below-investment-grade corporate securities have risen, particularly those with the lowest credit ratings (see Figure 2-7). Issuances of new corporate debt have fallen noticeably, as have those for asset-backed corporate paper. The interbank market for short-term loans also continues to experience problems; despite efforts by the Federal Reserve and some foreign central banks to shore up this market, the spread between the three-month

[8] ABX.HE indexes are calculated by the Markit Group Limited. ABX index values are based on the up-front premiums for credit default swaps on underlying subprime MBSs. The values of ABX indexes move inversely with the cost of ensuring that the holder of an MBS will receive all principal and interest payments.

[9] Mortgage-backed securities are repackaged in tranches, or securities of different seniority, in payment from the MBSs. An MBS with higher seniority, such as the most senior of the AAA-rated tranches, is entitled to payments before those in tranches with lower seniority, such as a less senior AAA tranche or any lower-rated tranche. In other words, a less senior tranche realizes a loss on an MBS before a more senior tranche.

[10] Usually it is the most junior tranche of a given credit rating that is selected for the index. There are no indexes for MBSs based on subprime securities originated in the second half of 2007 because almost no such mortgages were originated.

[11] See Congressional Budget Office, *The Budget and Economic Outlook: Fiscal Years 2008 to 2018* (January 2008), Chapter 2, for a fuller discussion of recent problems in financial markets.

Libor rate and the expected federal funds rate has moved upward recently (see Figure 2-8).[12]

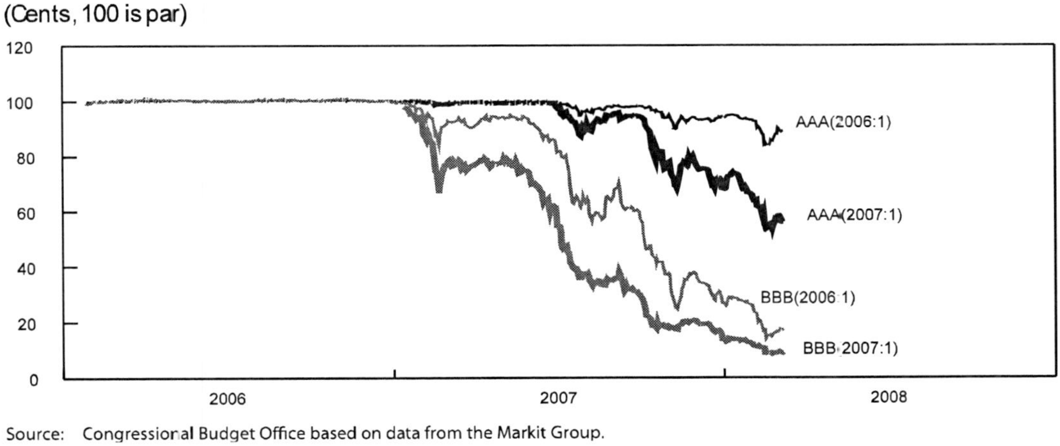

Figure 6. Inferred Prices of Subprime Mortgage Tranches
Source: Congressional Budget Office based on data from the Markit Group.
Notes: Prices are inferred from the Markit ABX.HE index for the BBB (next to the lowest investment grade) and AAA (highest investment grade) tranches of mortgage-backed securities. The 2006:1 vintage reflects mortgages available for securitization from July 19, 2005, to January 5, 2006. The 2007:1 vintage reflects mortgages available for securitization from July 19, 2006, to January 5, 2007. Data are daily and are plotted through March 28, 2008.

The Potential for Mortgage Losses. The ultimate volume of defaulted mortgages, which will affect both homeowners and investors, depends in part on the overall performance of the economy and on the size of the remaining gap between house prices and sustainable levels. A severe recession would result in larger mortgage losses than a mild recession or a short period of slow growth because a substantial recession would further depress house prices and homeowners' ability to finance their mortgages. Similarly, to the extent that house prices have farther to fall, losses will be larger than if prices have already declined to close to sustainable levels. The wide range of estimates of losses quoted in the media is due in part to the great uncertainty about the outlook for the overall economy and the ultimate level of house prices.

With sluggish but continued economic growth or a mild recession, as well as further declines of roughly 10 percent to 15 percent in average national house prices by mid-2009, the value of all mortgages that will enter foreclosure without further policy action could be about $500 billion to $600 billion over the next two years.[13] The ultimate losses on those

[12] The spread between those two rates is an indicator of credit risk. The three-month Libor provides funding among participants who may not have access to Federal Reserve liquidity facilities. Federal funds, in contrast, are overnight and shorter-term funding between banks with access to the Federal Reserve discount window. They typically have higher collateral standards than for Libor.

[13] The $500 billion figure is calculated by CBO from estimates in David Greenlaw and others, "Leveraged Losses: Lessons from the Mortgage Market Meltdown" (U.S. Monetary Policy Forum Conference Draft, February 2008). That figure represents 4.6 percent of the value of outstanding mortgages. The $600 billion figure was calculated on the basis of the statement of Mark Zandi, Moody's Economy.com, "The Looming Foreclosure Crisis: How to Help Families Save Their Homes," before the Senate Committee on the Judiciary (December 5,

mortgages will be smaller, possibly in the range of $100 billion to $250 billion, because some of the houses will not end up being repossessed. Also, considerable value will probably be recovered from new agreements worked out between borrowers and lenders and from foreclosure sales, for example. However, the recovery rate will most likely be lower than it has been in the past, particularly in some areas of the country, and sales of foreclosed properties may take several years to materialize.

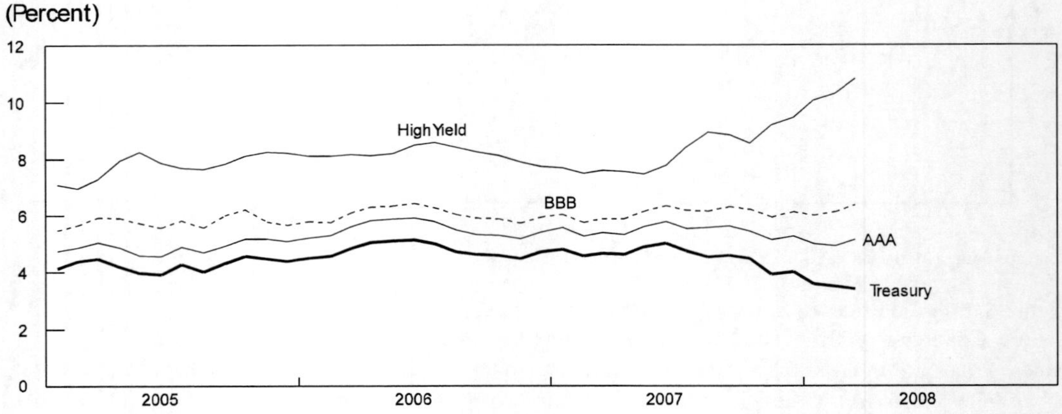

Figure 7. Yields on 10-Year Bonds.
Sources: Congressional Budget Office; Bloomberg.
Note: Data are monthly and are plotted through March 2008.

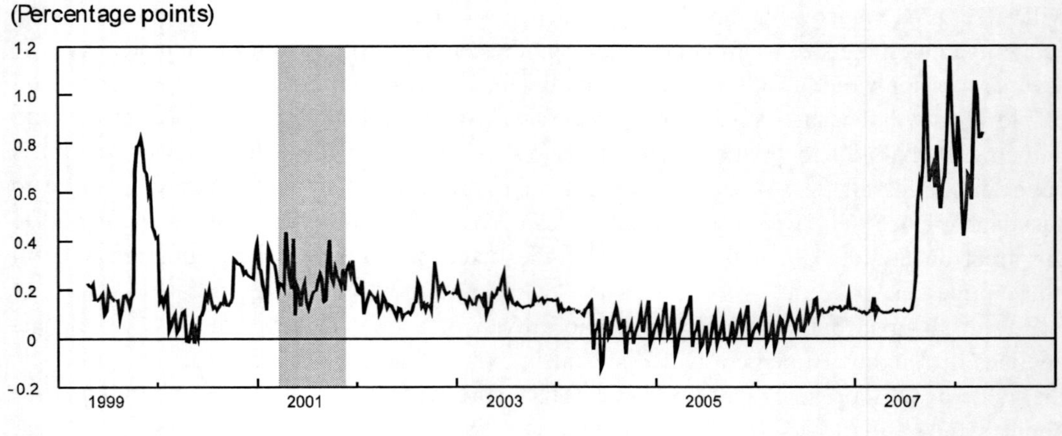

Figure 8. Spread Between the Three-Month Libor Rate and the Expected FederalFunds Rate

Financial institutions worldwide have already recognized about $230 billion in losses from the broader credit problem that began last year in subprime loans.[14] The International Monetary Fund recently estimated that total losses to all financial institutions around the world would approach $1 trillion, with more than half of that coming from residential

2007), in which the author estimated 2.8 million mortgages, or over 5 percent, would enter foreclosure through 2009.

mortgages and the rest coming from commercial mortgages, credit card loans, and automobile loans, among others. That amount would represent a notable loss of capital among the world's financial institutions, enough to significantly reduce the availability of credit.

Risks to the Financial System. The existence of substantial unrealized losses and uncertainty about which institutions are exposed to such losses may further impede the flow of credit in the United States and abroad. The possibility of large undisclosed losses has driven investors away from both the long-and short-term obligations of financial institutions. For the same reasons, financial institutions have become increasingly wary of lending to one another. In addition, institutions with assets of uncertain value on their balance sheets are likely to find it difficult to raise capital until the true value of those assets has been recognized because new investors will not want to share possible losses with current shareholders.

So far, problems in financial markets have not become severe enough to create a complete breakdown in the credit system. Such a breakdown could occur if lenders felt that they could not determine the risk they would be taking by lending to other entities: In that case, lending would stop, at least for a time. In such a scenario, even creditworthy borrowers could find credit difficult to obtain. Markets are still able to distinguish between those institutions that are creditworthy and those that are less so, as evidenced by sharp differences in the movement of stock prices of different banks. However, the near collapse of another major financial institution would further undermine the market's confidence and could severely cripple the financial system. That possibility is why the Federal Reserve has taken extraordinary actions to prevent such a failure.

Government Actions to Support Economic Activity and Stabilize Financial Markets

Both monetary and fiscal policymakers have taken significant steps to contain the economic damage caused by the turmoil in financial markets, but it remains unclear whether even those actions will prove sufficient to avoid a major recession. Fiscal policymakers have adopted an economic stimulus package whose effects should begin to manifest themselves late this spring. In addition, and perhaps more important, the Federal Reserve has taken extraordinary measures in addition to rapidly reducing the federal funds rate. In essence, the Federal Reserve has used its unmatched credit rating and large lending capacity to serve as an intermediary among financial institutions.

Fiscal Stimulus

In February, lawmakers enacted the Economic Stimulus Act of 2008.[15] That law provides tax rebates of up to $600 to individual filers, up to $1,200 for couples, and $300 per child. In addition, the law allows businesses to take additional deductions for accelerated depreciation and immediate expensing of capital purchases. That legislation will add an estimated $152 billion to the federal deficit in 2008 and another $16 billion in 2009. Overall, the

---

[14] Bloomberg LLC, Asset write-downs and credit losses table,April 1, 2008.

[15] Public Law 110-185; 122 Stat. 613.

Congressional Budget Office estimates that the law's provisions will add about 0.7 percentage points to the growth of real GDP in 2008.[16]

Actions by the Federal Reserve

The Federal Reserve instituted several actions in March to quell a crisis of confidence in the markets. The most extraordinary of those were creating a Primary Dealer Credit Facility and facilitating the acquisition of Bear Stearns by J.P. Morgan Chase.

The Primary Dealer Credit Facility allows all primary dealers to borrow funds overnight directly from the Federal Reserve.[17] Previously, that privilege was extended only to deposit-taking commercial banks. That step implies that the Federal Reserve is taking responsibility for ensuring liquidity not just to commercial banks, but also to a much broader swath of the financial market. In less unsettled times, ensuring that commercial banks have enough liquidity would be sufficient because those banks could then lend to the rest of the market. The need to provide liquidity directly to primary dealers is an indication of the breakdown of the usual flow of credit.

In another such indication, during the week ending Friday, March 14, other financial institutions lost confidence in Bear Stearns, the nation's fifth-largest investment bank, creating a potential liquidity crisis. Over that weekend, the Federal Reserve was involved in negotiations for J.P. Morgan's acquisition of Bear Stearns. The Federal Reserve lent $29 billion to J.P. Morgan against a portfolio of $30 billion of Bear Stearns' less liquid assets. In the event of losses on those assets, J.P. Morgan would be responsible for the first $1 billion in losses, and the Federal Reserve Bank of New York—and ultimately taxpayers—would absorb any remaining losses. (Taxpayers would be involved because any such losses would diminish the amount of the Federal Reserve's surplus that is turned over to the Treasury and recorded as federal revenues.)

The Federal Reserve has also continued to use its conventional tools. At the March 18 Federal Open Market Committee meeting, the federal funds target rate was reduced by 75 basis points, to 2.25 percent. The spread between the discount rate and the federal funds target rate was reduced to 25 basis points.[18] In its continuing effort to reduce strains in financial markets, the central bank has also enhanced its mechanisms for lending funds to financial institutions against illiquid collateral (investments that cannot be readily converted into cash). The Federal Reserve enlarged the amount of funds available to be lent under the twice-monthly Term Auction Facility from $30 billion to $50 billion. It also announced that it would lend up to an additional $100 billion to primary dealers in the form of 28-day repurchase agreements— another step to provide liquidity to that market.

---

[16] The law's provisions will subtract about 0.4 percentage points from growth of real GDP in 2009, CBO estimates, as most of the stimulus is removed.

[17] Primary dealers are banks or securities broker-dealers who may trade directly with the Federal Reserve System.

[18] The discount rate is the rate paid by banks borrowing from the Federal Reserve. The Federal Reserve sets a target rate for the federal funds, the rate banks charge each other for overnight loans. The Board of Governors of the Federal Reserve System can cut discount rates only when it has a request to do so from a Federal Reserve Bank. By March 20, all banks had requested cuts to a new spread of 25 basis points over the target for the federal funds rate. (A basis point is one-hundredth of a percentage point.)

Following those actions by the Federal Reserve and other central banks, short-term interest rates have fallen, but the perceived riskiness of the interbank loan market has not changed greatly. The spread between the cost of three-month Libor funding and the expected federal funds rate over the same period did narrow, but only modestly, and that spread remains well above typical levels.

POLICY OPTIONS

Policymakers have already taken steps to help the housing and mortgage markets cope with the effects of the end of the housing boom, and additional actions are under consideration. Some of those actions involve new ways of promoting the modification of troubled mortgages, while others involve having the federal government directly provide or guarantee credit to mortgage markets. Such actions would help avoid foreclosures and ease the downward pressure on house prices, helping the market adjust in a more orderly manner.[19] Many policy options, however, would also significantly shift the risk involved in mortgage losses from current lenders and investors to taxpayers. (Policymakers are also considering new supervisory guidelines and regulations for financial institutions to address weaknesses that contributed to the problems in financial markets. Those issues are not addressed in this paper.)

Considerations for Policymakers

Several possible short-term goals could motivate policy interventions:

- Assist borrowers who unwittingly overcommitted their income to mortgage payments. Many of those borrowers may have lacked sufficient financial sophistication to understand the nature of the risks they were undertaking. A related objective could be to lessen the social costs of having large numbers of people move out of their houses and into others.
- Avoid excessive declines in asset prices—house prices as well as prices of mortgage-related assets. That task may be very difficult to achieve because of the near impossibility of determining fair values in current markets. House prices, in particular, are expected to continue to fall for at least a year because of the over hang of unoccupied units, and such an adjustment is necessary to allow the housing market to function again. However, there is a risk that the price adjust ment may get out of hand in some areas, as forced or panic selling causes prices to decline too much.
- Reduce the costs of loan modification, refinancing, or foreclosure.
- Stimulate the economy as a whole in order to avoid or mitigate a recession. The housing market's troubles affect the rest of the economy by reducing activity in the housing market itself, by decreasing homeowners' wealth (which gives them less

[19] Six of the largest mortgage servicers, accounting for 50 percent of the mortgage-servicing market, announced on February 12 a plan called Project Lifeline, which specifies the conditions under which a mortgage borrower who is 90 days or more delinquent may be allowed an extra 30 days to work out a loan modification.

collateral for borrowing and tends to constrain their spending), and by con tributing to problems in financial markets.

- Support credit markets to mitigate turbulence in financial markets. Financial markets play a crucial role in a modern economy, and intervening to keep them working smoothly may help mitigate broader costs to the economy.
- Facilitate the cleaning up of balance sheets. The availability of credit to financial institutions, and hence to businesses and households that borrow from those institutions, could be limited if assets on their balance sheets are difficult to value. Moreover, institutions will have greater difficulty raising capital because potential investors will not know what they are buying and will not wish to share losses on current assets with existing shareholders.

Those goals are not always mutually compatible, and different policy interventions may fulfill some objectives but not others. For instance, supporting financial institutions in difficulty to prevent broader problems in financial markets may conflict with the goal of recognizing losses as quickly as possible to clean up balance sheets. Keeping homeowners in their houses may delay the necessary revaluation of the housing stock.

Whatever policymakers' goals, a key consideration is to avoid policies that distort incentives excessively. For example, homeowners who otherwise are capable of making their payments might take on additional debt or miss mortgage payments in order to create an impression of financial difficulty if doing so qualified them for mortgage assistance. Pressuring lenders to modify existing contracts may appear to benefit current borrowers, but such action could also ultimately raise interest rates on future credit transactions and thereby harm future borrowers.

One contribution that federal policymakers can make is to encourage a standard package for restructuring mortgages, including such things as how to determine what monthly payment the borrower can manage and how to distribute losses among first- and second-lien holders. Such a standard package, if it is sufficiently realistic, could be useful even if it is voluntary and even if it does not provide any federal monetary support. In that case, it could reduce the number of decisions that need to be made in a restructuring, speeding up the process. In addition, having a standard for restructuring could help gain assent from the various stakeholders—including second-lien holders and holders of low-ranked MBS tranches. Having rules for the restructuring is essential if there is to be a federal monetary commitment.

Loan Restructuring

A number of proposals aim to facilitate the restructuring of existing mortgages to help homeowners avoid foreclosure and stay in their current residences. Loan restructurings fall into two broad but not mutually exclusive categories: reducing the principal of a mortgage and changing the terms of a mortgage. A goal of many of the proposals is to make loan repayment more attractive to borrowers while providing lenders with a greater return than that realized from foreclosure (see Box 3-1).[20]

Box 3-1. The Costs of Foreclosure

With house prices falling in most areas of the country, some mortgage lenders are likely to suffer substantial losses from defaults and foreclosures. Estimates of the losses when a house is repossessed range from 30 percent to 60 percent of the value of the loan.[1] About half of those losses occur prior to the foreclosure process—that is, from the decline in the price of the house, missed interest payments, and unpaid property taxes.[2] The other half of the losses reflect the costs of preparing the house for sale (which includes lost interest payments during the time it is on the market); the expense of selling it; and, if the house is foreclosed, associated legal expenses. Those latter costs are the primary costs of foreclosure itself. (Any missed loan payments and any decline in the price of the house before foreclo sure are not considered costs of foreclosure.) Lenders typically are unable to recover such losses. The losses will be realized regardless of whether the homeowner leaves voluntarily or through foreclosure.

In addition to those costs, in foreclosure the lender loses the opportunity to share in the potential appreciation of the house. Although it is difficult to value that opportunity, a reasonable expectation might be 3 percent of the value of the house.[3] That calculation implies that 50 percent to 55 percent of the loss to lenders might be avoided under alternatives to foreclosure—in other words, about 20 percent to 25 percent of the outstanding balance of the mortgage.

1. That range comes from Charles Capone, *Providing Alternatives to Mortgage Foreclosure: A Report to Congress* (Department of Housing and Urban Development, March 1996). An estimate in March 2008 by consultant organization Clayton Holdings set the average loss from delinquencies on first-lien subprime and alt-A loans at about 40 percent. A third estimate, which used a 50 percent loss for all mortgages, comes from David Greenlaw and others, "Leverage Losses: Lessons from the Mortgage Market Meltdown" (U.S. Monetary Policy Forum Conference Draft, February 2008).
2. Amy Crew Cutts and William Merrill, "Interventions in Mortgage Default: Policies and Practices to Prevent Home Loss and Lower Costs" (Freddie Mac Working Paper, March 2008).
3. The 3 percent estimate is based on the price of an at-themoney call option that expires after five years on an asset with an expected price decline of 1.5 percent per year and a volatility of 6 percent.

Impediments to Voluntary Loan Restructuring

There are several legal and economic reasons that lenders may be reluctant to use loan restructurings to resolve mortgage repayment problems. Legal impediments arise in cases in which borrowers have a second mortgage or have a mortgage that has been securitized (that is, sold as a part of a mortgage-backed security). Economic impediments include imperfect information about borrowers and the perverse incentives that can be created for some borrowers by restructuring the loans of other borrowers.

[20] Hope Now, an alliance of various participants in mortgage markets, reports that since July 2007, it has helped more than 1 million borrowers, about 640,000 of whom have subprime credit ratings. Loans were modified for about 25 percent of the borrowers assisted by Hope Now.

Legal Impediments. One impediment to restructuring mortgages occurs when the borrower has a second mortgage. During the housing boom, a significant percentage of borrowers took on second mortgages. In February 2008, about 30 percent of subprime and alt-A loans had second mortgages.[21] The holders of the first mortgage and the second mortgage often have substantially different interests and bargaining powers. Given the decline in house prices, the market value of many second mortgages has often disappeared, and they would be worthless under foreclosure. Second-lien holders in such situations would seek to avoid foreclosure or a short sale because either would eliminate the potential for their loans to regain value if prices recovered in the future.[22] (In effect, second-lien holders have a call option on the value of the house—if the value goes down, they are not subject to further losses, but they will gain if prices recover.) To avoid the costly foreclosure process, the first-lien holder may have an interest in reducing the payment obligation of the borrower or permitting a short sale. Because the priority of liens generally follows the order in which they are recorded, for a refinancing lender to have the senior lien, a second lien must also be repaid or resubordinated.[23]

The second-lien holders, however, may withhold their consent to resubordination (if required) or threaten foreclosure to bargain with both the homeowner and the first-lien holder. In many cases, the ability to help borrowers having difficulty may first require coordination and agreement between the holders of the first and second mortgages.[24]

A second impediment concerns securitization. In some cases, complex interests inherent in securitization could impede the ability of a loan servicer to modify loans that belong to a securitized pool. To receive favorable tax and accounting treatment, the special-purpose entities that issue MBSs must avoid becoming active managers in a technical sense defined by the tax laws. Many mitigation efforts are permissible under current law because the Internal Revenue Service (IRS) and the Chief Accountant of the Securities and Exchange Commission (SEC) determined that as long as servicers follow a certain set of industry guidelines (the ASF Framework), their actions would not jeopardize the tax and accounting status of the special-purpose entities.[25] Proposals for mitigation efforts outside the ASF Framework, however, must address how to maintain the current tax and accounting treatment.

---

[21] In some cases, borrowers took out two mortgages: a first mortgage (or lien) at 80 percent of the value of the home and a second mortgage for as much as the remaining 20 percent of the home's value. The second mortgage financed some or all of the down-payment and allowed borrowers to avoid paying mortgage insurance on the first lien.

[22] A short sale is a sale at a price that is lower than the total value of the mortgages on the house.

[23] Priority among lien holders is determined by state property law. A minority (but growing) view among the states is that a previously subordinate lien will be resubordinated as a matter of law unless the new loan modifies the obligations of the borrower in a way that is materially prejudicial to the holders of the junior liens. Examples of modifications that may be prejudicial include increasing the principal of the first lien or increasing the interest rate. See Restatement (Third) of Property: Mortgages §7.6 (1997); *Bank of America v. Prestance Corp.*, 160 P.3d 17, 21 (Wash. 2007); and Grant S. Nelson and Dale A. Whitman, "Adopting Restatement Mortgage Subrogation Principles: Saving Billions of Dollars for Refinancing Homeowners," *Brigham Young University Law Review* (2006), p. 305. The majority view is that a previously subordinate lien will not be resubordinated if the refinancing lender has actual knowledge of the other liens. The remaining states would withhold resubordination if the refinancing lender has even constructive knowledge of the other liens or if the refinancing lender is a volunteer to the transaction.

[24] The transaction costs associated with obtaining such agreement are avoided in states where second liens are automatically resubordinate.

[25] The ASF Framework is the American Securitization Forum's "Statement of Principles, Recommendations, and Guidelines for a Streamlined Foreclosure and Loss Avoidance Framework for Securitized Subprime

In addition, contractual terms may sometimes restrict servicers' actions.[26] For example, pooling and servicing agreements may prevent the exchange of an existing loan for a new loan, such as one that allows participation in equity appreciation in exchange for modification of existing terms. Most recent pooling and servicing agreements give servicers authority to modify securitized loans if that action is in the interest of maximizing the value of the loan pool, but some agreements may be more restrictive. Pooling and servicing agreements can be amended with the consent of investors. However, investors in different tranches of mortgage-backed securities share losses unequally, which may limit servicers' ability to obtain permission to engage in additional mitigation actions.

The Congress is considering various proposals to protect servicers of securitized loans who agree to restructure mortgages (through modifications, partial discharge of principal, or short sales)—if the servicers believe that such restructuring will increase the value received on the loans over that which would be received through foreclosure.[27] Proponents argue that by providing servicers with legal certainty, the proposals would increase the number of mortgages that servicers chose to restructure. Opponents argue that the proposals are unnecessary because servicers already are protected if they compare all of the loss-mitigation options and choose the one that maximizes the return to the loan pool.

Economic Impediments. Lenders may be unwilling to adjust a loan's balance, despite the potential benefits, for two reasons. First, although some borrowers walk away from their homes when the home's value drops below the mortgage balance, more do not.[28] There is no workable way to distinguish between those types of borrowers ahead of time, and the cost of reworking every distressed loan would be far greater than dealing with the foreclosure expenses of only those borrowers who walked away. Moreover, offering a reduction of principal to "distressed" homeowners might encourage people who were otherwise capable of making payments to attempt to qualify for the benefit by taking on additional debt or missing several mortgage payments to suggest financial difficulties. Second, lenders would have no confidence that a borrower whose mortgage was rewritten would not choose to walk away if house prices fell even lower. Although Federal Reserve Chairman Ben Bernanke has urged

---

Adjustable Rate Mortgage Loans." See Rev. Proc. 2007-72, 2007-52 I.R.B. 1257; SEC Office of Chief Accountant letter, January 8, 2008, available at www.sec.gov/info/ accountants/staffletters/hanish010808.pdf. The ASF Framework applies to first-lien subprime residential adjustable-rate mortgage loans that have an initial fixed-rate period of 36 months or less (including "2/28s" and "3/27s"); were originated between January 1, 2005, and July 31, 2007; are included in securitized pools; and have an initial interest rate that resets between January 1, 2008, and July 31, 2010.

The framework provides a fast-track procedure for modifying loans and details the criteria for determining which loans are eligible for the procedure. In a fast-track modification, the interest rate on the affected loan will be kept at the existing rate, generally for five years after the date on which the rate would have reset had the modification not occurred.

[26] Most of the pooling and servicing agreements were executed before the IRS and the Chief Accountant of the Securities and Exchange Commission reached their decisions regarding the ASF Framework. Consequently, some of those agreements may contain provisions that are more restrictive than what could now be permitted under the framework.

[27] See H.R. 5579, the Emergency Mortgage Loan Modification Act of 2008, and the amendments intended to be proposed by Senator Specter (No. 4408) and by Senator Reid for Senator Clinton (No. 4492) to H.R. 3221, the New Direction for Energy Independence, National Security, and Consumer Protection Act.

[28] Until recently, borrowers had faced taxes based on the loss forced upon the mortgage holder when the lender took back ownership of the home. That served as a disincentive to walk away. However, the Congress temporarily excluded from taxation the gains on certain mortgage debt forgiven on principal residences and extended the deduction for premiums paid on private mortgage insurance in the Mortgage Forgiveness Debt Relief Act of 2007 (Public Law 110-142; 121 Stat. 1803).

loan servicers to consider reducing the principal on outstanding loans, voluntary reductions are likely to be rare.

Proposals to Facilitate Changing Mortgage Terms

A number of plans would keep a borrower's mortgage principal unchanged but lower the monthly payment for a possibly limited time. Under those plans, lenders would voluntarily negotiate such payment forbearance on a case-by-case basis. Most proposals have focused on preventing an increase in the interest rate on adjustable-rate subprime loans that are scheduled for their first interest rate reset in the next two years. (The decline in short-term interest rates engineered by the Federal Reserve has sharply reduced the size of any increase in initial resets and may even lower rates for some ARM borrowers this year.) Some proposals would lower payments both for adjustable-rate loans even when their rates have not changed and for fixed-rate loans. Lenders would find such proposals more attractive if borrowers' missed payments were added to their principal. If lenders bear the cost of the lower payments, such proposals are in many ways similar to reducing the loan principal.

Rate Freezes on Adjustable-Rate Loans. The Administration reached a voluntary agreement with some lenders in December 2007 to freeze interest rates for generally five years on certain types of subprime loans.[29] Eligibility is limited to subprime borrowers who face an initial adjustment to their mortgage interest rate between January 1, 2008, and July 31, 2010, and meet the eligibility criteria of the ASF Framework (see footnote 7). Although lenders would bear losses from the lower-than-agreed-upon interest rate, those losses might not be recognized immediately (unlike a principal reduction), depending on the accounting treatment. With the reduction in short-term interest rates, this freeze may have little impact in the coming year but may be more important when economic activity recovers and those rates rise.[30]

Other proponents have offered broader freezes. Some proposals would freeze rates on all subprime loans for up to seven years regardless of borrowers' equity or payment history. Others would go beyond subprime loans and would freeze rates for all adjustable-rate loans. Although broader plans would help more needy borrowers, they also would offer a windfall to borrowers who were not in difficulty at the expense of the holders of those mortgages. Convincing lenders to freeze scheduled adjustments of interest rates for a wider range of borrowers without adequate compensation would probably require some compulsion or financial inducements from the federal government. To the extent that lenders perceived a broad-scale freeze as a significant change in contractual terms (which is more likely under a compulsory change), the result would probably be higher interest rates on mortgages and other credit transactions in the future. In particular, lenders would require some compensation

---

[29] That agreement was arranged by the Treasury Department and the Department of Housing and Urban Development, with lenders, servicers, mortgage counselors, and investors.

[30] In "The Potential Effect of Rate Freezes on S&P-Rated U.S. First-Lien Subprime RMBS" (December 14, 2007), Standard & Poor's estimated that about 20 percent of the 1.2 million subprime adjustable-rate first mortgages would be eligible for fast-track modification. In March, it was reported that the Clayton Group expected about 50,000 of those loans eventually to be modified under terms of the voluntary agreement.

In "The Mixed Impact of Falling Rates on U.S. Alt-A and Subprime Borrowers," Standard & Poor's (March 26, 2008), the authors found that because of the sharp drop in the Libor, subprime borrowers facing an interest rate reset will on average pay a rate just 1 percentage point higher than their initial "teaser" rate. They also found that the lower Libor had "virtually eliminated Alt-A payment shock."

to protect against the risk that policymakers would again freeze interest rates or intervene in some other way.

If the goal of interest rate freezes is to help borrowers remain in their homes, the success would depend in part on their net equity in the homes as well as other factors, such as the borrowers' ties to their homes and costs of moving. In the current environment of lower short-term interest rates, borrowers' equity in their homes may be a more important determinant of the likelihood of foreclosures and walking away from homes with burdensome monthly payments.[31] As long as the market value of the house exceeds the mortgage balance, a borrower has an ability and an incentive to sell or refinance the home rather than walk away, even when payments are perceived to be onerous.

Other Ways to Lower Mortgage Payments. Some proposals would mandate that lenders allow borrowers to lower their payments in exchange for a greater stake in the equity of the home or an increase in the mortgage balance. That is, the restructuring would substitute a shared appreciation loan or a negative amortization loan for the current loan. A shared appreciation loan entitles lenders to receive a share of any increase in the value of a house in exchange for giving the borrower a below-market interest rate (thus lowering the monthly payment).[32] Borrowers who do not have much initial equity in their homes are better off with the lower payments when house prices decline. Negative amortization or deferred-interest loans offer lower payments and capitalize the shortfall into a larger principal balance. Borrowers have the option to make a minimum payment, one that is less than the original interest due. The amount that the payment falls short of the interest owed is added to the principal. Negative amortization loans might make sense for borrowers expecting their income to increase in the future, but such loans would merely defer problems for borrowers whose loan amounts exceeded what they could afford in the longer term. Some proposals to modify bankruptcy law also would allow changing mortgage terms.

Proposals to Facilitate the Reduction of Mortgage Balances

Proposals to reduce mortgage balances aim to help people stay in their homes, which may also help stabilize the current housing market. Those proposals provide incentives to dissuade homeowners whose loan balance is greater than the current market value of their homes from walking away from their mortgages when they can afford to pay them.[33] Studies have shown that the greater the shortfall between the value of a house and the amount of a borrower's mortgage, the greater the likelihood that the borrower will default on his or her mortgage.[34] Under certain conditions, lenders might prefer to voluntarily rewrite a mortgage for the current value of a home rather than have a borrower walk away, especially in a declining

---

[31] Kristopher Gerardi, Adam Shapiro, and Paul Willen, "Subprime Outcomes: Risky Mortgages, Homeownership Experiences, and Foreclosures" (Federal Reserve Bank of Boston Working Paper, December 2007).

[32] Proposals for shared-appreciation loans must ensure that the obligations would be legal, valid, and binding and receive the intended priority in foreclosure and bankruptcy proceedings.

[33] Borrowers would face some consequences by defaulting: a lower credit rating and, in some states, an attempt by lenders to gain title to some of their other assets (although recovery of that type has been rare so far).

[34] Gerardi, Shapiro, and Willen, "Subprime Outcomes." Borrowers have what essentially amounts to a put option—if the value of the house falls below the amount owed, they may be better off abandoning the house. See, for example, Ronel Elul, "Residential Mortgage Default," *Business Review* (Federal Reserve Bank of Philadelphia, 2006); and Michael LaCour-Little, "Equity Dilution: An Alternative Perspective on Mortgage Default," *Real Estate Economics* (September 2004).

housing market. Rewriting the principal balance of the loan avoids a costly foreclosure in a depressed market and gives the borrower an incentive to continue repaying the loan.

Determining the fair value of a house, and hence the appropriate write-down of the mortgage principal, may be difficult in the current circumstances, however. The national housing market is not likely to stabilize for some time, and house prices will probably continue to fall. That process of moving to stability is not likely to proceed evenly—some regions experienced larger price increases and building expansions than others, and thus they may take longer to adjust. In some neighborhoods, home prices may even dip below levels needed to stabilize the market when there are a large number of foreclosures or panic sales.

Some proposals involve changing federal bankruptcy law to allow bankruptcy judges to restructure certain mortgages on principal residences under Chapter 13, by limiting a mortgage to the current value of a home, for instance, or by changing the terms of a loan. Under current law, Chapter 13 halts foreclosure proceedings by lenders, giving homeowners an opportunity to restructure their financial situation. While Chapter 13 gives courts leeway to adjust many financial obligations, it currently does not generally allow the terms of a mortgage on a principal residence to be modified.[35] Changing that provision of Chapter 13 would allow bankruptcy courts to treat mortgages on a primary residence in the same way as secured debts on other items, such as motor vehicles, vacation homes, investment properties, and personal businesses. (In practice, bankruptcy judges seldom restructure mortgages on vacation or investment properties.)

Allowing a bankruptcy court to modify the amount or terms of mortgages changes incentives for both borrowers and lenders. It gives borrowers an incentive to file for bankruptcy as a way to lower their mortgage payments and avert foreclosure. Consequently, lenders would have a greater incentive to restructure loans voluntarily. Lenders would also have a greater incentive to be more prudent in making loans, which could help avoid future excesses in the mortgage markets. In doing so, lenders might raise mortgage rates, particularly for high-risk borrowers, to offset any expected greater losses from loan modifications in bankruptcy. However, there are divergent views on how much mortgage interest rates would rise.[36] The increase may be limited in part because lenders might also change other lending terms to reduce their exposure to losses. Changing the bankruptcy law could also add to the caseload of the bankruptcy court system.[37]

---

[35] 11 U.S.C. §1322(b)(2). Furthermore, the Supreme Court held that even when the value of the debt exceeds the value of the property—a partially secured debt—courts may not modify that debt. See *Nobleman v. Am. Savings Bank*, 508 U.S. 324 (1993). Conversely, when a second (or third) mortgage is wholly unsecured because the value of the property is insufficient to satisfy the first mortgage, such subordinated debt may be discharged; *Tanner v. FirstPlus Fin. Inc.* (*In re Tanner*), 217 F. 3d 1357 (11th Cir. 2000) announced what has become the dominant view among the circuit courts of appeals. Hence, the claims of partially secured creditors are protected by bankruptcy law, but the claims of unsecured creditors are not.

[36] See Adam J. Levitin and Joshua Goodman, *The Effect of Bankruptcy Strip-Down on Mortgage Markets,* Business Economics and Regulatory Policy Working Paper No. 1087816 (Georgetown University Law Center, February 6, 2008).

[37] Congressional Budget Office, cost estimate for H.R. 3609, the Emergency Home Ownership and Mortgage Equity Protection Act of 2007, as ordered reported by the House Committee on the Judiciary on December 12, 2007 (February 5, 2008).

Federal Assistance to Participants in the Mortgage Market

Although private participants in mortgage and financial markets will probably try to address the problems in those markets on their own, some plans would have the government (that is, taxpayers) contribute resources to encourage certain types of outcomes. Indeed, the government has already begun to do so, through initiatives involving the Federal Reserve and agencies involved in housing. Proposals for increasing that intervention revolve around extending federal credit or insurance to new and existing borrowers or mortgage lenders. The existing regulatory framework permits some expansion of federal housing and banking agencies' activity without Congressional action. Alternatively, a new agency could be created for the purpose, as it was during the Depression and in the thrift crisis of the 1980s. Finally, some proposals would rely on state and local governments.

If policymakers conclude that some commitment of resources is appropriate, they also will have to determine who should benefit from such resources. Acquiring loans in order to refinance them would directly assist borrowers and could help them avert foreclosure, thus limiting the likelihood of a downward spiral in house prices. Purchases or guarantees that were targeted to relieve lenders or mortgage pools of the risk from the most troubled loans would provide investors with more confidence in mortgage-backed securities and financial intermediaries. Providing credit to lenders without intervening in mortgage arrangements would help them keep their doors open and could be used as an incentive for lenders to work out a solution for their at-risk borrowers.

All such proposals, however, have downsides (beyond their budgetary costs). In the short term, extending credit to borrowers or lenders in a precarious financial position might encourage borrowers who were able to pay their debts to stop paying them in order to qualify for federal assistance. In the long run, some observers are concerned that expanding the federal role in mortgage markets risks undermining incentives for lenders and borrowers to make prudent decisions. If the federal government is expected to step in when economic times are bad, then lenders and borrowers do not need to consider the possibility of bad times when making decisions. The inability of current risk models to anticipate such bad times contributed to the present economic situation. Narrowly targeting federal interventions and ensuring that borrowers and lenders bear a substantial share of the costs could minimize the distortion of incentives to consider extreme risks.

It is also important to recognize that although those types of policy interventions may attenuate pricing pressures and allow a more orderly correction in the housing market, no feasible policy intervention is likely to completely stabilize house prices and mortgage markets. The main reason is that the extraordinary size of the housing market (see Table 3-1) and the magnitude of the problem would require a massive increase in the federal commitment to housing.

Large-scale federal intervention in housing markets could lead to a less efficient allocation of capital in the future. Increasing federal credit subsidies for housing would drive loan capital toward housing and away from investments that are more productive (see Box 1-1).

Table 3-1. Measures of the Size of the Housing Market

	2006	2007
Annual Housing Sales (Trillions of dollars)	1.9	1.4
Housing Sales as a Share of		
Owner-Occupied Housing (Percent)	9	7
Total Housing Wealth (Trillions of dollars)	19.5	20.2

Source: Congressional Budget Office based on data from the Bureau of the Census, the National Association of Realtors, and the Board of Governors of the Federal Reserve System.

Note: This table compares the state of the housing market in 2006, before the credit crisis began, with the state of the market in the second half of 2007, after the crisis had taken hold.

a. Data are from July through December.

Recent Activity by the Federal Government and Government-Sponsored Enterprises

A number of federal institutions and government-sponsored enterprises have already increased their participation in housing finance or been given more flexibility to do so.

Federal Reserve. The Federal Reserve has already started to take on some mortgage risk. On March 11, the Federal Reserve announced that it had created a new program, the Term Securities Lending Facility (TSLF), which will make loans to the 20 banks and securities firms that trade directly with the central bank. In the current situation, the Federal Reserve has found that it cannot simply provide liquidity to the overnight interbank market and expect it to flow smoothly into other parts of the financial markets. In the TSLF, the Federal Reserve offers to lend up to $200 billion of Treasury securities for 28-day terms against collateral including privately issued mortgage-backed securities.[38] The Federal Reserve has also extended through the Federal Reserve Bank of New York a loan of $29 billion to J.P. Morgan, backed by $30 billion worth of Bear Stearns' less liquid assets, in order to facilitate the acquisition of Bear Stearns by J.P. Morgan.[39]

Fannie Mae and Freddie Mac. These two large federally regulated participants in the mortgage markets have recently been given more flexibility to assume additional mortgage risk. The institutions buy up pools of conforming mortgages and securitize and sell them to the secondary mortgage markets. They also hold both conforming and nonconforming mortgages as part of their portfolios. Although federal regulations restrict conforming mortgages to a certain size and creditworthiness, the size limit was recently increased from $417,000 to 125 percent of the median house price in each region (an amount up to $729,750). In addition to that temporary increase, regulators in mid-March reduced the capital

---

[38] Details of the program are available at the Federal Reserve's Web site, www.federalreserve.gov/monetarypolicy/tslf.htm.

[39] A press release states that the Federal Reserve Bank of New York "will take, through a limited liability company formed for this purpose, control of a portfolio of assets valued at $30 billion as of March 14, 2008. The assets will be pledged as security for $29 billion in term financing from the New York Fed at its primary credit rate. JPMorgan Chase will bear the first $1 billion of any losses associated with the portfolio and any realized gains will accrue to the New York Fed. BlackRock Financial Management, Inc. will manage the portfolio under guidelines established by the New York Fed designed to minimize disruption to financial markets and maximize recovery value." See the Federal Reserve Bank of New York's "Statement on Financing Arrangement of JPMorgan Chase's Acquisition of Bear Stearns," available at www.newyork fed.org/newsevents/news/markets/2008/rp080324.html.

reserves that the two institutions have to hold against their own portfolios of loans. According to OFHEO, that reduction is expected to provide up to $200 billion of liquidity to the MBS market.

Although a larger role for those government-sponsored enterprises helps borrowers, much of the additional underlying risk is implicitly shifted to taxpayers. Markets have taken note of the precarious financial position of Fannie Mae and Freddie Mac; the cost of purchasing insurance against default on their obligations has risen severalfold since June 2007.[40] Prices in the credit-default swap market imply about a 7 percent probability of default over the next 10 years (versus about 3 percent last June).[41] Moreover, Moody's has placed one of the key GSE credit ratings on review for possible downgrade. Nevertheless, the borrowing advantage of the GSEs over ther corporations is likely to have increased since last summer, a demonstration of the value of the widely perceived implicit federal guarantee of their obligations.

Federal Home Loan Banks. Another set of GSEs, the Federal Home Loan Banks (FHLBs) have also intervened to support the banking industry and mortgage markets in response to the turmoil. The 12 Federal Home Loan Banks provide liquidity in housing finance markets by extending credit to various financial institutions. They take as collateral residential and commercial mortgage loans, MBSs, agency and government securities, small-business loans, and agricultural loans. During the second half of 2007, when the turmoil unfolded, FHLB advances to member financial institutions increased by $235 billion to a year-end level of $875 billion; loans to the 10 largest borrowers (including Citibank, Washington Mutual Bank, and Countrywide Bank) increased by $103 billion, to a level of $327 billion. In March, the Federal Housing Finance Board voted to double the FHLBs' authorized holdings of conforming Fannie Mae and Freddie Mac securities; the board believes that action could provide more than $100 billion to the MBS market.

Federal Housing Administration. The Federal Housing Administration (FHA) insures loans made by FHA-approved lenders and is the world's largest insurer of mortgages. It has a long tradition of assisting borrowers who would generally be considered candidates for today's troubled subprime and alt-A loans.

The economic stimulus package enacted in February increased the cap on the size of mortgages FHA may insure. That increase will allow the FHA to insure loans up to a maximum value of $729,750 in certain areas of the country.

To aid subprime ARM borrowers facing foreclosure, the Administration introduced FHA Secure in August 2007 and announced plans to expand the program in April. Originally, FHA Secure offered FHA-insured refinancing to borrowers with non-FHA adjustable-rate mortgages who were current on their loans up until the date of their first rate reset (if that reset occurs between June 2005 and December 2009). Through early April, only 2,500 mortgages of the 154,000 that FHA had refinanced since the creation of the FHA Secure program belonged to a borrower who had missed one or more payments on the previous mortgage. The remaining borrowers would have been eligible for FHA refinancing assistance

---

40 The cost of $10 million of protection has climbed from about $8,000 in June to about $45,000 as of early April.

41 A credit default swap is a contractual arrangement in which the buyer pays a premium at periodic intervals in exchange for a contingent payment in the event of the default of some third party. The size of the premium paid relative to the contingent payment generally increases with the likelihood of default.

that was available before the inception of FHA Secure. The program did little to assist borrowers who had missed a payment before their first reset;[42] could not afford to repay the outstanding balance under the new loan terms; or had insufficient equity in the property to meet FHA's maximum loan-to-value ratio of 97 percent.

The expanded FHA Secure program will broaden eligibility to subprime ARM borrowers who have missed up to three monthly mortgage payments irrespective of whether their inability to pay was associated with an interest rate reset. In addition, borrowers who have negotiated a reduction of loan principal with their current lender can qualify for FHA Secure insurance. For borrowers with no more than two missed monthly payments in the previous 12 months, the current lender will need to write the loan down to 97 percent or lower of the appraised value for the borrower to qualify for FHA insurance on the new loan. Borrowers with three missed monthly payments in the previous 12 months would be eligible if their loans had been written down to 90 percent or less of the currently appraised value. (See the discussion of this and related refinancing proposals under the heading "Facilitating Refinancings," below.)

Expanding the Role of the Federal Housing Administration

As the federal insurer of mortgages for nonprime borrowers, the FHA is an obvious candidate to implement an increase in direct credit intervention in the troubled sectors of the mortgage market. (Box 3-2 contains a discussion of the budgetary treatment of federal housing loan guarantees.)

Box 3-2. Credit Reform and Federal Housing Loan Guarantees.

The budgetary treatment of actions that the federal government may take to influence housing or mortgage markets would depend on the nature of the action. Any proposals involving the direct purchase of mortgages or the issuance of insurance for privately held mortgages would follow the treatment specified in the Federal Credit Reform Act of 1990 (FCRA). Since enactment of FCRA, the federal budget has reflected the costs (or savings) from most government credit transactions on a present-value basis. For budgetary purposes, it would not matter if mortgage purchases or guarantees were made by an existing agency or a new agency created to deal with the current problems. Nearly all other (noncredit) transactions are recorded in the budget on a cash basis.

Under credit reform, the estimated net cost to the federal government of a direct loan or loan guarantee over the entire life of that loan is recorded as an outlay in the year that the loan is disbursed. The "subsidy" cost for a credit program in a particular year is the estimated net present value of all future cash flows associated with loans made during the year. Present-value calculations, known as discounting, are used to reflect the fact that the value today of $1 to be received in a future year is less than the value of $1 received now. FCRA rules require the calculation of present values by discounting expected cash flows

[42] For adjustable-rate subprime mortgages made in 2006, about 10 percent had defaulted in the first 12 months. See Board of Governors of the Federal Reserve System, *Monetary Report to the Congress* (February 2008).

at the interest rates on Treasury securities (the rates at which the government borrows money). The individual discounted cash flows, representing federal expenditures and receipts anticipated during each year of the expected life of the loans, are then summed to determine the total cost of the loans.

The Federal Housing Administration's (FHA's) Mutual Mortgage Insurance Fund is an example of a program subject to FCRA rules. Through the program, FHA provides a federal guarantee of mortgage loans funded through private lenders and state and local housing finance agencies. At the start of the 2008 budget year, FHA's portfolio of guarantees for mortgages on single-family homes was $322 billion, of which $98 billion (or 30 percent) was for mortgages that had been refinanced.

The subsidy estimate for FHA loan guarantees is calculated on the basis of the contract terms of the loan guarantee and a projection of future loan terminations from prepayments and defaults. Contract terms for FHA loan guarantees include the fees charged to borrowers and the default-related expenses of lenders that FHA will reimburse. The effects of proposals that would adjust those terms—such as an increase in loan-to-value ratios, a change in equity sharing, or a strengthening of collection mechanisms—would be reflected in the estimated cash flows and subsidy rates.

Legislative proposals that would expand FHA's authority to take on risk would increase the subsidy cost of its programs (measured on a discounted present-value basis), unless additional fees were charged to offset that cost. In contrast, the full amount of grants to nonfederal entities, such as community-based organizations, state housing agencies, or government-sponsored enterprises (for example, Fannie Mae and Freddie Mac), would be recorded as outlays at the time of payment, even if such grants were ultimately used to refinance mortgages. Proposals that would allow states to issue tax-exempt bonds would affect revenues because an increase in tax-exempt state borrowing would result in a loss of federal tax collections.

Increasing FHA's Maximum Loan-to-Value Ratio. FHA is currently limited to insuring mortgages with a loan-tovalue (LTV) ratio of at most 97 percent. That means FHA cannot insure restructured mortgages with no borrowers' equity. Allowing FHA to insure no-money-down mortgages might increase the resources flowing to that portion of the market.

Doing so would increase the risk to the FHA's portfolio—not because no-money-down mortgages would be significantly riskier than mortgages with a 97 percent loan-to-value ratio, but because moving into that portion of the market would increase the number of high LTV mortgages insured. That increased risk could be offset by charging higher premiums on the riskier loans.

Facilitating Refinancings. FHA could also be used to facilitate the refinancing of outstanding mortgages that are most likely to enter a costly foreclosure. The expanded FHA Secure program announced on April 9, 2008, is one such plan. Several more expansive proposals also have been discussed. Some proponents suggest that the federal role would be largely administrative, simply taking the actions that private parties would have taken were it not for impediments to sales and renegotiations in a distressed mortgage market. Others suggest that any intervention will have little effect on foreclosures without a serious commitment of taxpayers' funds. (The viability of such programs, like that of the private-sector solutions described in the previous section, would depend on the ability of servicers to gain the agreement of all parties, including second-mortgage holders.)

In one version of those proposals, mortgage servicers would put up for sale and restructuring a set of problem mortgages (which may be in mortgage pools); FHA-insured lenders would purchase those mortgages and then issue new mortgages with lower principal balances and payments that borrowers could afford. The expanded FHA Secure program will operate in a similar way, although loans need not be sold to facilitate the write-down of principal to a lower value. In another version, mortgage lenders (presumably through servicers) would themselves restructure the loans, including both first and second liens.[43] Instead of the liens, borrowers would have a new first mortgage and an interest-only loan, with the latter carrying an FHA guarantee.

The money to finance those restructurings could come from four sources. One is the investors in the current mortgages in recognition of the decline in the value of the home—the collateral for the mortgage. A second is the mortgage servicers and investors in terms of the additional costs they would have to bear from other routes to restructuring, such as foreclosure. The third is the federal government in the form of subsidized insurance from the FHA. Finally, another source of financing is the value of possible future increases in the price of the house. That is, some of the gain from a higher price when the house issold could be assigned to the lender or taxpayers, as in a shared-appreciation loan. Lenders would be more willing to write down their loan in exchange for a share of future appreciation in the property. Assigning some of the future gain to taxpayers would reduce the cost of the federal subsidy.

The number of borrowers that could be assisted by such proposals would depend directly on the amount of mortgage insurance subsidy that the government provides. With moderate refinancing fees, as embodied in most recent proposals, the federal subsidy would probably amount to less than 5 percent of the new loan principal, on average. Given that scale of subsidy, CBO expects that perhaps several hundred thousand borrowers would benefit from expanded FHA-insured refinancings over the next few years. Generating higher levels of participation would require substantially deeper subsidies, which would in turn significantly increase the federal budget cost. (Under current law, any subsidy costs for FHA loan guarantees are subject to appropriation of the necessary funds. Annual appropriation acts also generally limit the dollar amount of new federal loan guarantees that FHA can enter into for a given year.)

The creation of borrowers' equity is important to such proposals. Mortgages for which the outstanding balance exceeds the value of the property are most likely to go into foreclosure because borrowers who have no equity will find few options for refinancing and will be more willing to walk away from a mortgage that they are struggling to pay. Restructurings with no federal involvement are not likely to involve any significant borrowers' equity, either. Indeed, many would leave borrowers with lower monthly payments but negative equity in the house. Unfortunately, even restructurings that create positive equity may not be a permanent solution. In a declining housing market, such equity may be evanescent, and the risk of redefault is thus likely to grow until house prices stop falling.

Distribution of Benefits. The benefits of any resources that the federal government provides to support the restructuring of mortgages (such as subsidized FHA guarantees) are

---

[43] Mark M. Zandi, Richard Jaffee, and Daniel Melser, *Home Appreciation Mortgage Plan,* Moody's Economy.com, March 2008.

likely to be shared among borrowers and lenders. While borrowers whose loans are restructured will not have to move from one home to another and will have lower mortgage payments, some might get approximately the same benefits from a lender-initiated restructuring without federal intervention. Lenders (through their ser-vicers) have strong incentives to avoid defaults and foreclosures. Lenders will receive a windfall on those loans that they would have restructured without federal assistance. Despite that, lenders will be willing to restructure more mortgages with federal subsidies than without them.

The distribution of benefits will have an impact on the decision of borrowers and lenders to participate in the program. In a purchase and refinance program, the government would separately set the level of assistance to borrowers and lenders. Those levels would need to be carefully chosen to ensure that borrowers and lenders had enough incentive to participate. For example, the government might offer a write-down for certain types of loans, and lenders would choose to offer eligible loans for sale at that write-down. Lenders will only offer up loans where they anticipate that the terms of sale exceed the value of the best alternative for dealing with each loan. Similarly, the assistance offered to borrowers would have to be generous enough to ensure that their new loan was affordable.

In a loan restructuring program (one that does not involve loan sales), the distribution of benefits would be decided by negotiation between borrowers and lenders, subject to any constraints imposed by the program's regulations. If regulations were to mandate, as a condition of federal support, a restructuring package that was too generous to borrowers, lenders might offer few mortgages for restructuring. If the restructuring package was not generous enough to borrowers, lenders might fear that the restructuring would not be effective at preventing further defaults. Moreover, borrowers might decide to walk away rather than accept the package. And even if regulation simply mandated that lenders use a single restructuring package—for example, writing down all loans by the same percentage below market and setting mortgage payments on the basis of the same interest rate—fewer loans might be restructured than if the lender could tailor the package to the borrower's credit and the lender's expectations of future price declines in the local housing market.

Price of a Loan. The price offered to holders of the existing mortgage (or mortgages) could be established by either a fixed write-down of the appraised value of the property or via an auction in which federally approved bidders would pay for pools of mortgage loans put up for sale by current servicers. Proponents of an auction argue that it could help reignite the secondary market for non-prime loans and enable a more efficient process of refinancing loans in bulk. The benefits of bulk refinancing might not materialize, however, as servicers would still need to decide on a case-by-case basis whether to offer loans into the program, and borrowers would still need to participate in the drafting of new loans.

Loan servicers will only sell a mortgage if they perceive that the price offered exceeds the price a private buyer might pay for it, the value of renegotiating the loan privately with the borrower, and the net proceeds from foreclosure. Servicers will be willing to take a substantial discount on the amount owed on loans for which foreclosure is the best alternative because of the high costs of foreclosure. One concern for taxpayers in a program that has a fixed write-down of the appraisal value is that it would give existing mortgage holders incentive to offer mortgages that were only worth less than that value. That adverse selection would impose higher costs on taxpayers for a given volume of guarantees.

Eligibility of Borrowers. The program would need to maintain a delicate balance between assisting borrowers who are unable to refinance or repay their current loans and excluding those borrowers who can. Screening borrowers using established affordability criteria would help, but borrowers would have incentives to understate their ability to pay. To discourage borrowers who do not need government assistance, the terms of the refinanced loan must be made sufficiently unattractive to make that loan desirable only to those with a true inability to pay. Such measures could include restricting program participants from taking second mortgages on the property, or forcing borrowers to share any equity gains in their loans with taxpayers.

Additional restrictions and provisions could be applied to refinanced loans to minimize the cost to taxpayers. FHA could compel borrowers to provide adequate documentation to certify that they can afford their new loans. Federal assistance might also be limited to owner-occupied principal residences. However, because verifying a claim of principal residence is difficult, many investors may be able to take advantage of such programs unless the process of verification is more stringent than the current underwriting process.[44]

Many loan restructurings will end in default. To help reduce the cost of those defaults to the federal government, the program could specify that borrowers who subsequently default be subjected to stronger collection mechanisms, such as those in the Treasury Offset program. In the Treasury Offset program, an individual's federal transfer payments—such as Social Security payments and federal income tax refunds—can be used to pay down delinquent federal loans or guarantees. Such an approach would be a more severe collection program than borrowers would typically face from private lenders: In some states, lenders have no legal recourse to assets or income beyond the value of the property; and even where recourse is legally available, lenders often do not pursue it for subprime borrowers, who are not expected to have significant assets beyond the mortgage collateral.

Further Expanding the Role of Fannie Mae and Freddie Mac

The Congress could also consider mandating that Fannie Mae and Freddie Mac play a larger role in supporting the financing of subprime mortgages.[45]

The GSEs could be required to securitize subprime loans—a requirement that would offer the GSEs the opportunity to make money from guarantee fees, which would reflect the risk of those securities—or to hold more subprime or alt-A mortgages in their portfolios. Various legislative proposals also have been made to have the GSEs contribute to affordable housing funds, which would support lower-income subprime borrowers.

Minimizing the risk to taxpayers of such an increase in the GSEs' portfolios would require an increase in the GSEs' capital. Both housing GSEs have experienced recent governance, financial, and accounting control problems as well as large losses on their subprime mortgage holdings. Taxpayers have been protected from having those losses shifted to them, however, by the GSEs' capital. Even though financial markets are distressed, the GSEs are likely to be able to raise new funds for subprime mortgage lending. With the support of an implicit federal guarantee of their debt and other liabilities, Fannie Mae and Freddie Mac have privileged access to funds in the capital markets. During times of financial

---

44 Over the past several years, many mortgages for owner-occupied property were actually obtained by investors.

45 Lawrence Summers, "This Is Where Fannie and Freddie Step In," *Financial Times,* August 26, 2007; and statement of Alex Pollock, resident fellow, American Enterprise Institute, "Legislative and Regulatory Options Regarding Mortgage Foreclosures," before the House Committee on Financial Services (September 20, 2007).

turmoil and uncertainty, when there is often a "flight to quality" by investors, the securities issued by those entities tend to be favored investments.

Working through the GSEs, however, would give the government less control over the use of taxpayers' money. The federal government could not dictate the terms of assistance as readily as it could if it expanded one of the federal agencies (such as FHA), because of the GSEs' for-profit charter.[46] Thus, there is a significant possibility that taxpayers might take on additional risk through the GSEs' expansion, but not all the value of that additional risk-bearing would go to the desired borrowers.

Expanding the Role of Federal Home Loan Banks

A less direct way to support the mortgage markets would be to follow the lead of the Federal Reserve by increasing the provision of liquidity to banks using the Federal Home Loan Banks as a conduit. The additional liquidity could be made conditional on banks' meeting specified refinancing, forbearance, or loan-modification objectives. That approach would put the onus on banks to devise specific strategies for resolving problems in the mortgage market. It would also make use of the banks' capital cushions, thus reducing the risk to taxpayers.

To do that, the FHLBs would need either more capital or reduced capital requirements. As with Fannie Mae and Freddie Mac, reducing capital requirements would increase the risk that taxpayers could be embroiled in a costly bailout if one or more of the banks failed.

Increasing Federal Assistance to Community-Based Organizations

Another approach would increase federal assistance to community-based organizations, such as community development corporations and community development financial institutions that provide services, counseling, and foreclosure protection to households.[47] Among other things, counseling may help steer borrowers to prime markets and away from subprime markets and may also be used to make delinquent borrowers aware of alternatives to foreclosure. In 2008, the Congress appropriated $50 million for the Department of Housing and Urban Development's Housing Counseling Assistance Program. The program provides counseling services to eligible homeowners and tenants, including home purchase, financial management, and rental counseling. (The Home Ownership and Equity Protection Act of 1994 has no provisions requiring counseling; however, some states require lenders to notify borrowers of counseling opportunities.) In addition, the Congress provided $180 million to the Neighborhood Reinvestment Corporation for mortgage mitigation activities.[48] A bill passed by the House would require lenders to alert delinquent borrowers to counseling opportunities, some of which could be provided by housing advocacy groups.[49]

---

[46] See Douglas W. Elmendorf, "What Should Be Done to Help Households Facing Foreclosure?" (Brookings Institution, November 2007), available at www.brookings.edu/opinions/ 2007/11_mortgages_elmendorf.aspx

[47] Edward M. Gramlich, *Subprime Mortgages: America's Latest Boom and Bust* (Washington, D.C.: Urban Institute Press, 2007).

[48] Consolidated Appropriations Act of 2008 (Public Law 110-161; 121 Stat. 1844).

[49] H.R. 1852, Expanding American Homeownership Act of 2007.

Creating a New Agency

Instead of using existing agencies, the government could create a new agency, either to buy subprime mortgages or to make loans directly to borrowers.

Although an existing agency could be given the same responsibilities as a new agency, a new limited-purpose agency would have a focused charter and could be set up to "sunset" (expire) after a reasonable amount of time. By contrast, expanding the scope of an existing agency's mission to include providing subsidies would force the new program to compete for resources and management time with the agency's other responsibilities. Moreover, the new responsibility could become regarded as part of the permanent mission of the agency, thus making it harder to end when the urgent need was over.

Setting up a new agency, however, is usually complicated and time-consuming. A recent example is provided by the Resolution Trust Corporation (RTC), which was created to address the thrift crisis of the 1980s. Although it was a new, independent agency, the RTC was staffed by employees from other federal agencies, mainly the Federal Deposit Insurance Corporation. During the six years it operated, the RTC resolved 747 failed thrifts with $394 billion of assets.[50] In its first 5 months, the RTC took over 318 failed thrifts but resolved only 37 of them. The situation for the RTC improved in the subsequent 12 months, and the RTC was able to resolve 315 institutions. The RTC's experience highlights two challenges with setting up a new agency. Policymakers faced significant difficulties in providing additional funding for the RTC after its initial $50 billion in funding proved insufficient. The agency also faced persistent criticism—some founded, some unfounded—about its operations and the complex management structure of the corporation and its oversight board.[51] Moreover, the RTC was in a situation that differs significantly from the current one: It was created to accelerate the breakup of the thrifts because, as long as they continued to operate, they were taking on ever-riskier investments.[52]

Buying Subprime Mortgages. A new agency could purchase problematic loans at steep discounts. That approach was used by the Home Owners' Loan Corporation, when it exchanged bonds for defaulted mortgages with lenders and investors at a discount and adjusted the loan terms to help borrowers during the Depression.

Proponents believe that such a program could put a floor on the prices of subprime mortgages and allow market participants to price the assets of financial institutions. The agency would aim to sell the mortgages at higher prices when financial markets were better able to price them and were more amenable to undertaking the risk. That would still leave the agency exposed to the risk of a delayed recovery in the housing market, which could keep mortgage prices depressed for many years and, hence, offer a poor return on investment to taxpayers.

---

[50] Resolving the 747 failed thrifts cost the RTC $83 billion, financed by $76 billion from the U.S. Treasury and $7 billion from the private sector. See Timothy Curry and Lynn Shibut, "The Cost of the Saving and Loan Crisis: Truth and Consequences," *FDIC Banking Review,* vol. 13, no. 2 (2000).

[51] See Lee Davison, "The Resolution Trust Corporation and Congress, 1989–1993 (Part I and II)," *FDIC Banking Review,* vol. 18, nos. 1 and 2 (2006).

[52] Note, however, that deposit insurance transactions are reflected in the budget on a cash basis, unlike the costs of federal loans and loan guarantees, which are recorded on a present-value basis.

Making Direct Loans to Borrowers. Instead of buying mortgages, a new agency could make loans directly to borrowers at affordable rates.[53] Borrowers would use the proceeds from the more affordable loans to prepay a fraction of their outstanding mortgage (or mortgages, if they had a second lien). That approach could get around the difficulty of obtaining agreement for mortgage restructuring from second-mortgage holders and MBS investors, since it would go through the procedures for prepayment established under the terms of their original mortgage contracts, including any penalties for early repayment.[54]

The number of borrowers with troubled mortgages who would be willing to take a federal loan would depend on the terms offered. Borrowers would have to be able to afford to make their combined monthly payment on the new loan and the remaining portion of the old loan. For the payment to be affordable for borrowers, the federal loan may need to offer below-market interest rates and a long term to maturity. In addition, the loan would need to replace a large enough portion of the original unaffordable mortgage.

Loans made at below-market terms to borrowers with negative equity in their property would be costly to taxpayers. The combination of negative equity and a history of missed payments on the original mortgage suggests that the probability of default on a direct loan would be high. A federal loan would be likely to have lower claim on the property than the borrower's preexisting loans. The government could strengthen the enforceability of the direct loan by making it nondischargeable in bankruptcy and subject to stronger collection mechanisms than privately issued loans. If the federal loan and original loans were adjustable-rate mortgages, affordability problems could resurface if short-term interest rates increased from their present historically low levels.

Like a purchase and refinance program, a direct lending program would face a similar challenge in restricting eligibility to borrowers who could not afford their existing mortgage but could afford their new mortgage. If the new loans carried interest rate terms that were significantly below those on prime mortgages, then borrowers of all types would be clamoring to participate.

Providing Mortgage Assistance Through States

Federal assistance to borrowers might also be channeled through states. Options for financing such assistance include expanding authority for tax-exempt bonds or providing direct grants to states. Less directly, federal grants to states might finance programs to help borrowers navigate through the process of restructuring their loans.

Currently, state-based housing agencies are eligible to issue tax-exempt bonds to finance new mortgages for first-time homebuyers. Tax-exempt debt allows states to finance at interest rates that are significantly lower than the rate on comparable taxable debt, the benefits of which can be passed on to borrowers. Expanding states' borrowing authority to refinance mortgages, however, would reduce federal income tax receipts.

Comparatively, tax-exempt financing is a less cost-effective means of transferring resources from the federal government to state and local governments. Because of the

---

53 Martin Feldstein, "How to Stop the Mortgage Crisis," *The Wall Street Journal,* March 7, 2008.

54 As of February 2008, about 70 percent of subprime loans and about 40 percent of alt-A loans featured prepayment penalties if the loan was prepaid within an initial period of generally two to three years, according

progressive structure of the federal income tax, the revenue loss to the federal government from those tax-exempt bonds exceeds the debt-service savings to states and localities. More direct means of transferring resources, such as grants, deliver more aid at smaller cost to the federal government.

to tabulations made by researchers at the New York Federal Reserve Bank from a sample of loans in First American Loan Performance's database.

INDEX

A

B

C

D

J

K

L

M

N

S

T